D1521885

when words sing

SEVEN CANADIAN LIBRETTI

when words sing

edited by

Julie Salverson

Playwrights Canada Press
Toronto

First edition: May 2021
Printed and bound in Canada by Imprimerie Gauvin, Gatineau

Jacket design by Kisscut Design

Playwrights Canada Press
202-269 Richmond St. W., Toronto, ON M5V 1X1
416.703.0013 | info@playwrightscanada.com | www.playwrightscanada.com

LIBRARY AND ARCHIVES CANADA CATALOGUING IN PUBLICATION
Title: When words sing : seven Canadian libretti / edited by Julie Salverson.
Names: Salverson, Julie, editor.
Description: First edition.
Identifiers: Canadiana 20210138343 | ISBN 9780369101242 (softcover)
Subjects: LCSH: Operas—Canada—Librettos. | LCSH: Libretto. | LCGFT: Librettos.
Classification: LCC ML48 .W567 2021 | DDC 782.1026/8—dc23

Playwrights Canada Press operates on Mississaugas of the Credit, Wendat, Anishinaabe, Métis, and Haudenosaunee land. It always was and always will be Indigenous land.

We acknowledge the financial support of the Canada Council for the Arts, the Ontario Arts Council (OAC), Ontario Creates, and the Government of Canada for our publishing activities.

 Canada Council
for the Arts
Conseil des arts
du Canada

 ONTARIO ARTS COUNCIL
CONSEIL DES ARTS DE L'ONTARIO
an Ontario government agency
un organisme du gouvernement de l'Ontario

 Canada

 ONTARIO CREATES | ONTARIO CRÉATIF

I would like to dedicate this volume to Wayne Strongman.

Contents

Foreword

Barbara Hannigan

I needed the words!

In my early teens, it was the words that were the clincher for me, as I was making the decision to concentrate on piano, oboe, or voice as my main instrument. I must have been fourteen or so, saying to my parents, "It *has* to be singing, because I want to *talk* to the audience!" Now, some thirty-five years later, the music I've sung has given me the words I so badly needed, reaching back to Greek myth, Homer's *Odyssey*, and Japanese Noh plays, Shakespeare and Racine, from da Ponte to Wilde, Wedekind, and Strindberg, and has imported the words of living writers Martin Crimp and Paul Griffiths into my musical soul.

Am I ever glad I chose singing! My "job description" includes languages ranging from the traditional operatic tongues of French, German, Italian, Russian, and more recently, English, to Ancient Greek, Finnish, and Tibetan. Not one to subscribe at all to *Prima la musica, poi le parole* . . . I've never felt a hierarchy. The genre of opera and classical vocal music demands partnership and flow between librettist, composer, and eventually, production team and performers. That's what makes this art form so special: the composer has been inspired by the words to create music, the words have required her to decide on tempo, rhythm, inflection and pitch, and surrounding harmonies; they have gotten him up in the morning or woken her in the middle of the night, with urgent ideas about how to best tell this story as a contribution to our rich and strange world. The director and her team, on and off stage, take the opera to birth. But in the beginning (or very near the beginning) were the words!

In my role as singer, it has been a privilege to pronounce the text as the composer has set it, in fact, I consider much of the inflection already taken care of, since the composer has already interpreted it through her text-setting. It is my responsibility to incorporate the text into my voice, psyche, body—to taste the words. To feel the difference between the legato voiced consonant and the explosion of an unvoiced consonant, the soaring flight of an open vowel and the tightly coiled compression of a closed one, the fine tuning of diction, which gives the word extra spin, and the inflection, which gives subtext to a phrase. It can also be a struggle! I remember explaining the difference between open and closed vowels to composers in lectures I'd give on "Writing for the Voice," demonstrating how an open vowel on a high note had a much better chance of being understood than a closed one. I told them how I wished the words "two weeks," which one composer had set for my voice on repeated high Cs, were instead the words "one month." Why? The former are closed vowels, which require the mouth to be, like the vowels, closed. The latter, open vowels, which encourage an open mouth. Just try it. Find a note in your range that is really high for you, and then try to sing these four words! Vowels are migratory creatures, and have different homes (and comfort zones) depending on where they find themselves within the singing tessitura.

I won't forget seeing and hearing *Beatrice Chancy* when it played at the Citadel Theatre in Edmonton back in 2001. I'd premiered several of James Rolfe's earlier, more edgy and angular vocal works and was surprised to hear the music George Elliott Clarke's libretto brought out of James, so different from his previous music. It was fascinating to read James's explanation of that process, in his contribution to this book. I can still feel the buzz around *Nigredo Hotel* when it played to sold-out audiences in Toronto almost thirty years ago when I was just beginning my career. That gritty piece of music theatre was a real game-changer for the Canadian opera scene. I remember a few years ago from my home base in Europe reading a review of *Dog Days* in the *New York Times* with immense curiosity. And I felt I was a bit of an insider as *Shelter* came to audiences, having had many conversations with writer Julie Salverson about the piece at various moments of its life. Julie and I were roommates, back in the late 1990s in Toronto, and twenty years of friendship and bouncing ideas off one another has given delicious food for thought as we've been cooking in our various kitchens all these years. I was honoured when Julie asked me to write the preface for *When Words Sing*.

Each chapter of this anthology is a cliffhanger. We have the libretti themselves—beautiful and bare, haunting, funny, heartbreaking, full of possibility—accompanied by insights and reflections from the librettist and composer, and vivid commentary from the creative team. By the end of each chapter, I feel I've experienced each opera in a new way. Most of all, I realize what a gift it is to come back to the words, the reason why I chose to become a singer.

Editor's Preface

Julie Salverson

The first time I was invited to Tapestry Opera's Composer-Librettist Laboratory, LIBLAB, I never got the message. Someone had dropped out and Jennifer Stein recommended me as a replacement. When I didn't reply to the phone call, they moved on. That wouldn't have been difficult. Canada has a lot of writers. What most of them don't know is that opera has a place for them. I hope this book proves that.

I was lucky. The LIBLAB accepted me the following year with the early notes for what became *Shelter*. The first assignment was to create our own version of Euripides's Greek tragedy *Medea*. Why would a contemporary woman murder her children? The singers didn't yet have anything to rehearse, so I invited them to join composer Sean Ferguson and me while we foraged for an idea.

I asked soprano Tamara Hummel what she loved most about singing. She thought for a moment. "The feeling of my breath going through my body." What sprang into my mind—and it chilled me—was a recent newspaper article. A woman had jumped from a subway platform with her newborn infant in her arms. Could I try something with this unbearable story? Sean grimaced. "Go for it."

I sat alone on the floor of the church gymnasium, wondering what the words for an opera were supposed to look like. The enormity of it froze me. I pushed away everything except what Tamara had said. As she stood on the edge of the platform, what would this woman's breath feel like going through her body? And I began.

There is nothing like hearing your words sung by opera singers. Just nothing. I cried the first time, and I have cried since. All the words in this book are infused with music; they only come alive when conducted and played and sung. Because of this, it is the music that history has paid attention to in opera. But one day, browsing through a pile of Canadian plays at a book fair, I asked myself, "Why aren't there any libretti here?" Fortunately, Annie Gibson at Playwrights Canada

Press thought it was an interesting enough question to commission this book. I told her I couldn't find any collections of contemporary libretti in English. None. "It's either a great idea or a terrible idea," one of us said.

Wayne Strongman once told me, "The birth of new work is all about relationship." Everyone involved in *When Words Sing* has been generous. I am grateful to all the contributors. It is no small thing to put your work into a form it is not meant for. When you read these libretti, please remember that they are meant to be sung. I am beyond grateful to Annie and to Blake Sproule for taking the risk to make this happen and for including the words of composers, directors, designers, and producers. I thank Jessica Lewis for telling the world this book is coming, Blake for pulling it together at the worst of times, and Bill Penner for his brilliant editorial eye. The responsibility for the selection of the libretti is entirely mine—I was given carte blanche. There are many powerful Canadian librettists whose work is not in here. Maybe we can do a second volume! I owe a huge debt to Linda Hutcheon, who was the midwife for this book. She talked and emailed with me for hours, days, years, and was the creative sounding board I needed. I am a newbie to opera. When Juliet Palmer and I were commissioned by Tapestry, we went to all the operas we could find. I'm sure I was the only one in the balcony entranced by *La traviata* who didn't know how it ended.

This book is being edited and launched during the pandemic. If frontline workers and health providers are saving our bodies, creativity is saving our souls. As a global reckoning sends us home to face ourselves, the wild cry of what being alive really means erupts from the stories we speak, paint, sing, breathe, and dream. The seven stories here rage, howl, accuse, adore, and rejoice. They remind us what being alive is. I hope we listen.

Thanks to R. Murray Schafer for the title. Forgive us the theft. We borrow in admiration.

Introducing the (Canadian) Libretto
Michael and Linda Hutcheon

In the Beginning

By the time Samuel Johnson famously decried opera as an "exotic and irrational entertainment" in the mid-1700s, the musical dramatic art form had already been around for well over a century and would continue to thrive to our present day. We realize that our personal affection for this art form has a lot to do with the fact that it brings together music, literature, and dramatic spectacle. Opera is not only an extravagant but also a resolutely collaborative art form, and that's what makes it so complex and so intriguing for us. Opera is what Nelson Goodman calls an "allographic" art, one that requires many artists to bring it into existence. Unlike a painting, where we see what the artist places directly on the canvas (making it an "autographic" art), an opera is not just its printed literary text (or libretto) and its musical score.* It is the sum of the work of both a librettist and a composer, but it is given life on stage by a phalanx of other artists: singers, musicians, directors, and designers. Opera is the combination of what Kier Elam refers to as both its "dramatic texts" (score, libretto) and its "performance text" (the live production).** But it all begins with the libretto (literally, in Italian, the "little book"), the dramatic text whose words are written to be set to music by the composer.

---

* Nelson Goodman, *Languages of Art: An Approach to a Theory of Symbols* (Indianapolis: Bobbs-Merrill, 1968), 113.

** Kier Elam, *The Semiotics of Theatre and Drama* (London and New York: Routledge, 1980), 2.

We soon realized that an opera libretto is not really like a screenplay, though some may read like one. Nor is it a play, though it is a dramatic text. It has its own forms and conventions peculiar to opera. At times during its long history, the libretto has been a free-standing published literary work (as in the Baroque period), while at other times it has been published along with the musical score. Often it was printed as a separate book, to be read by audience members before or even during a performance. Here in this volume, though, seven diverse contemporary Canadian libretti are published in a new anthology that allows for both discovery and comparison. They are helpfully accompanied by framing comments by the librettists, composers, and designers, as well as by prefatory contextualizing essays.

And Then There Was Chamber Opera

All of these libretti were written in a modern form that we now call "chamber opera," conceived and created for smaller musical forces and often performed in smaller, non-traditional spaces—resulting in an intimacy, immediacy, and intensity difficult to achieve in an enormous opera house with a large orchestra. And this is where and why we personally got "hooked." Unlike full-length operas or musicals, chamber operas are usually shorter, but like both, they are meant to be music-driven theatre, with the emphasis on the theatrical. Some of the motivation for the spread of this form in the twentieth century was clearly economic: with smaller performance spaces and fewer musicians and singers, chamber operas cost less to produce. In the 1940s, for example, the English Opera Group was therefore able to tour many of Benjamin Britten's chamber operas throughout the UK and bring them to new audiences; in Canada, in 2013, Queen of Puddings Music Theatre took Ana Sokolović's *Svadba* to Calgary, Edmonton, and Vancouver, after a European tour (Dublin, Orleans, Paris, and Belgrade). (Financial support for both commissions and touring from the Canada Council and other arts funding agencies made this expansion possible.)

Their relatively smaller scale also makes chamber operas quicker to create and produce, and thus more easily and more rapidly responsive to issues of the day.

That is most certainly the case with the Canadian chamber operas whose libretti appear in this volume. But just as important has been the explosion both in the number of new operas—especially chamber operas—in recent years and also in the number of smaller chamber opera companies that have commissioned and produced them. In Toronto alone, where we live and enjoy opera, there arose eleven independent opera companies by 2020, including two well represented in this anthology: Tapestry Opera, one of the first to appear, and Queen of Puddings Music Theatre. But new chamber operas have been created all over the country, from St John's, Newfoundland, at Opera on the Avalon to Vancouver at City Opera. And their libretti have been commissioned from Canadian novelists, playwrights, poets, filmmakers, dance scenarists, actors, and . . . librettists. Because the libretto is a unique musico-dramatic genre with its own conventions and history, its form has to be learned and perfected—and that takes time and practice. Happily, the flourishing Canadian operatic culture has created ample opportunities for both.

The "Little Book" Fights Back

There have always been music-oriented critics who have denigrated the libretto as a literary art form, calling it repetitious, simplified, often absurd in its plotting, and literally of no value until it is transformed by the music. Indeed, as Arthur Groos, a serious scholar of the form, laments, "libretto-bashing has a distinguished tradition in the blood sport of opera."[*] But any opera begins with a libretto text, just as any art song begins with a poem. These are the precise words that the music is written to—and for. The librettist is the composer's enabling co-creator; without the dramatic text there would be nothing to set to music, much less to inspire creativity.

The relative status of these two artists in an operatic collaboration has changed over time. Librettists have gone from being recognized poets and dramatists (Apostolo Zeno and Pietro Metastasio, in the early years) to being demoted to lesser artistic roles and duly ordered about by imperious composers. By the

---

[*]   Arthur Groos, "Introduction," *Reading Opera*, ed. Arthur Groos and Roger Parker (Princeton: Princeton University Press, 1988), 2.

nineteenth century, they sometimes had even these roles taken over by the composers themselves. Some, like Richard Wagner and Hector Berlioz, did so in the search for full creative control. In what came to be called *Literaturoper*, pre-existing texts were set by composers almost verbatim, again pre-empting the librettist. Ideally today, however, composer and librettist are individual artists, expert in their different fields, working together to create something neither could do alone.

Operatic Subjects

What, exactly, attracts such operatic co-creators to particular subjects on which to build their works? Historically, we know that in the beginning, in Renaissance Italy, the tale of Orpheus, the musician-poet, proved usefully appropriate for this new art form that aimed to bring together literature and music, but the myths and legends of antiquity offered popular narrative materials for opera well into the eighteenth century. In other words, adaptations of familiar stories provided librettists with a wealth of subject matter. With the rise of a literate middle-class audience and a growing European literary culture came operatic adaptations of literary romances, popular novels, epics, short stories, melodramas, and stage plays. What was important was that the work chosen for adaptation be popular and well-known. Canonical writers like Shakespeare, Schiller, and Walter Scott were always in fashion in the nineteenth century.

Given the high cost of production, opera has tended to rely on the tried and tested, rather than the new. The familiarity of the stories and the cultural capital of their status are what have provided both box-office appeal and aesthetic legitimacy. In more recent times, though, popular films, comic strips, television shows, and news stories, not to mention celebrity biographies, have made their way onto the operatic stage: *A Wedding, Jerry Springer: The Opera, Malcolm X, Jackie O, Nixon in China,* and in Canada, the historical tale of *Pauline* (Johnson), by Margaret Atwood and Tobin Stokes. Of course, original stories are also always possible, but may well present financial risks, because they are untested as "hits." In other words, audience expectations and desires are never far from the co-creators' minds. As will be clear from the libretti collected here, however, this is countered by the appealing invocation of current political issues—such as racism and sexism

(*Beatrice Chancy; Missing*), climate change (*Dog Days*), and war (*Shelter; Ours*). These timely topics also provide ample fodder for chamber operatic texts today. So too do important moral and psychological concerns of our day, from trauma (*Nigredo Hotel*) to autism (*Rocking Horse Winner*) to PTSD (*Ours*).

The Conventions of the Opera Libretto

What makes an opera libretto read differently on the page than a screenplay or a drama? In short, the particular conventions of opera. While varying according to the historical period, conventions came into being early in opera's history as a way to make the new art form easier for creators to write and for audiences to understand.* They arose as practical ways, in other words, to make opera recognizable as a form, as well as accessible and enjoyable for audiences. In some periods, librettists had to conform to specific conventions of poetic structure (metre, rhyme, stanza form), mostly because it was this that determined the rhythmic and harmonic structure of the music to be written. Everything from the number of characters and scene changes to the positions on stage of singers was often also codified by convention. For much of opera's history, the dominant musico-dramatic form was what was called the "number opera." This regulated the succession and alternations of (conversation-like) recitatives and (soliloquy-like) arias with ensembles (duets, trios, and so on). The librettist therefore could use two simultaneous temporal dimensions: one "naturalistic," in which events unfold and characters converse (in recitative); and the other, more "psychological" or "emotional," as characters stop and reflect upon their emotional and mental states (in arias and ensembles).**

Today, the conventions of opera have loosened up considerably. As can be seen in the seven libretti in this volume, some are written in poetic verse, others

---

* Carolyn Abbate and Roger Parker, *A History of Opera: The Last Four Hundred Years* (London: Allen Lane, 2023), 21–22.

** Michael Halliwell, *Opera and the Novel: The Case of Henry James* (Amsterdam and New York: Rodopi, 2005), 28.

in prose. Almost all take advantage of the introspective potential of arias, set in contrast with the action or conversation allowed by more recitative-like passages. But all librettists have to deal with the obvious fact that the music to which their words will be set is a "retarding" agent:* it slows down narrative time, in part because it takes so much longer to sing than to speak (much less read) a line of text. What this means is that whatever story the librettists want to tell, adapted or original, it must be concise and tightly focused; to this end, drastic selection and compression are often required, but always without damaging comprehension or dramatic impact.

The Librettist's Challenges

Librettists have to make important decisions, some of them simple but crucial, such as choosing how many principal characters to include. Therefore, they may have to resist subplots and their distracting characters. If they are adapting a prose fiction text, as some do here, the task of the librettists will be to render what they select from those texts into equivalences in order to dramatize rather than narrate, that is, to show rather than tell—and to do so concisely and to maximal dramatic effect. Events and characters can be shown (materialized and dramatized) or talked about and described in dialogue (in recitative). Actions can be delineated in stage directions, and the setting can be established with stage set directions or by what characters say or sing about it. But economy and concision must never be at the cost of emotional impact; librettists cannot leave all the affective work to the composers, performers, and production teams. It is also true, however, that librettists begin their work in full knowledge that those other artists will also be working to bring the opera to life on stage. Therefore, they have to take that future collaboration into account even as they begin working. In other words, elements like rhythm and pacing, visual and even emotional impact are not the sole task of librettists. As is the case with almost all the libretti published in this volume, librettists and composers often work closely together; through workshops, the

---

*   Leonard Rosmarin, *When Literature Becomes Opera: Study of a Transformational Process,* ed. M. Bishop (Amsterdam: Rodopi, 1999), 49.

rest of the production team and all the performers and musicians can also have creative input into the final opera. The introductory remarks by composers, librettists, and designers of each work in this collection give a strong sense of how this process worked in individual cases.

Not only do these seven libretti share a cultural context (recent Canadian chamber operas about currently relevant themes), but they also differ in significant and telling ways. As we have noted, some are written in prose, others in verse; the language of some is colloquial, but that of others, more "literary" and formal. In some libretti, sounds are as significant as words, conveying meaning beyond the semantic. All are in English, though *Missing* is in significant part in Gitksan. Some (*Ours*; *Beatrice Chancy*) are more or less naturalistic dramas, while others (*Shelter*; *Missing*; *Nigredo Hotel*; *Dog Days*) deploy supernatural or surreal techniques to suggest something beyond the realistic. Some of the dramas are close to those of their adapted texts (*Dog Days*; *Rocking Horse Winner*), while others veer off in different directions, with new ends aimed at and attained.

In short, there is (happily) no simple single rule for how to write a libretto today, in Canada or elsewhere. Opera is a flexible, protean art form, and always has been, and that's why we adore it. The growing number of new chamber operas has simply sped up the changes and increased the number of varieties available. One important sign of this ramped-up operatic creativity is the existence of this volume, making these Canadian opera libretti finally available to readers, producers, performers, and . . . the curious.

Beatrice Chancy

Libretto by George Elliott Clarke

Composed by James Rolfe

Recovering (Hi)stories Through Opera

Michael and Linda Hutcheon, Opera Scholars

What a difference an anthology makes! Back in the early '90s, Canadian composer James Rolfe was considering writing more vocal music and, to that end, bought a collection called *Poets 88*,[*] in which he discovered a young poet named George Elliott Clarke, a self-described "Africadian"—of African, Acadian (and also Indigenous) descent. A poem by Clarke called "Look Homeward, Exile," in Rolfe's words, "leapt off the page, as if possessed."[**] He was immediately attracted, as he later put it, to "its strong rhythm, heightened language, and high stakes."[***] The poet, then a graduate student at Queen's University, quickly agreed to collaborate with Rolfe on an opera, and eventually suggested one about the often neglected history of slavery in Canada, to be set in the Annapolis Valley in Nova Scotia in 1801 when slavery was still legal in the British colony. This preface tells the story about how *that* poetry anthology ended up provoking the libretto you can read in *this* anthology.

As you will see from Clarke's eloquent comments in this volume, the tale that he so passionately wanted to tell—and that became the chamber opera called *Beatrice Chancy*—is "based on a true story," as they say, specifically the story told by the Romantic poet Percy Bysshe Shelley in his dramatic narrative about the

---

[*]   Bob Hilderley and Ken Norris, eds., *Poets 88* (Kingston: Quarry Press, 1988).

[**]   James Rolfe, cited on his webpage: http://www.jamesrolfe.ca/category/music/operas-stage/.

[***]   James Rolfe, email, 29 Dec. 2019.

historical Roman woman, Beatrice Cenci. But Clarke's adapted version of this story was decidedly and pointedly Canadian, for it was seen through the lenses of both the early enslavement of Africans in our country and the traditions of the slave narrative.[*] Given this, as he tells us here, he wanted his libretto to be "gutsy and gritty, hellish and highfalutin, dirty and dreamy." Composer James Rolfe, writing his first opera ever, felt outside of his musical comfort zone, as he candidly admits in his remarks here, but set to work to "make the words sing," as he so poetically and perfectly puts it. He composed the piece for six voices and seven musicians, including a fiddler who sometimes played solo, on stage as part of the action.

The novice opera composer and librettist[**] had the chance to experiment and develop a few scenes of the opera together in the context of the Banff Centre's Composer-Librettist Workshop, as part of a new program led by John Hess and Keith Turnbull. The two creators were then commissioned to complete the work by Hess and Dáirine Ní Mheadhra, the artistic directors of the newly created Queen of Puddings Music Theatre in Toronto. What then occurred was the intriguing creation of two parallel texts. Clarke's verbal exuberance and dramatic expansiveness initially clashed with the demands of the libretto as a genre. Since it takes so much longer to sing than to speak or even read a line of text, libretti are by definition concise and concentrated dramatic narratives, as Rolfe knew. Quickly, the collaborators decided that Clarke would first write a full-length verse play version, and from that they would distill the opera's text. That play was subsequently published as *Beatrice Chancy* (Polestar Book Publishers, 1999), after being given a dramatic reading at Theatre Passe Muraille in Toronto in 1997.

In the process of distillation that resulted in the libretto, the number of characters would be reduced; certain scenes would be cut or merged; some of the

---

[*]   See also George Elliott Clarke, "Racing Shelley, or Reading *The Cenci* as a Gothic Slave Narrative," *European Romantic Review* 11.2 (2000): 168–85.

[**]   Both artists went on to produce an impressive array of operatic works. Clarke wrote the libretti for two other Canadian operas (thus far): *Québécité: A Jazz Fantasia in Three Cantos* (Kentville, NS: Gaspereau Press, 2003) and *Trudeau: Long March/Shining Path* (Kentville, NS: Gaspereau Press, 2007). Rolfe has become one of the most commissioned and performed opera composers in Canada, with *Fire* (1999), *Rosa* (2004), *Orpheus and Eurydice* (2004), *Elijah's Kite* (2005), *Swoon* (2006), *Aeneas and Dido* (2007), *Ines* (2008), *Europa* (2013), among others.

dense poetic diction would be altered for more immediate aural comprehension. Though stripped down and laser-focused, the libretto's text also saw additions suggested by the musical intertexts, both colonial and slave: ring shouts, hymns, blues, spirituals—and Nova Scotia fiddling. But the story, the politics, and all the characterization of the verse play would all remain intact.

While opera libretti in earlier centuries had also been written in verse, the poetry of Clarke's drama is particularly rich and complex, and thus not easy to adapt to operatic singing, except in emotionally gripping arias. In transposing his verse play into an opera libretto, Clarke claims to have sought "a homely, hard purity of line, a demotic that hurts, a black blank verse, a lyric sense eschewing broken music, postmodernist weeping."* Rolfe's eloquent and expressive music allows the libretto's searing words to be clearly heard.

The first workshop of Act One occurred in June 1996 and that of the whole work in December 1997. The creators acknowledged that these workshops were crucial to hearing and understanding what worked and what didn't. It also gave them the welcome opportunity to hear what Rolfe called "the fruit of our years of imaginative labour."** Queen of Puddings Music Theatre was equally encouraged and staged the premiere in June of 1998 at the Music Gallery in Toronto.

This full-length opera in two acts lasted one hundred minutes, and provided the twenty-year-old New Brunswick soprano, Measha Brueggergosman, as Beatrice with her professional operatic debut. The Toronto *Globe and Mail* reviewer, Urjo Kareda, noted "her rich passionate soprano on fire, her emotional investment in this woman total." He went on to say: "With *Beatrice Chancy*, I felt I was face to face with the future of opera—and its breath was hot."***

We can personally testify that for audiences experiencing that first production, in a small intimate performance space, the piece was electrifying. This potent, charged opera owed its impact to both the music and the libretto, obviously, as well as the deeply moving Queen of Puddings production, directed by Michael

---

* Clarke, "Charge," in "Beatrice Chancy: A Libretto in Four Acts," *Canadian Theatre Review* 96 (1998), 62.

** James Rolfe, website: http://www.jamesrolfe.ca/category/music/operas-stage/.

*** Urjo Kareda, "Opera Review: Beatrice Chancy: Beatrice Chancy a Triumph," *Globe and Mail*, 22 June 1999.

Cavanagh. This was one of the first chamber operas we had ever seen, but it would not be the last. In the Music Gallery, the singing actors and the musicians were so physically close that we could have touched them; their joys, passions, and pains were almost palpable. Their sung words were so immediate that it was as if they were heard in the aural equivalent of **BOLDED UPPER CASE** at all times, even when whispered. Our—and from what we could see, the rest of the audience's— emotional and intellectual immersion in the characters' story was total, as the music and the words together in performance worked their magic.

Given the opera's immediacy and impact, in no time the piece was reprised: June 1999 at the du Maurier Dance Theatre in Toronto; August 1999 at the Alderney Landing Theatre in Dartmouth, Nova Scotia; February 2001 at the Citadel Theatre in Edmonton, Alberta. That special operatic magic continued for us into our listening to the CBC Radio recording of the 1998 live Toronto production and further, into our viewing of the CBC TV adaptation of the opera, which aired in February 2001, during Black History Month. The first Canadian opera broadcast on television in more than thirty years, this attracted considerable critical and public attention, and with good reason. A minimalist production, it nevertheless maintained the brutal and moving power of the original stage version. As with the Metropolitan Opera's *Live in HD* productions today, cinematic close-ups were used, but in this case they served to mimic and recreate the intimacy made possible by the original small theatrical space.

Given the explosion in critical writing about postmodernism in the 1980s and '90s, we were primed to see *Beatrice Chancy* as engaging with the historical past, but through the distancing filters that time inevitably entailed. Rolfe clearly drew on multiple musical traditions—Indigenous, African, Scottish, English, Irish, Welsh, French—to create what we found to be a moving as well as historically resonant score. But the music was also an exciting and very contemporary hybrid mashup of past and present in its rhythms, harmonies, and melodies. Similarly, Clarke may have been adapting a nineteenth-century verse play, but that work's historically conditioned linguistic decorum was replaced by the librettist's distinctive poetic diction, which ranged from the brutal and frank to the biblical and soaring. Graphic descriptions and powerfully enacted depictions of violence— especially of a rape—replaced the offstage action of the adapted text.

In the opera version of the historical story, the rapist-slaveowner, Francis Chancy, is murdered by his daughter, Beatrice and her lover, aided and abetted by his wife/her stepmother; for this, they are executed by the state. This was yet another way in which the opera seemed to us to be invoking the postmodern and even postcolonial zeitgeist, for it recounted not the customary history of victors and oppressors, but rather that of the subaltern oppressed who seek to throw off their burden. This tells the history of Beatrice and the slaves of the place ironically known in the opera as "Paradise," and if Beatrice is hanged, it is because she has taken matters into her own hands to cast off the burden of slavery.

The libretto of *Beatrice Chancy* is dedicated to Marie-Josèphe Angélique* and Lydia Jackson, two enslaved and abused Canadian women who, like Clarke's Beatrice, however, had agency, as we say today. Slavery historically destroyed kinship relations, as Toni Morrison so powerfully taught us in novels like *Beloved* (1987). Perhaps that is why the crimes presented here are crimes against kin: parricide and incest. But they are also the historical crimes of the "true story" on which the work was based, of course. In adapting Shelley's version of that historical account, as inflected through slave narratives, Clarke (as he explains in this volume) was deploying history not only to inaugurate his own act of memory (and thus ours), but also to offer a new interpretation of what tyranny can mean in a different historical context, one closer to home. Or, as Maureen Moynagh asks, "What better way to make the point that slavery was an intimate part of the formation of Canada (however much myths of nation have sought to forget it) than to represent it as a family affair?"**

Opera may not at first seem like the most obvious art form in which to engage postmodern or postcolonial history with didactic intent. Nevertheless, it is its very stylization, its conventions, and its manifest artifice (as sung drama) that effectively work to make us all self-conscious and self-aware; it is what makes us stand back and question what history we remember and what we choose to elide, whose history we tell or do not, and to what end. Here, the true story on which *Beatrice Chancy* is based ends up reminding us of the painful part of our history that is Canadian slavery. And it is the heightened emotions that music brings to the words and drama that make this something we *feel* as well as intellectually understand.

---

* She is also the subject of Lorena Gale's popular play *Angélique* (Playwrights Canada Press, 2000).

** "'This history's only good for anger': Gender and Cultural Memory in *Beatrice Chancy*," *Signs*, 28.1 (September 2002): 110.

Finding Beatrice Chancy: *Excursions and Incursions*

George Elliott Clarke, Librettist

When James Rolfe approached me in the summer of 1992 to author him a libretto (Italian for "little book"), I'd no idea what one was. I just thought it'd be an interesting form to try. It is true, though, that I grew up with lots of opera—classical, Italian opera—in my boyhood home, for my father, Bill Clarke, loved classical music as much as my mom, Geraldine, loved rhythm and blues—or soul. Always, when Bill commandeered the stereo, we got to hear soundtracks, such as the Italian-American Henry Mancini (*Breakfast at Tiffany's* [1961] and *The Pink Panther* [1963]). Even so, his first love was classical, and so we heard Giacomo Puccini's *Madame Butterfly* (1904), but also Giuseppe Verdi's *Aïda* (1871). Still, I'd never really given much thought to opera—or their libretti, even though my accession to poetry had begun with my fancying myself a songwriter, beginning at age fifteen, when I knelt on the floor beside my bed (to use it as a desk), took up some coloured markers, opened a scribbler, and, as of Dominion Day 1975, began to write four songs per day. (I knew they were songs because they rhymed.) Then, to improve as a songwriter, and following the advice of various manuals, I began to study Bob Dylan, which led me to the blues and to Rimbaud and to Dylan Thomas and Baudelaire and Robert Hayden and LeRoi Jones (Amiri Baraka) and Gwendolyn Brooks, and so on. So that, by sixteen, I was trying to be a poet and was writing four poems per day. (I knew they were poems because they didn't rhyme.) Also at that age, while sitting in the back seat as my mother drove me to my Halifax high school, in fall 1976, I was leafing through *Poetry of Our Time* (1965), a schoolbook anthology, edited by Louis Dudek, when I came upon a translation, by Ezra Pound, from Japanese (but of a Chinese poet), namely, "The

River-Merchant's Wife: A Letter" (1915). The anglicized, Oriental poem seemed to exude the pathos of Mississippi blues. I knew I wanted to write just as raw and fresh and painful a poetic. The next sixteen years saw me work to achieve such a style. So I was most attuned to works that were visceral, earthy, sweat-producing. I knew, then, in 1992, that my libretto for Rolfe would be open to bodily fluids smacking folks full in the face—right in the midst of an aria.

The model for my libretto confirmed the poetics. I'd decided to adapt, for my purposes, Percy Bysshe Shelley's "closet" tragedy, *The Cenci* (1819), which treats the history of the actual noble clan, whose family members were practically exterminated by execution in September 1599 in Rome. I read it as preparation for my comprehensive examination in English literature as a doctoral candidate at Queen's University, of Kingston, Ontario. The play is atypical in Shelley's oeuvre. He is a poet of philosophy and fancy, airy thoughts and radical dreams. But, in this piece, he writes of blood, gold, guts, and dirt, of crime and sin, of drunkenness and homicide and sadism. (In a published article I argue that Shelley's play is actually a displaced slave narrative.*) The story—utterly unignorable—that Francesco Cenci raped his daughter, Beatrice, who then engineered his murder, and who is then, in turn, tortured and beheaded, together with her elder brother and her stepmother, is a tale that has enthralled centuries of writers and artists. When I read this play, which is so Gothic as to be a *giallo* (in fact, *gialli* director Lucio Fulci made a 1969 film of the story), I knew that I would fashion my own work out of it. I also knew, immediately, that my Beatrice would be mixed race, the slave daughter of her rapist-father and master, and that she would be executed after stabbing him to death and thus, simultaneously, liberating other slaves. The story would be transferred from Papal-State Italy to colonial Nova Scotia, the year being 1801.

Following Shelley's lead, my libretto had to be gutsy and gritty, hellish and highfalutin, dirty and dreamy. To flesh out the Italian descent of the work, back to Dante's *La Divina Commedia* and the *Inferno* I went, rereading it in multiple translations. US poet Henry Wadsworth Longfellow had the most ethereal account (1867), but the earthiest was John Ciardi's (1954), while Daniel Halpern's edition

---

* George Elliott Clarke, "Racing Shelley, or Reading *The Cenci* as a Gothic Slave Narrative," *European Romantic Review*, 11.2 (Spring 2000): 168–85.

(1993) featured translations by twenty living, twentieth-century poets. Yet, the English-language poet whose Italian predilections were particularly poignant for me was none other than Pound, who made homes in Rapallo and Venezia, and wrote his most emotive and intellectual work, "The Pisan Cantos," while in detention at Pisa, due to his having made pro-fascist propaganda speeches during the Second World War. *The Cantos*—his epic poem, begun in the 1920s and "completed" in 1966—is a partial attempt to update Dante by locating "Hell" in the wars inspired (as he believed) by bankers and arms merchants, and "Paradise" in "Renaissance" movements in Italy, China, and the early American Republic, or wherever art and culture won a measure of real public-or-private support and poets could be governors. In any event, Pound's Italian biography—the light and water and marble of Venezia—has been inspirational for me, and I have never failed to visit his grave on Cimitero di San Michele, just as I have never failed to critique his politics—to chastise his ghost, as it were. In writing *Beatrice Chancy*, I reread *The Cantos* annually, 1994 to 1999.

Yet, I also took to Italian opera and the *bel canto* tradition. I bought CDs of Verdi's *Macbeth* (1847), *Rigoletto* (1851), and *Otello* (1887) and Puccini's *Madame Butterfly* (1904) and *Manon Lescaut* (1893). I studied *Italian Art Song* (1989) by Ruth C. Lakeway and Robert C. White, Jr., but also, later, *Opera: Desire, Disease, Death* (1996), a study of opera and medicine authored by Linda Hutcheon and Michael Hutcheon. These works all helped me to pitch my "Africadian" diction, my knowledge of African-American (and colonial Canadian) slavery and *resistance* to same, into something like essential, Italo-operatic registers.

It was the manuscript for *Beatrice Chancy* that transported me to Italy, for the first time, in October 1998. New York City's Rockefeller Foundation deemed its completion worthy of a month-long stay for me at the paradisaical Villa Serbelloni at Bellagio. I prefaced my stay there by visiting Venezia for a week. As an introduction to Italy, it was—pun intended—"transporting." But grime and grit was Milano, while murk and miasma demarcated Venezia. Italy yields dramatic extremes— magnificence and squalor, both with classical economy and surreal romanticism. Its light is brilliant; its dark is opaque. I more or less did finish the libretto for *Beatrice Chancy* in Bellagio, on Lago Como, even while music from a summer workshop production of the opera played out of CBC Radio, far away from me, across the Atlantic.

But I also need to refer to the other major cultural tradition that was mine to draw on at will: the gutbucket and guttural, the blues and the spirituals, the narratives of slave insurrection and the annals of dastardly "massas" and their Gothic plantations. Along with McLaurin's recherché biography of a master-murdering rape victim, namely, *Celia, A Slave* (1991), I could reference works like *Bullwhip Days: The Slaves Remember, An Oral History* (1988), edited by James Mellon. In the latter work, any illusions about Dixie having been a pastoral Eden are shattered utterly via the testimony of ex-slaves, then very elderly, recorded in the 1930s by field researchers employed by the US Works Progress Administration. Frank and down-to-earth, their recorded memories include four-letter words used as festively as the n-word—and often in conjunction—along with the application of bullwhip and/or branding iron. These works informed me that, as much as *Beatrice Chancy* is a work of semi-borrowed imagination (from Shelley), the miseries and *violences** depicted in it, the curt and graphic and even vicious diction, all come out of actual history, including that of the Annapolis Valley in colonial Nova Scotia. Indeed, I recall reading, in some work of amateur, rural history, the tradition that a slave woman murdered her master because he had taken to playing William Tell with *their* children. Her neat administration of poison served to end the offender's hillbilly version of Russian roulette. And, according to that now-by-me-forgotten historian, this particular slave woman escaped hanging . . .

---

* See John Fraser, *Violence in the Arts* (Cambridge UP, 1974). Note also that the section divisions in *Beatrice Chancy* (1999), the verse-tragedy, are named for Fraser's chapter titles.

A Glance Back at Beatrice Chancy

James Rolfe, Composer

Looking back twenty years at *Beatrice Chancy*, what do I notice?

First of all, the story. When George transposed the tragedy of the Cenci family from Rome *circa* 1600 to Nova Scotia *circa* 1800, he grafted a classical tragedy with a tight structure and high stakes onto a little-known chapter of Canadian history—slavery in Nova Scotia. A cauldron bubbling with murder, torture, rape, racism, sexism, religion, money, and power was conjured up: a rich and nourishing operatic stew.

Sex and race were the hottest topics; they still are. With regard to sex, Beatrice overthrew both her oppressor and the operatic tradition of heroine-as-victim when she killed her father. Regarding race, the stories of African Canadians—and of Canadian slavery in particular—were rarely seen in theatre, and never in opera. This silence was shattered in Act One by the cries of Lead, a black slave being tortured by his white master Chancy. Confronted with the ugly truths of slavery and white supremacy in Canada, audiences seemed to have had the breath knocked out of them—only to have it knocked out again in Act Two, when Beatrice is raped by her own father and master, the same Chancy.

Next, I notice an exuberantly diverse musical landscape. Records of musical life in Nova Scotia at the dawn of the nineteenth century are scant, especially for the African Canadian population, but there are some evocative traces. For example, half the fiddlers in the Annapolis Valley were known to be African Canadian; this must have inflected the performance of traditional fiddle tunes. We also know that many cultures lived side by side: English, Scottish, Irish, African, American, French, Mi'kmaq, Welsh, and others. I ran with these clues, dreaming up dishes

fragrant with musical miscegenation. The 1990s were a time of burgeoning awareness of musical diversity: world music, ancient music, contemporary music, and
all kinds of popular music were disseminated through campus radio and new
and reissued recordings, radically broadening our collective musical imagination.
I loved and devoured it all: funk, reggae, medieval, avant-garde, hip hop, rap,
flamenco, fiddling—all fed into my imagination and were transformed into the
music of *Beatrice Chancy*. (I was hardly the first classical composer to do so: my
antecedents include people like Charles Ives and my own teacher John Beckwith,
with their use of North American hymn tunes and other historical popular music.)
It was exciting to throw open the doors to classical music and opera and let in
something fresh.

For me, something fresh was rhythm. Many other musical traditions are far
more rhythmically sophisticated and engaging than classical music; why not liven
things up a bit? And an opera about African Canadians that wasn't rhythmically
lively would be both a betrayal and a drag. In particular, as a white composer, I
felt a duty to get out of the way of the characters and "pass the mic," to let them
speak in their own voices, not with classical or operatic accents. The story and
characters of this opera lay well outside the mainstream; "same old same old"
would not cut it.

In light of the current availability of every imaginable genre and era of music
through the Internet, this approach hardly seems radical today. Yet at the time, I
felt perplexed and self-conscious about it. Opera was a medium well outside my
comfort zone, and I had never written music that sounded like this. My music
had tended to be stylistically unified, atonal, spiky. Some of my listeners were
baffled or alienated by this apparent change of direction, and I shared their discomfort. It took me years to accept my compositional choices as being artistically
valid. Then there was the story itself, which unleashed a power and charisma I'd
never experienced. The characters were larger than life and a bit out of control.
Audiences took sides, breathed and lived and died with them. I was swept aside
by what I thought was my own creation, but turned out to be much larger than
myself, larger than I could have imagined.

Finally, I notice English. For singers, English is full of booby traps. Italian,
the operatic mother tongue, has its round open vowels and smooth classical
metres; but English brims with awkward clumps of consonants, closed vowels

and diphthongs, asymmetrical rhythms, and blank verse. I felt strongly that the words should be as comprehensible and immediate as possible, especially as live surtitles were not usual at the time; it was essential to give back to these characters the voices which oppression had stolen from them. My job was to make the words sing, and to make them clear, starting with a rhythmically lively and natural setting. George's libretto already had a good deal of rhythmic life; I added my own rhythmic styles and structures to heighten pacing and characterization—slow and considered for the older preacher Moses, for example, and faster and more volatile for the young firebrand Lead.

How have the reception and context of this opera changed since its 1998 premiere? We still struggle with race and sex. Conversations about issues such as privilege, cultural genocide, reconciliation, and reparations have migrated from the margins into the mainstream. Our ears are more open to hearing non-classical music within a classical context, and less concerned with the purity of a work's operatic pedigree, or of distinctions between opera and music theatre. In these respects, *Beatrice Chancy* looked ahead, and perhaps even blazed a trail. As a first opera, and one with such an explosive story, it was an enormous risk for George and myself. Fortunately, we didn't realize that, or didn't care, and just followed our noses, unselfconscious about the operatic form, about what we should or shouldn't do. Twenty years on, this is perhaps the most precious memory of all.

Beatrice Chancy *Costume Design*

Diana Smith, Costume Designer

Most of my design work experience has been decidedly unconventional, having
collaborated for many years with Jerrard Smith and various directors on R. Murray
Schafer's *Patria* series of music theatre productions. I have designed costumes
for several dance and theatre pieces, including, of course, *Beatrice Chancy* but
my design approach has been largely shaped by my experiences working with
Schafer. This has meant working both indoors and outdoors, for both ambulatory
and stationery audiences and, when indoors, in mostly non-purpose-built venues
(e.g., Toronto's Union Station, the Ontario Science Centre). As a result, I've always
considered each production individually, rather than as belonging to a category
such as opera, dance, or play, especially as Schafer's works can include any or all
of professional and amateur child and adult singers, musicians, dancers, actors,

puppeteers (and puppets), and so on, and even audience and crew members, so I had to be ready for anything.

Coming to *Beatrice Chancy*, I had the script/libretto, music, discussions with the director and the other designers, historical period, the nature of the characters and their relationships, practical requirements of the cast—all elements I would have to consider in any production. Specific to *Beatrice Chancy* was the use of the Music Gallery space, which included a long alley-like stage with audience and costumed musicians on either side. This meant that performers would be seen from relatively close up so costuming, makeup, and hair had to be quite detailed and natural, not exaggerated as would be needed on a proscenium stage where the audience is seated at a distance. I think my happiest memory from *Beatrice Chancy* is being complimented on Measha (then Gosman) Brueggergosman's costume by her mother (who had always made her daughter's concert dresses).

Beatrice Chancy premiered at the Music Gallery, Toronto, from June 18 to 20, 1998, with the following cast and creative team:

Beatrice: Measha Brueggergosman
Francis: Gregory Dahl
Lustra: Lori Klassen
Lead: Nigel Smith
Deal: Lisa Lindo
Fr. Moses: Marcus Nance

Librettist: George Elliott Clarke
Composer: James Rolfe
Director: Michael Cavanagh
Music Director: Dáirine Ní Mheadhra and John Hess
Set and Costume Design: Jerrard and Diana Smith
Lighting Design: Paul Mathiesen
Producer: Leslie Lester
Stage Manager: Lesley Arbarquez Bradley

Characters

Beatrice Chancy, a slave

Francis Chancy, her master and father

Lustra Chancy, his wife and stepmother to Beatrice

Reverend Richard Moses, an enslaved Baptist

Deal, a house slave

Lead, a field slave and beloved of Beatrice

Slaves

Act One

Scene I

A plantation in the Annapolis Valley of Nova Scotia, ca. 1801. A mansion in the background; fields, gardens, and orchards flourish.

Carrying fiery, pitch-pine lamps, SLAVES *gather and circle counter-clockwise, leaping, shouting . . .*

MOSES: Massa Winter be dyin' now—
Our icy chains'll soon be no mo'.
Ain't sweet spring on th' horizon?
Ain't we gonna dwell in Zion?
Apple branches blaze with blossoms,
North wind burns fresh as freedom.
O sweet Jesus, won't we be free?
O King Jesus, won't we be free?
O King Jesus . . .

LEAD cutting in and picking up the tempo.

LEAD: One of these days
When the moon's like blood,
And the stars go dark,
We gonna be free—
Gotta be free—
Brothers, sisters,
Sisters, brothers:

Free like Moses,
Free like David.
If we kill Pharaoh,
If we kill Goliath,
Gonna be free.

DEAL: Praise the Lord!
Don't contradict
Almighty God—
His power and His glory.

LEAD: *(aside)* Power? We ain't got no power.

DEAL: The slayer of evil—
Almighty God—
Who rents us breath . . .

LEAD: He can stop mine right now:
This here life ain't no life—
We crawl around in shit
Like white maggots,
Smilin' as they whip us,
Laughin' as our flesh bleeds!

MOSES: I pray that God's gonna rain down fire
One of these days, hallelujah!

DEAL: Hallelujah!

LEAD: Why we always makin' God feel
Downright broken, pissed off, an' tired
With our sorry-assed, po'-mouthed prayers?
If prayer could bust iron, we'd be free.

DEAL: Quit howlin' yo' bo'n stupidness, Lead,
'Fo' ya make all 'em white pistols go off.

LEAD: Deal, I bet you's an expert on white pistols—
Ain't you felt 'em go off inside you mo' than once?

DEAL: When ya sees a cucumber, Lead,
I knows ya mus' be jealous!
At least I ain't no white folks's monkey,
Soaked in rum and nutmeg . . .

LEAD: Stuff yo' stinkin' mouth!

DEAL: Why don't you worry 'bout yo' li'l half-white gal?

LEAD: I'll kick yo' black ass till the colour come off.

MOSES: Long as we fightin' each other,
We ain't fightin' the jailer—
The folks who got us in chains.

DEAL: Amen, Moses!

MOSES & DEAL: Think on sweetness, Lead:
After three long years,
She'll be here, be yours, tonight!

LEAD: How can I love, how can I love,
When ma heart be all in chains?

DEAL, MOSES, & LEAD: How can I love, how can I love,
When ma heart's all in chains?

Enter LUSTRA.

LUSTRA: Why are you just gargoyling about?
You should be working! You should be sober!
Deal, can't you and these other chits
Try decent clothes?

DEAL: Give us decency, ma'am, and we'll wear it.

LEAD: *(aside)* Give us honour, else we take it.

LUSTRA: Quit your sassing! Do what I say.
Master Chancy tramps home—
He'll expect his feast table china'd
And laden with pig and liquor.

SLAVES: God ain't gone to some distant star.
Uh-uh, bruthuhs, uh-uh, sistuhs.
He's in the fields where us toilers are.
Uh-uh, bruthuhs, uh-uh, sistuhs.

Exit SLAVES, singing.

LUSTRA: My husband's only daughter,
His precious coloured girl steals home.
She mirrors a lyric of light
Upon a July-bright river.
To the convent I slipped Beatrice
To slip my husband's eyes from visions
Of her mother. But I've failed:
Our love is slipping; we're falling.

Enter BEATRICE.

BEATRICE: Dear Lustra, my second mother,
I joy to be home again,
After three long years . . .
How I longed to eye dark-passioned clouds
Sugar snow, rain, over the river.

LUSTRA: Your presents are so, so lovely!
And how lovely, how lovely you've grown—
So clear your sable mama's girl.

BEATRICE: I loved her well, before she . . .
How's our lord, how's my father?

LUSTRA: He's . . . he's . . .

BEATRICE: He's what?

LUSTRA: I can't say; shame cuts my tongue.

BEATRICE: Tell me, tell me! I'm your daughter.

A bell shivers the dusk.

LUSTRA: Our lord staggers home from the woods!
I must go to him.

LUSTRA exits quickly.

BEATRICE: Our Father who art in Heaven . . .
Why is dark fear shaking my breath?
Why is white pain sobbing through my bones?

For three long, empty years
I stooped in a nun's cell,
Weeping out my stark loneliness, hating
The strange city, warships huddled
Together in the harbour, mills
Fuming disease, fomenting war,
Markets splitting mother and child . . .
Where are you? I need you.

O Lead, O my love,
If we should fail, if our love should fail,
Air will sour, rain spill dull, language fold,
Sun ruin, destroy, what's left of me.
I hardly learned to say your name
Before I was gone.
I hardly learned to feel your love—
Then I was alone.

Crucified Christ, I call on Thee—
For succour and for sufferance.
Save my father from his foul sins,
Forgive my silly, foolish sins,
Teach me pity, teach me patience,
Sweet Lord, Amen.

    Enter LEAD.

LEAD: I wanna talk ta ya
By the mauve river
    Under the plum sky.

Walk by mauve water
    Near the orchard
        Under apple blossoms.

Under the plum sky,
   By the mauve river,
      I wanna talk ta ya.

BEATRICE: Talk.

LEAD: Have ya been good?

BEATRICE: Why need you ask?

LEAD: You remember what we was?

BEATRICE: Rubies . . . berries . . . buried rubies . . .

LEAD: I'm serious!

BEATRICE: So am I!

LEAD: Jes' tell me if our time be ruins!

BEATRICE: My love, you wrote me such letters,
Such raw, hurting words,
But your letters, your verses,
Were second scripture to me.
They still flower in me.

LEAD: Someone be ripe as blackberries
An' pretty as calico lace.
Your skin's like roses sunk in cream,
Milky as sheer silk rained upon.

LEAD & BEATRICE: Everything's beautiful with you.
Let's run away, let's marry, we'll be free.
Miz. Fine Brown / My sweet Lead, be my

woman/man,
We'll be as two lovers—we'll be free.

LEAD: Black pearl.
You're a dark, black pearl
Black strawberry, succulent to the eye.

BEATRICE: "Then the tree spoke unto her
And it began to bend,
Saying, 'Mary, gather cherries
From the uttermost limb,'
Saying, 'Mary, gather cherries
From the uttermost limb.'"

The amadoux lock again. A violet bell bleeds in the white wind.

Scene 2

A dining room in the mansion. LUSTRA, DEAL, LEAD, *and* MOSES.

LUSTRA: I wish he'd quit this slavery business.
It corrupts us.

SLAVES: Chancy's got everything but a son:
The Church'll grab his fortune when he dies.
He's drowning himself in bad rum and dirty thighs.

Enter Francis CHANCY.

CHANCY: My wife, my family, forget
Your soft troubles, your pains.
Make those fiddles quarrel like gulls,
Break out steps that stamp like rain,

Lori Klassen, Marcus Nance, Nigel Smith, and Gregory Dahl.
Photo by Guntar Kravis.

Sing with voices like wine

Pissing from a fat stomach,

Jupe and swing and whoop!

Now that daylight-down

And my daughter's come.

SLAVES: Ain't gonna grieve, ain't gonna grieve,

Ain't gonna grieve no mo',

Ain't gonna grieve, mistuh massa,

'Cos I found my Lord.

CHANCY & LUSTRA: Here's Grand Pré wine,

Annapolis cheese,

Windsor butter,

Madeira Portuguese;

Jamaican dark rum,

Adam's pale ale,

Pickled melon, chicken,

Biscuits, pigtails;

Oysters, scallops,

Gaspereaux, an' clams,
Wild blueberries,
Sides of ham;
Black coffee, sweet cream,
Chokecherry pie,
A good kick of whisky,
Newfie screech, rye.

LEAD: Grasshopper settin' on a sweet p'tato vine,
Sweet p'tato vine, sweet p'tato vine,
Turkey gobbler snuck up right behin',
An' snapped 'im off a sweet p'tato vine.

Irritated, CHANCY *cuts* LEAD *short. Enter* BEATRICE.

ALL: Welcome home, Beatrice, welcome home.

CHANCY: Beatrice, my daughter,
Come here, be closer.

ALL: Our vanilla, country Helen,
No older than sixteen Aprils.

CHANCY: I sent you to Halifax
To make you more like us—
Wise, modern, beautiful.

BEATRICE: *(joining* CHANCY*)* Our father, Lustra, and all my folk,
I love you through and through.
If I should miss Heaven when I die,
This memory will be my Zion.

ALL: Was ever a lass so lovely
As Annapolisa Beatrice?

CHANCY: Your gold-skinned beauty ravishes night;
You're glitteringly pure—like bright steel.

BEATRICE: Father, why don't we say a prayer?

CHANCY: To see you standing here,
You'd almost forget your tropic
Mammy was too my sable slave,
Darkest buckwheat honey, I loved
To spread upon my sheets.

BEATRICE: Sir, save such language for your wife.

LUSTRA: *(aside)* His softness for her mother stabs me:
I feel a knife cut through my throat.

BEATRICE: Father, your wife blanches with shame.

CHANCY: It shames me this minx is barren.
Where's my son, my son,
The son who'd gild my days?

LUSTRA: I pray that God will open my womb one day.

CHANCY: With what? A key? A knife?

LUSTRA: My darling husband, hear! Beatrice
Wants to be an honest man's beloved . . .

CHANCY: What's this, Beatrice? What news is this?

BEATRICE: Father, I was tutored well to be
A faithful wife; I am in love.

CHANCY: And who is this man you want to love?

LEAD steps forward meaningfully.

(hissing) What? You, you love this slave?

BEATRICE: I've grown a woman, and do love this man.

CHANCY: And I thought you thought
Yourself to be lucky to be partially my flesh,
Not some slut, so low as to go lusting
For the pawings of some half-ape.

BEATRICE: Father, you don't know what you're saying.

CHANCY: You'll not mock my love
By embracing such filthy,
Tar-plastered dung!
You're nobody's slave but mine!

LUSTRA: Chancy, she's your own daughter!
Please don't jest about such things.

CHANCY: No, I don't jest about such things—
For slaves and women are things;
And you and Beatrice have things
Not made for thick, black things.

BEATRICE: Father! You've drunk too much!

CHANCY: You've got too much mouth.

*CHANCY seizes BEATRICE. LEAD bolts forward. CHANCY draws his pistol
and knocks out LEAD with its butt.*

BEATRICE: Lead! Lead!

CHANCY: So you're the cur my daughter loves?
I'll iron, collar, you with chains!

BEATRICE: You'll not do it!

CHANCY: Silence, you whore!

> *Slaps* BEATRICE *hard, and thrusts her behind an adjoining door, locking it.*

You pickaninnies—back,
Back to your stinking huts!

> *SLAVES conceal themselves onstage.* LEAD *is now bound with chains.*

LUSTRA: She meant nothing, my lord . . .

CHANCY: Nothing is what you mean to me!

> *Shoved out by* CHANCY, LUSTRA *exits.* LEAD *awakens.*

LEAD: Where's Bea? What's—

CHANCY: Close your black mouth, you crumb of shit!

> CHANCY *lights a cigar, then draws it close to* LEAD'S *face.*

You can crave what you'll never have—
My hot, tight, sweet, nigger ginger.
But I'll decide on love and death—
And on pain—which is all you're worth.
'Tis a sickness to be black.

If I loved you. I'd die.
So I must hate you.
Good night, good night.

> *Exit* CHANCY. MOSES *and* DEAL *come out of hiding, and try to comfort* LEAD.

MOSES & DEAL: I must walk my lonesome valley,
I got to walk it for myself.
Nobody else can walk it for me:
I got to walk it for myself.

Act Two

Scene I

CHANCY's library. BEATRICE waits, locked inside, her gown tattered.

BEATRICE: Lord, don't abandon me. Help me! Save me!
Why does flesh that made me hate me?
What have I done? What is my sin?
Oh, Father, who art in Heaven,
Deliver me from my father.

Knocking.

Who's there?

LUSTRA: Our master has left a bit of food.
Come, eat.

BEATRICE: Where's Lead? Does my love still breathe?

LUSTRA: He breathes yet.

BEATRICE: But—

LUSTRA: But Chancy whipped Lead till his back was red,
Then lavished saltwater on his wounds.
Lead howled, howled enough to burst his ribs.

BEATRICE: God hates our planet
And all who creep beneath His gaze.

LUSTRA: Like all mulattas, you speak too hotly.

BEATRICE: Would my words scorch! My singed skin
Tells white men I'm their whore,
Tells black men I'm their serf.
I'm shunned by white women and bludgeoned
By my sisters' blunt talk and hard looks.
They pick me apart.

LUSTRA: You think yourself a martyr, Beatrice,
But your passion's unruly.

BEATRICE: Lustra, you treat me like some pet,
Stroking my smooth hair, my light skin.
But I am the colour of trials.
My sufferings sue my mother's,
Who worked her gold flesh to white bone,
Whose sweat nourished these orchards
Where apples flourished upon her pain.

LUSTRA: She was a born strumpet!

BEATRICE: Jealous you were of her! Jealous,
So jealous you bolted her outdoors
One dark, frigid December dawn!

LUSTRA: Don't blame me if she was almost naked!
She had no business in my bed.

BEATRICE: It was your beloved husband
Who brought her to your bed.

LUSTRA: A wife has rights!

BEATRICE: Did she have rights?

LUSTRA: I didn't know convents were schooling
Defiant trollops nowadays.

BEATRICE: They haven't changed since you were there.

LUSTRA: Say what you like! To men, we're all slaves.
Often, I feel I'm no true wife,
Just the queen slave of his harem.
My chains are invisible and silent,
But they weight me, they press me down.

BEATRICE: Then he's the same?

LUSTRA: The very same:
He lunges after sin, pursues it.
He sluices down to cesspools of lust
Seizes pleasure from lush, open females,
Whose only perfume is sweat of manure,
Later to bed, lugs their smell—
An aroma of saffron that hennas everything
So I can hardly breathe—
The moaning scents of coloured women—
Like pungent, burnt orange,
The heavy, smoked taste of despair.

BEATRICE: I hurt for you, Lustra.
Your sorrows wound my heart.

LUSTRA: It's women's fate to endure
Dishonour, injury, pain.

BEATRICE: Ask Governor Wentworth to send troops
To end our daily crucifixions.

LUSTRA: Practice mercy, Beatrice, and forgive him.

BEATRICE: Let's ask that Wentworth send troops
To strengthen our mercy with steel.

LUSTRA: Depend on English graciousness,
Our English justice.

BEATRICE: Depend on a few good soldiers.

Scene 2

Night. LEAD and MOSES conspire.

LEAD: The two-legged dog comes, pantin',
Smellin' of piss and bad wine,
Sniffin' up our mamas'
An' our sistuhs' dresses.
Our fathers be dead in the grass;
Our children be bones in the grass.
Our people be driven and whipped.
Our saviours be beaten and burnt.
I'll take no mo' shit! No mo' shit!

MOSES: Easy, Lead, easy. God's justice will be done.

LEAD: We're far from justice here, Moses.
Massa whipped me like I was a horse.
My wounds hurt; so must he.
Either we'll die first or he will.

MOSES: Boy, I tell ya, put your anger to flight.
God resents our puny human rage!
Why don't you watch, wait, and run away
With sweet Beatrice?

LEAD: Hell, I can't wait!
I had a dream of vengeance,
A black man with an axe, cleaving
White bodies in God's holy name.
Soon, soon, a black army will march—
And cut and stab and burn—
And make white Nova Scotia howl.

MOSES: Vengeance is mine, saith the Lord.

Scene 3

A chapel. BEATRICE *is kneeling in silent prayer.* CHANCY *enters silently.*

CHANCY: *(aside)* God, Beatrice, if you only knew how much I suffer!

Your perfume on my face
Is like fallen apples in an autumn grove.
I'll speak so lightly,
My words'll touch you like dew
Brushing grass at dawn.

I'll discover your verse—
Wet, shining, under a black bush,
Black fragrance in a black vase—
Sex instigating the black rasp of knives—
To be darkly entered, the vicious prize,
Sap-eating triangle, housing noxious buzzing of incestuous
Insects busy at sex.

Oh God, if you exist . . . Oh God!

BEATRICE: Father!

CHANCY: My beloved girl, I want to show
My love, prove my love under God.
We're one flesh, and should stay one flesh.

BEATRICE: I've prayed, but never thought
I'd hear your friendly words again.

CHANCY: I hate everything, everything in this world, but you.

BEATRICE: God loves us, father.

CHANCY: Yet, you must obey me.

BEATRICE: Yes, but never to sin.

CHANCY: To kiss your father's no sin.

BEATRICE: On the cheek, no.

CHANCY: On the lips, dear.

BEATRICE: When I was a girl, I'd do so.
Now I've grown a woman, I shan't.

CHANCY: A Christian kiss is all I ask—
To prove you love me, Beatrice, as you claim.

BEATRICE: Forgive me, father. I knew not your meaning.

BEATRICE hesitates, then kisses CHANCY lightly on his cheek.

CHANCY: I saw you, crushing plump
Raspberries against your lips, juice
Splashing red 'gainst your creamy skin.
Desire cut me to the bone; I still bleed.

CHANCY pulls BEATRICE against him by her long hair.

BEATRICE: Stop hurting me!

CHANCY: You hurt me more:
The sharp scent of your virtue,
Wafting from your breasts and hair—
It inflames me, it burns my eyes.

BEATRICE: If your eye hurts thee, pluck it out,
Lest your whole body burn in judgement!

CHANCY: Ah, Beatrice, you will lead me to Heaven.

BEATRICE: What've I done to you?
I was born—that's your fault.

CHANCY: Everything that comes puking
From between a woman's legs is corrupt.

BEATRICE: Then, I'm nothing: Drop me, toss me aside.
I've done nothing. Nothing! I'm innocent!

CHANCY: Your innocence is your pride—
And pride rideth before a fall!

BEATRICE: What is my great crime? That I'm a woman?
That I'm black?

CHANCY: Your lean thighs justify your slavery.

She thrusts a nearby candle into his face. He bats it away. Screaming, struggling.

Act Three

Scene I

A sitting room. BEATRICE *staggers, bedraggled.* LUSTRA *shadows her.*

BEATRICE: *(wildly)* I was black, but comely. Don't look
Upon me: this flesh is dying.
I'm perfumed, bleeding carrion,
My eyes weep pus, my womb's sopping
With tears; I can hardly walk: the floors
Are tizzy, the sick walls tumbling,
Crumbling like proved lies.
His scythe went shick, shick, shick and cut
My flowers; they lay in heaps, murdered.

> *As if awakening, tearing her hair.*

His sweat infests my hair!
Get a knife! I'll hack it off!
He dug his lips upon my breasts:
Hand me a knife, I'll slice 'em off.
His breath panted upon my thighs—
Draw me a bath of boiling pitch.

LUSTRA & DEAL: O God!

BEATRICE: Ha! Don't dare utter that name:
I want nothing more to do with him!

I feared God. He feared nothing.
I knelt and prayed. He pried out my heart.
I built a home. He built a fire.
I was pure. He was powerful.

LUSTRA & DEAL: Peace, Beatrice!
I'll wash your wounds.

    BEATRICE smashes the water jug.

BEATRICE: Don't give me water;
I can't be cleansed!
His smell's still on me.
It'll take a razor
To cleanse the real filth—
My very skin!
Black, blackened, blacker . . .
All I gotta do is die.

DEAL: The sun burns us,
The rain soaks us.
Our bones bend in pain,
But don't break;
No, they don't break.

The dew chills us,
The wind shakes us.
Our eyes writhe in pain,
But don't weep;
No, they don't weep.

Scene 2

The garden. SLAVES, *sunflowers, stars, sparks.*

DEAL: Y'all shoulda seen how she looked—
Half-dead, hippling, bloody . . .
She be our sistuh—
What we gonna do now?

LEAD: Fix that bugger like a porcupine:
Catch 'im, burn 'im, skin 'im,
Gut 'im, boil 'im!

MOSES: Oh God, where are You? If You's tired
Of watchin' folk drag chains through fields,
Bustin' their teeth, gettin' crushed like mice,
O show Your face now!

LEAD: While we're bowed down, with our eyes shut in prayer,
White men taste our daughters and our women.

LEAD & DEAL: The white man's Heaven's the black man's Hell!

DEAL: They loves us, they say,
Yes, they say they loves us,
And beats and rapes and kills us to prove it.

LEAD & DEAL: The white man's Heaven's the black man's Hell!

LEAD: They tell us that we're animals;
They even tell us we're dirt.
Then, they tell us to be Christians.

LEAD & DEAL: The white man's Heaven's the black man's Hell!

DEAL: We own nothing but our breath—
Nothing but our breath—
An' massa even poison that.

LEAD & DEAL: The white man's Heaven's the black man's Hell!

Enter BEATRICE, *clapping, singing.*

BEATRICE: Jesus, lance down the valley,

CHORUS: Jerusalem! Jerusalem!

BEATRICE: Jesus, lance down the valley,
Lest the white man sell me,
For a sack of potatoes,
Prevent me to marry,
Steal me from Nova Scotia,
Slay me that awful day,
Slay me that awful day.

I had a dream,

CHORUS: Jerusalem!

BEATRICE: I had a dream,
And in this dream,
I saw Jesus,
I saw the Lord.
He was standing there,
That pale corpse.
I killed Jesus,

I stabbed him,
All bloody and red.
I stabbed Jesus—
Again and again and again . . .

MOSES: Murder's a sin, murder's a crime!

LEAD: He must die; I'll stab him!

DEAL: You bes' know what you're doin'.

MOSES: Bow down to God! You're too proud!

BEATRICE: Strength doesn't come from surrender.

MOSES: Fix your eyes on the dove!
You've worshipped the wrong God too long.
Fix your eyes on the dove!
You've mixed in hatred with love.

BEATRICE: If my words frighten you, I'll go.
But I'll not go on, appeasing his lust.

Exit BEATRICE. LEAD *follows quickly.* DEAL *lingers, then exits slowly.*

MOSES: May God grant mercy to you, Beatrice!
May God grant mercy to us all.

Can't move no stone
To let my saviour out.
Can't move your heart
If I start to doubt.

Can't find no love,
Gotta find my saviour first.
Can't get your love:
I damn well must be cursed!

Can't move no stone
To let my saviour out.
Can't move your heart
If I start to doubt.

Exit MOSES, *magisterially. Rain, thunder, lightning.*

Act Four

Scene I

CHANCY's study. He lies drunk and senseless—as if dead. LUSTRA sits nearby.

LUSTRA: I'm not myself, but a stranger,
Blundering in shadows.

Once this man loved me. I remember:
He'd seem gigantic, falling over me.
But his love quailed: snow wept for us.
Our love broke up like ice.

What happened to our love?
We forgot that kiss that drove us into the grass
So hard the stars fell.
Yet, I feel terrified and phoxed and wholeheartily in love with him;
And I hate him and want to kill him now; all at once.

What happened to our love?

Ah, tell me, Lord, tell me . . .

CHANCY stirs, awakening.

CHANCY: Who's there?

LUSTRA: I bring you roses, darling,
Rare roses from our garden . . .

CHANCY: These flowers gangle tawdry, mongrel,
Bad-tempered: pouting crimson
Snatches foaming slugs.
They smell like false women
Come from diseased gardens.

LUSTRA: Husband, they are only nature.

CHANCY: Nature is a gross machine of eating and fucking.
We hunger, thirst, sleep, wake,
Grey, wrinkle, palsy, die,
And have no vote in the business.

LUSTRA: You have a brain fever. Sleep, sleep.

CHANCY: A man knows death before he feels it,
He swears and drinks too much of abomination,
He giddies to bed, feeling cold, the cold of sheets,
The cold of moonlight executing his neck,
The cold of the woman beside him,
His love turned to ice, gelling his heart.

She's poisoned the stones of the earth against me.
I'm afraid of her forensic gaze,
Her scissored gash, negotiated,
Stabbed, yes, but stabbing back.
In smutting her, I smote myself.
Ah, but I love her, I love her,
Even down, even down, to death.

He falls unconscious.

LUSTRA: You frighten me, my husband.

Enter BEATRICE *and* LEAD, *bearing a dagger.*

BEATRICE: When he's dead, he'll sleep better.

LUSTRA: Hush! He's your father!

BEATRICE: Call him what you like.
I call him my raper.

LUSTRA: You don't know your father.
He kissed his cross at supper;
I believe he wants to turn to God.

BEATRICE: Yet, you begged to feed him opium'd tea.

LUSTRA: Husbands and wives share
  mysteries of forgiveness
I wouldn't expect you to understand.
That laudanum was a wife's last gift to
  her husband.

LEAD: Time for compassion's gone:
I'll massacre every piece of his white
  flesh.

LUSTRA: He was so, so, tender
  tonight
When we caressed, sweetly tender.
I almost fell in love again . . .

Measha Brueggergosman and Lisa Lindo.
Photo by Guntar Kravis.

BEATRICE: Damn your sissified dreams!
You've wifed him for the last time.
Be glad. Your divorce is nigh.

LEAD: Slave days is over!

LEAD approaches the sleeping CHANCY.

LUSTRA: Have you lost your compassion?

BEATRICE: He will be stabbed, then pitched down—
As if fallen—into an apple tree.

LUSTRA: I look at you and I see a gallows.
How can he die and we live?
Murder's unforgivable, Beatrice.

BEATRICE: To destroy love, that's unforgivable.

LEAD returns.

Huh? Done so soon?

LEAD: My fist was set to strike . . .
Then he started mutterin',
Moanin' to God in his sleep.
I figured he might wake . . .

LUSTRA: A sign! A sign! Don't death him now!

BEATRICE seizes the dagger from LEAD.

BEATRICE: Men are brave, women braver.
Slave days is over!

Lights down, except on LUSTRA. *She cowers.*

LUSTRA: O what have we done?

Lights up. BEATRICE *and* LEAD *are blood-spattered.*

Oh my sweet Lord, oh my husband!
My husband—he lies out there—barbed in branches.
Thanksgiving, and we've harvested
Just one fruit . . .

BEATRICE & LEAD: We're free! We're free.
We'll live no more like beasts.
We'll eat cornbread, gulp wine, and drink
As much light as our eyes can hold.

MOSES & DEAL: *(off)* Oh Mary, doncha weep, doncha moan:
Pharaoh's army got drowndèd.
Oh Mary, doncha weep.

LUSTRA: Why are they singing?
Some evil has happened.

LEAD: Who's there? Who is it?

He rushes out to see.

MOSES: Slavery and Chancy has died.
Hallelujah! Praise God!

DEAL: Mistah Chancy—he dead! Soldiers
Be draggin' Chance, scratched up, gory,
From a bust up apple tree.
Look t'yo'selves. Troops troop.

BEATRICE: Soldiers? We don't need their justice now.

LUSTRA: Why did you have to mangle an old man?

BEATRICE: Old man? He was a devil.

LUSTRA cries.

LEAD bursts in.

LEAD: The mouth of the Church Road
Is blocked up with white men.
Wentworth's soldiers be lookin'
To chain and hang us!

LUSTRA: Oh my God, oh my God!

BEATRICE: Let them hang me! I'll not cry out!
My whole life has been a prison.
Soon I will be free.

LEAD: Let me die like Samson!

LEAD dashes out. Shouts, screams, shots. He staggers back in, shot, dying.

BEATRICE: Lead! Oh my sweet Lead!

LEAD: Air will sour, rain spill dull,
Language fold, worms ruin
Destroy, what's left of me.

BEATRICE: Lead, Lead, if I have to destroy
This whole world to let you live . . .
To let love live, I'll do it!

A soldier blocks the entrance to the room.

Light darkens, rests, then flares again.

Scene 2

BEATRICE *and* LUSTRA *stand before two nooses. Ex-*SLAVES *gather around them.*

LUSTRA: Every bit of evil on earth
Has found its way to us.

BEATRICE *cradles her stepmother's head against her breasts.*

MOSES: Give us this day our daily bread
And our lost children
Crushed like eggshells.

DEAL: I'm chasin' the moon, chasin' the moon:
No more auction block for me.
Moonlight's branchin' through the trees:
Many thousand gone.

ALL: Is death the price of happiness?
Must we hate before we love?

A soldier binds the arms of LUSTRA *and* BEATRICE.

LUSTRA *weeps.* BEATRICE *comforts her.*

BEATRICE: Lustra, don't weep!
We'll breach Paradise today:
Tears'll be no more.

My kin, my people, lay us down
Under stars so thick, we breathe
Fresh grass and shout in tongues.
Remember that we craved only love,
That we were the light that blazed as love died.
Beloved Jesus, take my blood,
Use it all to scour away our sins.
Lustra, my brave kin, dearest Lead,
I love you, I love you, l love you.
I'll keep the warmth of our love
Deep in the tomb. It's all but all.

Drumrolls. Darkness. BEATRICE *and* LUSTRA *are hanged.*

Illumination again. MOSES *begins to sing, and is joined by the cast.*

ALL: Oh freedom, oh freedom,
Oh freedom over me.
And before I'd be a slave,
I'd be buried in my grave,
And go home to my Lord and be free.

Fin.

Dog Days

Based on the Short Story by
  Judy Budnitz

Libretto by Royce Vavrek

Composed by David T. Little

What Makes Us Human?

Beth Morrison, Producer

Dog Days is a powerful, pull-no-punches work of opera-theatre that premiered in 2012 in a production by my company, Beth Morrison Projects, and PEAK Performances at Montclair State University. With music by David T. Little and a libretto by Royce Vavrek, *Dog Days* became the breakout piece for this premiere team of opera authors. Indeed, it became the breakout piece for Beth Morrison Projects. Robert Woodruff, the director of the piece, served as a dramaturge in the creation of the work. His input as a veteran and iconic theatre-maker was invaluable in the shaping of the libretto.

Working from a short story by Judy Budnitz, Royce and team crafted a libretto that got to the heart of the question, "What makes us human?" Through interactions with the non-singing role of the dog, played brilliantly for the premiere by iconic NYC theatre artist John Kelly, the "humans" in the story are forced to face the darkest parts of their beings. Who is this man in a dog suit? What has made him drop out of the accepted societal structure to troll the piles of garbage behind the family's house on his hands and knees looking for food scraps? While we never receive the answer to that question, we learn quickly that the family is on the verge of starvation. There is a war being waged on American soil, likely WW III, and most people have moved to the coasts. But the father, Howard, keeps his family at home—somewhere in the Midwest—and battens down the hatches. His decision changes life as they know it forever. They only receive food in the form of government rations dropped from a helicopter that, over time, disappear. The family resort to eating grass and dandelions from the yard. Howard tries to hunt, but even the animals have disappeared.

Why won't Howard move the family? Why is he so stubborn? These questions are at the heart of the drama. Howard's refusal to make decisions that would improve things for his family leads to their demise. *Dog Days* was written well before Donald Trump's presidency was even an inkling of a possibility in the us. The lead-up to his election, however, saw many white, working-class men losing their jobs in factories: jobs that used to provide a stable income upon which families could be supported. As manufacturing increasingly moved to Mexico, China, and other countries where it was cheaper to create goods, more and more families lost their livelihood. Trump's promise to "Make America Great Again" spoke to these men, who pined for a time gone by. I believe that Howard is one of those men.

Howard's pride and his nostalgia for a previous time leads to his stubbornness and ultimately his downfall. In his daughter Lisa's first aria, she recounts the following:

My dad cries in his sleep.
I've never seen him
But I hear him.
Mom sleeps through everything,
So she doesn't notice.
But I do.

Gone are the nights he'd spend in front of the tv.
Hours and hours and hours when the plant closed down.
Mom nagged:
"Gonna get off the couch?"
But he knew it was no use.
So he sat staring off into space,
A wall of beer cans piling up at his feet.
His face big and red
His eyes like two lost polka dots.
His face big and red
And lost, and afraid.

Royce has set up a scenario where the men are portrayed as giving in to their basic instincts, but the women, particularly Mother and Lisa, demonstrate the heart of the piece. Mother sacrifices and lets the boys eat the majority of her rations: they are "growing boys." She experiences signs of starvation well before the others and is not able to look out for the family. Mother is the only character who doesn't have a name, putting her more into the iconic Mother role than a specific one. Mother assembles the family together for dinner every night, hanging on to that ritual, even if dinner is just blades of grass. She is trying to keep some semblance of normal despite the unimaginable circumstances. *Dog Days* was written long before the global pandemic, but one can't help but draw parallels with the many heads of families who have lost their jobs and are struggling to put food on the table, all the while trying to keep some sense of normalcy for their children in the most abnormal of times.

It is Lisa who demonstrates what is best in humanity in *Dog Days*. She is a nurturer, a friend, an innocent. Lisa sneaks rations to the Dog Man, befriends him, names him Prince, and continues to look out for him. She risks her father's ire; Howard chases Prince away on several occasions. Something about Prince is an affront to Howard's manhood. His very existence provokes Howard's rage. Does he see himself in Prince? Can a man really be just a step away from becoming *that*? Could Howard become *that*? These are his deepest fears.

One of the opera's pivotal moments arrives in Act Two with Lisa's "Mirror Aria." Lisa admires the boniness of her frame. She feels like a model because she is so thin! This is a tragic commentary on the psyche of a typical American teenage girl, wanting to be skinny and rail-thin like the supermodels in the magazines. "Pain is beauty. Hunger is beauty. Hunger made me," Lisa sings into the mirror.

For the final twenty minutes, there is no text. We watch as Lisa lays out her mother's body. In the libretto it says that she collects snow from outside; there is no running water. In Woodruff's production, Lisa uses her own urine from a bucket as she performs the ritual of cleaning the body of her mother. The music becomes a deafening noise scape. Father and sons enter covered in blood from their feast. They have done the unthinkable. This is what war has brought; this is the result of war—a suppression of empathy, of sympathy, of our basic human qualities.

At the end of the opera, Lisa chooses love. She chooses salvation. She chooses hope. Lisa shows us that it is possible to remain human in the direst of circumstances and, in so doing, she holds us all to that higher standard.

Writing Dog Days

Royce Vavrek, Librettist

A career as a librettist isn't an obvious path for a farm kid from Grande Prairie, Alberta. I grew up in a family that had the local country radio station playing near-continuously in our home, and my father was known to sit down at our upright piano and play a handful of songs by ear, including his rendition of "The Beer Barrel Polka." My mom and dad understood and valued music, enrolling me and my siblings in piano lessons from a young age, and supported me through additional music lessons when my interests branched out to singing, choir, and musical theatre lessons.

It was when Jonathan Larson's *Rent* became a cultural touchstone that I became aware of opera. I was in love with musicals (a love that would lead me to graduate studies in musical-theatre writing at New York University), and here was a blockbuster Broadway hit that was based on a canonical opera. At the local bookstore in Grande Prairie, I found *The Rough Guide to Opera*, a handbook that went through the history of the art form, offering profiles of famous figures, scenarios of important works, and reviews of recordings, among a host of other things that painted a remarkably vivid picture of the world of classical music drama. I was sure that, with a little digging, I too would find an opera plot on which to base my own new musical. Little did I know that this search would be the first portal for me to pass through in my personal journey to becoming a full-time opera librettist.

While my undergrad studies found me at the Mel Hoppenheim School of Cinema at Concordia University in Montreal, my graduate studies brought me back to writing for the stage, after a rather prolific high school spell of writing, producing, and performing my own plays for competitive festivals around Alberta. After my formal studies, it was through American Lyric Theater's Composer Librettist Development Program (now grown to also nurture dramaturges) that I really found myself in the driver's seat co-authoring operas. As part of that program's first cohort of nine resident artists, we were given assignments to write arias, duets, and one-act operas, mentored by the American composer-librettist Mark Adamo. It was at the presentation of these short operas, that I met David T. Little, who would become one of my main collaborators and dearest friends. Months later, when David was offered a commission to write a twenty-minute excerpt for a young artists' concert at Carnegie Hall, he asked me if I'd be interested in fashioning a libretto for the opportunity. We settled on *Dog Days*, based on a short story by Judy Budnitz, as the source for our project, and set out to write a few excerpts that we hoped would lead to an opportunity to complete the full opera.

Dog Days was the perfect first full-length opera libretto for me to write. It was undeniably contemporary in every way, requiring an honesty and directness in the language, and it had characters that spoke like me and my family (both biological and artistic). In many ways it felt autobiographic, or at least allowed me to interpolate autobiographical nuances, for instance, the Cheez Whiz aquariums that Lisa sings about in her first act aria "Friends" was based on memories of creating ecosystems in jars in elementary school; the reference to poplar branches in the aria "What are the Odds?" recalls the shelterbelt of trees that protected the perimeter of the yard of my family's home quarter. Even the family makeup in the opera of a mother and father and their three kids—two older brothers and a younger sister—was the same as mine. There was something in the familiarity of the landscape, physical and emotional, that allowed me to find my way into the text in a way that would inform the way I write every new opera.

I am often asked what the telltale qualities of a Royce Vavrek libretto are. Those are always difficult for me to put my finger on, and probably best left to the analysis of others. But I can say that I am a synthesis of the millions of stories that have passed through my eyes and ears, and the influences that I hold extremely dear to my artistic sensibilities. I think you'd be hard-pressed to find any artist who isn't a manifestation of past art that ignited and captivates their imagination. Though there are too many to name, today I feel like a handful of my foundational inspirations must include the cinema of Atom Egoyan, Lars von Trier, and Catherine Breillat; the literary fiction of Miriam Toews, Richard Ford, and Thomas Hardy; the musical lyricism of Kathleen Edwards, Dolly Parton, and Martha Wainwright; and the theatre of Martin McDonagh, Caryl Churchill, and Neil LaBute. This would seem to be the recipe for a contemporary librettist . . . at least this one.

On the Origins of Dog Days and "Little & Vavrek"

David T. Little, Composer

As a graduate student, I got into the habit of composing each morning with a TV on in the background. I would wake up a little later than I like to admit, and have my morning coffee while watching the previous night's *Daily Show*. It was 2003, and pre-*Colbert Report*, so as the half-hour ended and the caffeine worked through my system, I'd switch to the Independent Film Channel (IFC), mute the TV, and start composing. Throughout the day, if I needed a break from the notes and rhythms, I would unmute the TV and watch a few minutes of whatever happened to be on before returning to work.

On one particular day, I looked up to see a black and white film in which a young girl talked with a man wearing a homemade dog costume. The image was so odd, and the film so beautifully shot, I couldn't look away. Before I knew it, I had watched the rest of the film, rapt for all of its remaining twenty minutes. I think I barely blinked. As the credits rolled, I wrote down the name "Ellie Lee," reflected for a moment, then muted the TV again and returned to composing.

In that moment it didn't occur to me that *Dog Days* could ever be an opera. In 2003, I was just on the cusp of sorting out how opera could interact with my creative life. At the time the form still felt hopelessly antiquated to me, though it was a question I was wrestling with. But opera or no, something about the world that Ellie Lee had conjured wouldn't let me go.

The following year I composed "After a Film by Ellie Lee" as part of my *Songs of Love, Death, Friends, and Government*. Based on my own text, it sought to evoke the atmosphere and landscape of Lee's film, with a non-specific reference to its plot. I was living in Boston at the time, studying with Osvaldo Golijov who, seeing this collection of songs, said they felt to him like little studies for operas. That comment—and a chance encounter at the New England Conservatory with a performance of "If I Loved You" from Rodgers and Hammerstein's *Carousel*— would be revelatory. The following fall I would return to my native New Jersey and begin work on my first opera, *Soldier Songs*.

* * *

I met Royce Vavrek four years later, following a performance of one of his works at Symphony Space in New York City. From our first conversations, it was clear that we had a lot in common. We had both grown up in rural farming communities—he on a farm, and I in a farm town—and each had made a leap into writing opera and theatre somewhat blind; we shared a love for auteur filmmakers like von Trier, Kaufman, and Solondz; we had encyclopedic knowledge of classic musical theatre. To say we hit it off is an understatement.

Not long after that initial meeting, I was invited to participate in the Dawn Upshaw/Osvaldo Golijov Workshop for young composers and singers at Carnegie Hall. They specifically asked me to write a *scena* for five singers. Of course, a *scena* needs words, and while I had written my own libretto for *Soldier Songs*—a monodrama—this new piece was to have multiple characters, who would need to interact. Not feeling I could handle dialogue, I reached out to Royce to see if he would be interested in collaborating. He was.

Royce has reminded me that in those earliest days I said I wanted to explore the "poetry of the every day." With this as a broad conceptual frame, we began brainstorming ideas for a topic. In the course of these discussions, I remembered *Dog Days*. Though we couldn't find a way to watch Ellie's film, the original story by Judy Budnitz was printed in *The New York Times* and I sent it to Royce. He loved it. After securing permission from Judy, we got to work.

We premiered *Scenes from Dog Days* in May 2009 at Carnegie Hall. The recording from this performance served as a kind of demo, which our conductor Alan Pierson brought to the attention of PEAK Performances at Montclair. PEAK would commission the completion of the work, and would also connect us with the legendary director Robert Woodruff. I would later bring producer Beth Morrison and my ensemble Newspeak into the *Dog Days* family as Royce and I dug in to finish the work.

For months Royce, Robert, and I met to workshop the libretto; tearing it apart and putting it back together every few weeks. Once Royce finished the "composing draft," as he calls it, I got to work. As I composed, the text continued to evolve depending on what the music was telling us: a new scene might be added, or an existing scene cut; requests for word replacements would be debated, sometimes granted, sometimes defended. Ours is a lively, deeply collaborative, and sometimes messy process, but I'm always thankful that Royce is open to it. Not all librettists are. But I think the most artistically successful operas are made this way.

Dog Days premiered in September 2012 at PEAK Performances at Montclair. It was a massive hit; an improbable success for two artists who, at the time, had basically no track record. It landed on several major best-of-the-year lists, and was called one of the best new operas in twenty years. But for us it was just a piece we felt passionate about making; rendering characters we cared for deeply in the context of a story that we felt needed to be told. We were fortunate to have people in our lives willing to support what to others might have seemed like a fool's errand. It was a life-changing experience. But most importantly, it brought us together as a team. *Dog Days* was the first story we told together, but we've told many since, and have countless more to tell.

Designing Dog Days

Vita Tzykun, Designer

In the following conversation, designer Vita Tzykun responds to written questions from Bill Penner.

BILL PENNER: Since many readers may not be familiar with the designer's process, perhaps you could write a bit about your overall approach, and how opera may differ from designing for a play, dance performance, or a television or film project.

VITA TZYKUN: When designing for opera, everything starts with the music. First, I read the synopsis of the opera so that I have a general understanding of what the piece is about, and then I listen to the music without concentrating on the words and write down my first raw emotional impressions from it. They can be very abstract, but they will colour my work from that point onward.

Next comes the detailed look at the words. First, I read the libretto without stopping, like I would read a poem or a novel, and try to formulate my first impressions from it in one sentence. What is the spine of the story? What are the core questions? I see it almost like a painting with music being the colours and the words being the drawn lines. Both are complex on their own and are interwoven with each other. After that, as any designer would do, I create what we call a "character/scene breakdown." It's essentially a road map of the piece that tells us details about which character does what, when, and where. From that document, rhythms and patterns emerge that allow us to dig deeper into the story. It's a kind of investigative work, and one of my favourite parts of the project.

Then comes visual research, preliminary doodles, revisions, meetings with the creative team, and finalized designs. Altogether, that's fifty percent of the work. The remaining fifty percent is realizing the vision and bringing it to life on stage.

BP: What effect does the scale, the combination of live orchestration, the emotional strength of song, and the grand themes affect your design choices? That is to say, within the large ideas of the libretto, the power of the singers' voices, and the score, how do you decide what to show or not show in the elements of your design?

VT: It's all very intuitive. I think that we all share a fundamental understanding of composition, colour palate, and visual rhythm. As a designer, I use these tools to evoke emotions from the audience. When a moment feels exceptionally powerful in the music and libretto of the piece, it becomes very clear that a strong visual statement must follow. It doesn't mean that a huge scenic shift or a drastic costume change should happen, but the overall experience for the audience has to be seamless. All of the elements should be in tune with each other.

BP: In your discussions with the director what decisions did you make regarding the "era" of the *Dog Days*? It's dystopian for sure, and could be set in the immediate future, but there are elements in the script that suggest it could have happened in the past (no digital technology referenced, only a non-working television, etc.).

Dog Days
Prince (1)

pieces of cloth wrap his knees and elbows protecting him from the harsh pavement. messed up dirty hair and tangled beard. collar with a ripped chain on his neck. part of a fur collar from a torn coat wrapped around his torso. layers of dust cover his skin. sores and cuts.

Vita Tzykun

Dog Days
Prince (2)

same as (1) but with more
layers of found cloth covering
him. trying to keep warm as
much as he can. may be even
pieces of card board or old
newspapers stuck to the
old and ripped blanket.

Vita Tzykun
2020

Looking at the production photographs there are few clues to the time frame, for example, are they wearing reasonably current clothing, or old hand-me-downs because that's all that's left?

VT: Thank you for noticing that. One of the most difficult tasks for a designer is to create a design that can encompass a large swath of time. For *Dog Days*, I specifically wanted to design characters that look like they could have lived in a modern era or near future. When travelling around America, I noticed how recognizable contemporary fashion is here. Many Americans shop at chain stores like Gap and Old Navy, and those designs remain very consistent. Researching and emulating the generic "modern American" style is what allows me to design a look for the characters that the audience finds relatable.

BP: In the libretto Lisa is described as "a preteen girl." In the photographs she appears to be older. Was this a practical decision based on the challenges of presenting an adult performer as a child? Or did it evolve from the apparently more physical relationship between her and Prince?

VT: It's common practice for adult opera singers to portray children or young adults on stage because of the extremely complex and difficult demands of operatic singing. A preteen girl can't physically sing opera alongside adult professional opera singers as her vocal instrument has not yet fully matured. For example, characters in operas like Juliet in *Romeo and Juliet*, Cio-Cio-San in *Madame Butterfly*, and the title role of *Manon* are all noted in the libretto as teenage girls, yet are always sung by adult professionals.

BP: Was there a primary distinguishing feature that identifies/isolates the character of Prince that came out of the libretto?

VT: We knew from the start that it has to be very clear that Prince is a man that behaves like a dog. His character is ambiguous—we don't know how he got to this state. It was up to the clothing and the performer's physicality to tell his story. My design combined human clothes and pieces of fur that were connected together with rope and packing tape. This makeshift work-in-progress look was very clearly something Prince had put together himself. The purpose was not to "explain" Prince, but to respect the ambiguity that Royce inserted into the libretto.

The original designs had a broken chain around his neck, but as rehearsals began, it was removed. We realized that it presented too much of a backstory, which made him too specific. What we needed was an archetype; his character became mysterious and iconic without it.

Dog Days was commissioned by and first produced by PEAK Performances, Montclair, New Jersey, on September 29, 2012, with the following cast and creative team:

Lisa: Lauren Worsham
Howard: James Bobick
Mother: Marnie Breckenridge
Elliot: Michael Marcotte
Pat: Peter Tantsits
Captain: Cherry Duke
Prince: John Kelly

Librettist: Royce Vavrek
Composer: David T. Little
Based on the short story "Dog Days" by Judy Budnitz
Director: Robert Woodruff
Musical Director and Conductor: Alan Pierson
Scenic and Video Design: Jim Findlay
Costume Design: Vita Tzykun
Sound Design: Matt Frey

Characters

Lisa

Howard

Mother

Elliot

Pat

Captain

The Man in a Dog Suit/Prince

Prologue: A Man in a Dog Suit

A family, not unlike your own, sits in a house, watching a TV that isn't turned on. HOWARD reads the newspaper, while MOTHER sweeps the floor free of dead beetles, for what may be the fifth time today. LISA, a preteen girl, reads an adolescent-themed book, while her teenage brothers, PAT and ELLIOT, sit stoned in ratty T-shirts.

In front of the house walks THE MAN IN A DOG SUIT, who howls at the front door, hungrily. HOWARD, annoyed at the noise, immediately throws down his paper. He calls for his gun prominently hung on the wall . . .

HOWARD: Get me my rifle.

PAT and ELLIOT rush to grab the gun off the wall.

ELLIOT: Take care of it this time, Dad!

ELLIOT, PAT, and HOWARD exit the house in a huff, pointing the gun at THE MAN IN A DOG SUIT, yelling at him, scaring him away.

HOWARD: You get outta here!

ELLIOT: He's for real this time.

PAT: He'll shoot your paws right off ya!

ELLIOT: Stupid fuckin' mental case!

HOWARD, cocking the gun, gives a disapproving look to ELLIOT. THE MAN
IN A DOG SUIT *runs away.* PAT *and* ELLIOT *laugh, while* HOWARD *is visibly riled up.*

PAT: That takes care of that.

ELLIOT: Stupid shit for brains . . .
Stupid fucking . . . fucking thing.

HOWARD looks down the barrel of his gun.

HOWARD: Bet the squirrels are out today!

ELLIOT: There's nothing out there!

PAT: He's crazy!

PAT & ELLIOT: Take care of it, Dad.
Nothing out there.

HOWARD: *(yelling into the house)* Bet the squirrels are out today . . .
Going hunting!
Be back later.

PAT & ELLIOT: Nothing!

HOWARD exits, while PAT *and* ELLIOT *go into the house, and to the basement.* LISA *exits the house and sits on the stoop, taking in the mere hum of the town. She continues to read.* THE MAN IN A DOG SUIT *peeks his head around the corner of the fence, catching* LISA's *attention.*

LISA: Mom!
He's back!

MOTHER *walks to the door, sweeping dust out.*

MOTHER: Aw! Looks like he's starving.

THE MAN IN A DOG SUIT walks up to the stoop.

LISA: He stinks.

MOTHER: No collar,
Must be a stray.

LISA: He's a man in a dog suit, Mother!
A man in a dog suit.

MOTHER: Go get a plate.
See what you can dig out of the garbage.

LISA runs into the house, getting the plate and garbage.

(to THE MAN IN A DOG SUIT) Sit!

THE MAN IN A DOG SUIT sits.

Good dog.

*LISA returns with some scraps. THE MAN IN A DOG SUIT shoves his face
into the food, eats manically, and then licks the plate clean.*

Fetch!
Good dog.

LISA: He's a man!
Some retard weirdo!
He's a *man*!

MOTHER: Not a word to your father, Lisa.

> MOTHER *takes the empty plate to the kitchen.* THE MAN IN A DOG SUIT *and* LISA *remain outside.*

LISA: Sure is quiet.
No crickets, no katydids.
I bet you have fleas.

> *Inside the house* MOTHER *begins sweeping again, while* PAT *and* ELLIOT *smoke a joint while reading* Playboy *magazines in the basement.*

MOTHER: A mountain
Of beetle carnage.

LISA: Your fur's all matted.

MOTHER: Sweeping yields
An endless collection . . .

LISA: No crickets, no katydids.

MOTHER: . . . of dead insects.

LISA: Nothing.

ELLIOT: They say the little ones all ganged up.

LISA: No crickets . . .

PAT: Yeah, the little ones.
America's house of cards . . .

LISA: No crickets . . .

PAT: . . . is crumbling.

ELLIOT: It's crazy as hell.

LISA: . . . no katydids.

PAT: Well you can only be on top for so long, I guess . . .

LISA: I bet you have fleas.

ELLIOT: Whatever.

MOTHER: A mountain
Of beetle carnage.

ELLIOT: Shut up and roll the joint.

MOTHER: Sweeping, sweeping . . .

LISA: No crickets . . .

MOTHER: Sweeping, sweeping yields . . .

LISA: . . . no katydids.

MOTHER: . . . an endless collection . . .

LISA: . . . no katydids.

MOTHER: . . . of dead insects.

LISA, *still sitting with* THE MAN IN A DOG SUIT, *tugs on his ear. She hears* HOWARD *in the distance.*

LISA: You should get outta here.
Dad'll be back soon.
His hunting never lasts long.
He gets frustrated; discouraged.

THE MAN IN A DOG SUIT *doesn't budge.*

Get outta here!

She shoves him.

You're asking for it!

She kicks THE MAN IN A DOG SUIT *and then chases him off. He runs to the other side of the fence.* MOTHER *comes out, hearing the commotion.*

The sound of a helicopter is heard overhead. A large box of rations is dropped and breaks wide open.

Act One: Summer

Scene I: Dinner

MOTHER prepares dinner as HOWARD comes home dejected and without any food to feed his family. He sits at the kitchen table lost in thought as MOTHER places the cutlery and sets out the food.

HOWARD: Went down the southwest road
With those caragana bushes.
Went down the southwest road . . .
Nothing.
Not a print in the dirt.
Not a single print in the dirt.

MOTHER: Call the kids for dinner.
Call the kids . . . Howard.

HOWARD snaps out of it, bellows downstairs for PAT and ELLIOT, and upstairs for LISA.

HOWARD: Lisa!
Pat!
Elliot!
Dinner.

Back to his earlier stream of thought.

Where'd they go?

MOTHER: Boys've been home all day.

HOWARD: *(annoyed)* No.
The animals,
Where the hell did they go?
Couldn't have migrated,
A mass exodus
Fearing the extent
Of human failure.

> *LISA comes downstairs.*

MOTHER: You wash your hands, Lisa?

> *She turns around and goes back upstairs.*

HOWARD: Makes ya wonder . . .

MOTHER: Call the boys again.

> *HOWARD bellowing downstairs, impatiently.*

HOWARD: Boys!
Get up here!

> *A beat, then to his wife.*

No talk of it in the paper.
The extinction of journalism.

MOTHER: Could be hiding . . .

HOWARD: Don't be dumb.

ELLIOT and PAT come up the stairs without shirts on.

(to PAT and ELLIOT) Seem to have forgotten your shirts.

ELLIOT: It's a hundred goddamned degrees out there.

PAT: It's just . . . fucked.

MOTHER: *(reprimanding him)* Hey.

ELLIOT: Who cares about shirts anyway?

HOWARD: You'll both be wearing T-shirts
When you sit down at my table.

PAT: Shit.

PAT pulls ELLIOT back downstairs.

HOWARD: *(to MOTHER)* Stupid savages.

MOTHER is somewhat sympathetic to PAT and ELLIOT.

MOTHER: Howard, it's hot.

LISA enters, walks to the table but doesn't yet sit down.

Lisa, can you get some pickled carrots?

LISA: I'm sick of pickled everything . . .
Pickled carrots,
Pickled beets,
Pickled eggs,
Pickled . . . pickles.

MOTHER: *(sternly, while disappointed)* Go.
Please.

    LISA *goes.* PAT *and* ELLIOT *bolt up the stairs, fully dressed.*

HOWARD: *(to* PAT *and* ELLIOT*)* Better.

    Smelling his son's body odor.

You stink.

ELLIOT: Ran out of deodorant.

HOWARD: Use mine!

ELLIOT: Who cares?

HOWARD: I do!
We're the ones who have to sit here and smell you.
You do stink, you know.

ELLIOT: Bum deal.
Lucky to have allergies,
stuffed nose.

MOTHER: *(diffusing the situation)* Let's say grace.

    They take their seats around the table, bowing their heads, saying their
    version of "grace."

MOTHER, FATHER, LISA, PAT, & ELLIOT: We are thankful for this food.
And each other.
Lucky is the family
That sits around the supper table

Together.
We are thankful.

LISA: Will tomorrow . . . ?

HOWARD: Amen.

> *ELLIOT pops open the jar of pickled carrots as MOTHER passes a plate of flat bread and a small bowl of rice.*

MOTHER: *(to LISA)* Go easy on those carrots.
It's the last jar we have left.

LISA: *(with her mouth full)* Gee, wonder why!

MOTHER: Don't talk with your mouth full.

LISA: *(swallowing, with sarcasm)* I wonder why all the jars have disappeared.

MOTHER: Five mouths . . .

LISA: The boys sure seem to like their afternoon snacks.
Pat seems to be getting fatter
And there's nothing to eat.
And there's not a thing to eat.

PAT: You saying we're hording the cans?

LISA: I'm saying you're fat.
And you've eaten the entire cold storage room.

PAT: You're an idiot.

LISA: Fat Pat!

Fat Pat!

Fatty Fat!

PAT: A friendless idiot.

LISA: You're ugly.

PAT: Idiot.

LISA: Fat and ugly.

LISA and PAT their war of words climaxing.

LISA (& PAT): Ugly! (Idiot!)

HOWARD: *(intervening, slamming his fists on the table)* Stop.

PAT: She started it.

HOWARD: I finished it.

They all sit in silence for a few seconds.

PAT: Idiot.

PAT and ELLIOT have devoured their dinner and hop up from the table leaving their dirty plates.

HOWARD: Where do you think you're going?

ELLIOT: Downstairs.

HOWARD: *(angrily)* No.
We can have ten minutes.
Ten minutes around the table.
Ten minutes as a family,
For fuck's sake!

MOTHER: *(shocked)* Howard!

HOWARD: I want ten minutes with my family!

ELLIOT and PAT sit back down in an uncomfortable silence.

PAT: So . . . Dad . . . um . . .
Hear any more news?

HOWARD: Don't trust the news.

They continue to sit in tense silence.

Okay.
You can go.

PAT and ELLIOT scatter, leaving the rest of the family at the table. LISA, inconspicuously to her family, but conspicuously to the audience, places a few potato wedges in her pocket.

Blackout.

Scene 2: Friends

LISA excuses herself from the table. MOTHER begins to clear the table. HOWARD sits, lost in thought.

LISA: Gonna get some fresh air before curfew.

MOTHER: Don't go too far.

LISA: Where would I go?

LISA exits the house, stopping on her porch. She looks around for THE MAN IN A DOG SUIT who is hiding out of sight by the fence.

(in a stage whisper) Hey . . . dog-man.
I know you're here.

THE MAN IN A DOG SUIT pokes his head around the fence, looking at LISA.

Come here.
Hey!

He doesn't move. She gets a little bossy, like HOWARD.

Come here.
Hey!
You deaf or something?
Come here!

He still doesn't move. She digs in her pockets and pulls out two potato wedges, offering them.

You're not gonna turn these down.

He doesn't move for a second, but then can't refuse, running up to her and eating them ravenously. When he is finished, she wipes her hands on her pants. He sits, seemingly contented.

No man in his right mind
Could pass up wedges.
No man in his *retarded* mind
No man . . .
Not when he's starving.

We could be friends if you want,
Even though you're not normal.
But we could be friends, if you want.
After all, what's normal anymore?
What's normal anymore anyway?

Normal was stealing snapdragons
From old ladies' flowerbeds.
Normal was fishing out mosquito larvae with Marjorie
From the old dugout,
Making aquariums out of old Cheez Whiz jars.

Nothing's normal.
Nothing's normal anymore.

You got a family?
Everyone has a family.
Do you have a litter of puppies?
Little ones that were yanked from your doghouse,
And handed out to families
On farms on the outskirts of town?

He doesn't say anything, doesn't so much as bark.

You got a wife, dog-man?
Does she know that you're . . .
Does she know you're messed up?
Like the guys on afternoon talk shows
Who go crazy, then beg forgiveness.
Maybe she fell in love with a character from her drugstore romance.

Maybe . . .
Maybe she . . .
Maybe she didn't want to love a dog.
Maybe she *doesn't* want to love a dog.
Maybe . . .
Maybe she just doesn't want to love a dog.

A beat.

You want to know a secret?
My dad cries in his sleep.
I've never seen him
But I hear him.
Mom sleeps through everything,
So she doesn't notice.
But I do.

Gone are the nights he'd spend in front of the TV.
Hours and hours and hours when the plant closed down.
Mom nagged:
"Gonna get off the couch?"
But he knew it was no use.
So he sat staring off into space,
A wall of beer cans piling up at his feet.

His face big and red
His eyes like two lost polka dots.
His face big and red,
And lost and afraid.
And his eyes like two lost polka dots.

I'm gonna pet you.
But if I get a rash tomorrow . . .

> *She reaches out to him, petting him, cutting off the intimate moment is the curfew siren . . .*

Curfew.
You're a good listener, dog-man.
Crazy, probably,
But you listen.

> MOTHER *comes to the door.*

MOTHER: *(calling)* Lisa!

> LISA *patting* THE MAN IN A DOG SUIT's *head.*

LISA: I think we'll be friends.
Or not.
We'll be friends or we won't.

> LISA *turns away, going inside the house, stopping at the door.*

I think we'll be friends.

> THE MAN IN A DOG SUIT *runs behind bushes, hiding for the evening.*

Scene 3: Parents

Everyone readies for bed in their respective rooms (the brothers laying low downstairs). MOTHER *cries as she pulls the sheets back, unable to get into her side of the bed.*

MOTHER: I can't move.
My legs won't walk me into bed.
My joints have seized;
My bones now fossils.
Refusing to let me crawl under the blankets.
My legs won't walk me into bed.
Something slithers around the mattress coils.
Bleak, black.
My legs won't walk me into bed.
They know the white cotton
Can feel like death's satin.
But I beg them,
Walk me into bed.

HOWARD: Get in.

HOWARD enters casually.

MOTHER: We should've went . . .

HOWARD: Went where?
Problems everywhere!

MOTHER: My cousins went east.
And your sister.

HOWARD: We're best off . . .
Best off right where we are.
Here.
As a family.

MOTHER: I have a hard time recognizing my boys anymore:
Shattered childhood;
Broken minds.

HOWARD: The boys look . . .
The boys look . . . healthy.

A slight beat, enough for MOTHER *to give him a look.*

Healthy enough.

MOTHER: *(getting more upset)* Howard!

HOWARD: Healthy enough.

MOTHER: Who are you kidding?

HOWARD: *(an angry whisper)* You're getting worked up.
Gonna bust a vessel in your eye, again.

MOTHER: I'm tired.
And these rations are pathetic,
Stale crumbs.
We're beggars.

HOWARD: No.

MOTHER: We are beggars.
Beggars!

HOWARD: No!

MOTHER: Beggars with nothing to beg for.

HOWARD: I'm not . . .
We're not beggars.
That man in the costume . . .

MOTHER: Howard—

HOWARD: *That's* a beggar.

MOTHER: Just trying to talk to you.

HOWARD: We're not beggars.

MOTHER: Just trying to talk to you.

HOWARD: *I'm* not a beggar.

MOTHER: Just trying to talk to you.

HOWARD: I'm trying!
Don't you accuse me of not trying.

MOTHER: Just trying to *talk* to you.
Howard.

HOWARD: I go out every day.
Hunting,
Praying for a shot.

MOTHER: Please, Howard!

HOWARD: Don't you dare . . .
Don't you dare.

MOTHER: I didn't mean—

HOWARD: It's all I fucking think about.

MOTHER: Howard, we know you try.

HOWARD: You blame me.
Everyone is so goddamned ungrateful.

MOTHER: I'm starving,
And I'm tired.
By next week we'll be eating dandelions from the yard.

HOWARD: Fuck.

Then a memory . . .

Found a deer,
(a boy's adventure)
Fresh dead.

A curious boy . . .
I found a dead deer
Barely a fly on the carcass.
A fresh-dead deer
Pierced on jagged branches

Found a deer,
(a boy's adventure)
Fresh dead.
Barely a fly on the carcass.

Stared a mile deep . . .

PAT and ELLIOT join him, singing from their perch in the basement, singing in a strange back-up fashion.

PAT & ELLIOT: Stared a mile deep . . .

HOWARD: Stared a mile deep into its eyes . . .

PAT & ELLIOT: Stared a mile into their eyes.

HOWARD: . . . its eyes.
Stared a mile deep . . .
To the root of . . . death.
To the root of death.

Shaking the image from his head.

HOWARD: *(to MOTHER)* Get into bed.

He turns his light off. MOTHER stands as the attention shifts to the basement where ELLIOT and PAT pass a pinner between the two of them . . .

Scene 4: Brothers

PAT and ELLIOT's eyes glow in the dark.

PAT: Suck it back.

ELLIOT: You can't roll, man.
This is the worst fucking pinner I've ever seen.

PAT: Let's use your pipe then.

ELLIOT: No way.

ELLIOT takes a hit, exhales a large cloud of smoke.

PAT: There you go.

ELLIOT: Nice one.

ELLIOT passes the pinner.

You know
I got to thinking—

PAT: Bad idea.

ELLIOT: No no no.
Come on.
This is good.

Beat.

So,
When this is all done—

PAT: This?

ELLIOT: "This."

PAT: What?

ELLIOT: The predicament of the whole fucking world.

PAT: Oh, that.

ELLIOT: When this is all done.
It could be brutal.
A fraction of the people left behind.
Severely diminished population.
Just us and, a hypothetical,
Just us and some women.

PAT: Ideal!

ELLIOT: That's what I'm saying . . .

PAT: Oh man.

ELLIOT: That's what I'm saying . . .

(in a godlike voice) "Go forth and repopulate."
Our job to mate.
Prepare yourself, Patty-boy.
Go forth and repopulate
We'll be kings of the new world.

Our moment to copulate,
Row after row of heaving breasts,
With only one desire:
To be ours!

They beg us, "We need you!"
Who are we to say no?
Empty bodies need to be filled.

Go forth and repopulate,
Our job to mate,
For the good of humanity.
Ladies, we love you all.
Let us satisfy your hunger!

Scene 5: Letter

LISA's room—it's a bedroom suitable for a younger girl: very pink, very daddy's-little-princess. LISA writes in her diary, humming as she does so. Her text is projected on stage.

LISA: Dear Marjorie:
I made a friend today.
Some dog-man lunatic.
Kinda revolting, but kinda cute.
He listens.
And his eyes twitch.
He's got smokers fingers.
And grey in his beard.
I'll tell him about you tomorrow.
Tell him you're my best friend.
You're still my best friend, right?
I miss having a girlfriend.

A beat.

Every day it gets a little quieter.

A beat.

No crickets, no katydids.
Not anymore.
No crickets.
No katydids.
It's like noise never existed . . .

A beat.

xoxoxoxoxo,
Lisa.
P.S. Too bad you'll never read this letter.

Act Two: Fall

Scene I: Naming

A helicopter approaches as the family runs outside expecting their rations to be dropped. A box falls, but it disintegrates on contact, reduced to dust. The helicopter's noise fades away. HOWARD *looks at the gun on the wall. He knows that hunting is useless, but goes nonetheless.*

LISA *sneaks into* ELLIOT *and* PAT's *downstairs space, hoping to steal some of their stashed food, but they fight her off.*

MOTHER *walks down the gravel driveway to the mailbox. She plays with the flag, wondering if it still works . . . it does. Opening up the box, she peers inside. There is nothing but a dead moth and a few other insects. She sweeps them out with her hands and throws them to the wind.* MOTHER *latches the mailbox door and walks away, the gravel crunching beneath her feet as she walks.*

She grabs an ice-cream pail and begins filling it with grass and foliage for dinner.

LISA *goes outside to sit on the stoop, where* THE MAN IN A DOG SUIT *sits. She tries her best to patch up a hole in one of the man's sock-paws, though she's pretty clumsy with the needle and thread.*

LISA: Like car exhaust . . .
You'd think my brothers elected a new pope.
Can't go down there till they're high.
Otherwise they'll clobber me.

Dope makes them lazy,
So they tease me . . .
Sticks and stones . . .
Sticks and stones.

My brothers think they're princes.
Princes of what?

> MOTHER *comes around the house holding an ice cream pail that she is filling with grass and foliage.*

Mom?

MOTHER: Uh-huh?

LISA: How about Prince?

MOTHER: What Prince?

LISA: Prince as a name?
A name for a dog?

MOTHER: It's a perfectly fine name.

LISA: His name is Prince!

> HOWARD *returns from hunting. He holds his gun by his side, but he's ready to make a move if necessary.* MOTHER *sees this.*

HOWARD: What's this?

MOTHER: He's not hurting anyone.

HOWARD: Yet.

Not hurting anyone yet.

MOTHER: He keeps the other beggars away.

LISA: Like a guard dog.

I've named him Prince.

HOWARD: Even purebreds go rabid.

HOWARD takes a moment to decide. He walks up the steps, pushing the side of PRINCE's head with the butt of his gun.

LISA cuddles up to PRINCE. MOTHER walks around to the back of the house, picking grass. PAT and ELLIOT's faces can be seen in the basement window. They watch as LISA and PRINCE embrace.

MOTHER grunts and groans as she pulls the browning grass from the ground. On the other side of the picket fence she notices a single dandelion plant with flour flowers—a bounty that she pulls from the ground.

MOTHER walks into the house, where her family is waiting by the table, seemingly expecting dinner. She divides the food among them, giving each a dandelion plus a bowlful of grass. She doesn't get a dandelion. PAT and ELLIOT, starving, attempt to dig in, though HOWARD's glare stops them. They put their forks down as the family members bow their heads.

ALL: We are thankful

For this food and each other.

Lucky is the family

That sits around the supper table

Together.

We are thankful.

HOWARD, PAT, & ELLIOT: Our stomachs sing out . . .

In silence, the family begins to eat. Hungrily they dig into the grass,
though it is nearly inedible. LISA *eats as much as she can before her stom-*
ach gives out. She dashes from the table to the kitchen sink where she
vomits. Embarrassed, she runs upstairs to her bedroom. HOWARD *runs*
up after her, standing in her doorframe. LISA *knows he's there . . . but*
neither of them have anything to say.

After a few moments, HOWARD *retreats, grabs his hunting gun from the*
wall, and exits the house.

Scene 2: Alea

LISA *downstairs in the unfinished basement with her brothers.* PAT *and*
ELLIOT *lay on the floor, stoned, while* LISA *sits against a wooden post.*

LISA: It's getting closer.

ELLIOT: What is?

LISA: The war.
I can feel it.

ELLIOT: Oh, you don't feel anything.

LISA: I can feel it.
There's something in the air.
Something we can't see, or hear, lurking.
Even Prince has been acting strange . . .

PAT: You're crazy as hell . . .

LISA: I can feel it.

PAT: . . . they should lock you in the psych ward!

LISA gets up and peers out of the basement window.

LISA: I think everybody's moved away.
Haven't seen old lady Martingale peer from behind her curtains in so many mornings.
Haven't seen Mr. Davis get his mail in weeks.
Haven't seen anyone.

PAT: Everybody's dead, Lisa.

LISA whips her head around to listen to him, a tad scared.

Government comes in the middle of the night . . .

ELLIOT: Yeah, with trucks.
Clears 'em out
When we're asleep.

LISA: They break into people's houses?

ELLIOT: They can smell the bodies.

PAT: Yeah, the ripe ones.

LISA is disturbed by the idea.

LISA: Ripe?

LISA takes a moment to work it out in her brain. Is he teasing? Is he not? She turns back to peer out the window.

We'd know if they were coming in the middle of the night:
We'd hear the trucks,
We'd see broken doors.

PAT: You're so young.
So naive.

LISA: Oh, shut up, Pat!
Hey, Dad's outside.

PAT & ELLIOT: There's nothing out there!

LISA: And he's not even chasing Prince away for a change.
Everybody's acting weird.
Everybody's . . .

Outside HOWARD *is talking to* PRINCE. HOWARD *bends over to address him, refusing to get on his knees.*

HOWARD: *(angry, baffled)* A human being,
A goddamned human being!
A man no less,
A man
Just like me.

Gotta stand up like a man.
Gotta stand up like a man.
Gotta stand up!

Take off this Halloween costume bullshit . . .

Beat, shaking his head.

. . . pathetic.

Composing himself, looking around to see if anyone is listening in as he talks more gently to PRINCE.

Listen here, guy,
I'll give you a change of clothes,
My clothes,
If you just stand up like a man
Stand up and speak to me,
With the voice God gave you,
None of this barking shit.

PRINCE *responds, barking, sending* HOWARD *into a rage.*

Be a goddamned human being!
A goddamned human being!
Goddamned . . .

PRINCE *begins to run away.* HOWARD *runs after him.*

Come here, you!

LISA *at the window.*

LISA: Scared him away.
Dad needs to learn how to talk to people—
And dogs.

HOWARD *returns from chasing* PRINCE *away, enraged, almost inhuman.*

HOWARD: This . . .
Fucked.
This . . .
Fucking man in a goddamned costume.
Fuck you, guy.

Fucking sock ears hanging off his head.
Who the fuck does he . . .
Who the fuck does he . . .
Who the fuck does he think he is?

Fucking guy.
Barking, barking.
Fucking guy.

I can bark too, guy.
Barking, barking.
I can bark too, guy.

And I bite too, guy.
And I, I bite!
And I bite!
And I bite!

Thinks he's some sorta mutt.
This fucking . . .
Fuck you guy!
Don't you bark in my direction
You fuck!

> *He kicks over the coffee table.* MOTHER *jumps. He then kicks at the tele-*
> *vision, breaking the glass.* PAT *and* ELLIOT *dash up the stairs and watch*
> *their father in his act of rage. After his outburst,* HOWARD *falls on the*
> *couch,* PAT *and* ELLIOT *flanking him.* MOTHER *comes to clean the mess*
> *with a broom and dustpan.*

MOTHER: You feel better now,
Do ya?

HOWARD: No.

Just worse and worse and worse and more fucking worse.

Scene 3: Mirror

LISA stands at the bathroom mirror, opening it. She pulls out a bottle of Flintstones vitamins, eating one, relishing the flavor. Sitting on the toilet, she continues to eat the pills one by one until she can't contain herself and she dumps a handful into her palm and shoves them into her mouth. For a moment she feels entirely satisfied.

Out of the shadows downstairs, PAT and ELLIOT sneak out of the house. We see them slip into the nighttime.

MOTHER: Lisa . . .

You've been in there for half an hour.

LISA: Be out in a minute.

LISA puts the Flintstones bottle back in the cabinet, then exits.

MOTHER: You okay, Lisa?

LISA: Yeah, fine.

She goes to her room, shutting the door. She walks to her mirror and removes a pink pashmina that obscures the surface. She looks at herself for quite a while, introducing herself to the new image that stands before her. She takes off her shirt and stands in her training bra and a pair of boyish boxers.

LISA: Hello there, beautiful!
Hello there!
Skin stretched
Around a bony frame.
Angles, shapes, and corners
Revealed under baby fat.
It's happened, Lisa,
It's happened!

The face you always wanted:
With cheekbones
Jutting like boulders from a white sand beach.
Boulders!

Hello there, beautiful,
Hello, beautiful girl:

Ribs like an antique washboard,
I rub my fingers
Down and up,
Up and down.
I've lost count of the ridges . . .
It's happened!

Like corrugated cardboard.
The kind that Dad has piled up,
Waiting to be burned,
In the dead of winter,
When nothing's left but our shivers.

Hello there, beautiful,
Hello in there:

Collarbone necklace,
Legs like stilts,
Skeleton fingers for dainty rings.
It's happened . . .
It happened.

"You look just like a model, Lisa.
Look just like a model," you say.
"You flatter me!" I say.
"How'd ya do it, Lisa?
I want pointers—
I'm desperate here!"
I say, "It was simple!

No twelve-step program,
Cutting carbs,
No counting points,
No cigarettes,
No dope,
No treadmill . . .
Not even the old two-fingers-down-the-throat trick!"

Pain is beauty, they say;
Hunger is beauty, I say
Hunger builds beauty,
Hunger made me . . .

But my hair has lost its colour and shine.
My skin is dry,
My freckles fade away,
But I'm beautiful!

Marjorie?
Marjorie . . .

If I squint hard enough,
I can see you, Marjorie, deep in the mirror,
Sitting there on my bed.

If I squint hard enough,
So hard my head begins to throb,
I can see you, your silhouette,
Your feet dangle from the side of my bed,
In your hand-me-down running shoes.

Marjorie . . .

I miss our grass-blade duets,
The buzzing stems between our thumbs.
I miss hanging like baby possums
From the Martingale's oak tree;
The one we carved our names into
On the fourth tallest branch.

I'll carve Prince's name too.

Hello there, beautiful:
Hello!
Hello hello hello hello
In there.

Mirror, mirror, hello!

I wonder if I've already passed through . . .
Are the jabberwockies waiting?

What if . . .
What if I'm only beautiful on the other side?

> *LISA curls up in a ball, clutching her stomach . . . the Flintstones vitamins finally taking a toll on her.*

Scene 4: Rubicon

> *HOWARD sleeps in the reclining chair in the living room. A CAPTAIN and SOLDIER enter the house holding PAT and ELLIOT by their coat collars, their hands bound. The SOLDIER carries a machine gun, crosshairs fixed on HOWARD.*

CAPTAIN: These your sons?

HOWARD: Depends.

CAPTAIN: Boys've got imaginations
That got the best of them.

HOWARD: I'll straighten them out.
Goodnight.

CAPTAIN: I was hoping to have a word with you, Mr. . . .

HOWARD: . . . Howard.
The name's Howard.

CAPTAIN: Just a word, Howard.

> *Beat.*

It's not right,
Boys breaking into people's homes,
Staring blankly at the dead,
Howard.

HOWARD: Sure they didn't mean any harm.

CAPTAIN: Oh, I'm sure they didn't mean any harm.

HOWARD: Just boys with too much time on their hands . . .

CAPTAIN: Just the sort of kids we're looking for, Howard.

HOWARD: Best be looking elsewhere.

CAPTAIN: Service, Howard.
A good way to curb deviant behaviour.
Make positives out of negatives.
Howard, you get me?

Don't want to point fingers
No, I don't want to imply ignorance,
But I worry that you haven't thought this through.

There's a bright future,
A bright future beyond the bleakness of today.
There's a new community,
Waiting to come together:
To celebrate, to rebuild.

A bright future,
A bright future beyond the bleakness of today.
There's a new community,

Waiting to come together:
To celebrate, to rebuild.

You've watched this town disintegrate.
Homes sit with nothing but ghosts inside.
Folks vanished . . . vanished.
Howard, you were blindsided.

But there's hope, Howard.
You get me?
Wars get won.
We win, we start over.
We build, again.
A new community.
Like the mighty phoenix, we'll be reborn!

Your boys are crying out,
Reckless in their need to belong.
Rode their bikes for miles
Searching for something to hold on to.

Eyes caressing the dead.

HOWARD: Sure they didn't mean any harm.

CAPTAIN: Hungry eyes, caressing the dead.

HOWARD: Sure they didn't mean any harm.

CAPTAIN: Desperate boys out there scavenging
Like two ravenous ravens.

HOWARD: Goodnight.

CAPTAIN: Reap the benefits:
Food, Howard,
Security, Howard.
You get me?

HOWARD: Goodnight.

CAPTAIN: Howard!
You get me?

HOWARD: Goodnight!

CAPTAIN: I'll come back for them.
It's a matter of time.
You're not listening, Howard.
I'm trying to help you.

HOWARD: Thank you, Sergeant.

CAPTAIN: Captain.

HOWARD: But there's no way in hell . . .

SOLDIER: You can't control your children.
There's a training camp waiting for them.
I'll have them weapon-trained so fast,
They'll forget . . .
They'll forget you existed.

> *The* CAPTAIN *unties the boys' hands.* HOWARD *disciplines the boys. The* CAPTAIN *watches, pleased.*

HOWARD: We make choices.

We commit.

We plan.

We execute.

We suffer consequences.

We swallow hard.

We give in.

We make choices.

We commit.

We plan.

We execute.

We suffer consequences.

We swallow hard.

We give in.

We swallow hard.

> HOWARD *spits at the* CAPTAIN. *Unfazed, she shows herself out, noticing* PRINCE *on the stoop. She smirks, then exits.*

We swallow hard.

Act Three: Winter

Scene I: Odds

The sound of a helicopter, far overhead, passes over the family. No rations are dropped. MOTHER *in the kitchen, sweeping.*

MOTHER: What are the odds
When not even wind rustles the poplar branches?
When not even the usual hum
Exists in daytime, nighttime, anytime?

What are the odds
When our cheeks have sunken,
Our ribs ripple under our skin?

What are the odds
When nothing is left?
No food to feed our growling bellies;
Only fantasies to feed our souls.

What are the odds,
When he goes on his missions:
Hunt after hunt
Yielding nothing?

Twenty years spent with him.
Twenty years building up what war breaks down in
Days, minutes, seconds.

The shell,
The shedded skin
Of what he was before

Twenty years spent.
Rearing sons,
Once-little ones,
Who hide in the basement
Doing God knows what,
Though we both know, God and I, that there's nothing left to do.

(. . . so tired . . . go to sleep)
I make my bed:
Quilt from the cedar chest,
Afghan from the sofa.

(. . . so tired . . . but Lisa!)

Change the pillowcases,
The fitted, flat bed sheets—
Press them, press them, press them,
Muscle out the creases . . .

(. . . so tired . . . but Lisa!)

I make my bed.
I give in,
Submit.

What were the odds
That I was given this life
And not somebody else?

Scene 2: Endgame

A blizzard sets in. LISA *gets dressed up in her snowsuit and then exits to the porch to cuddle up to* PRINCE. PAT *and* ELLIOT *are forced upstairs due to the freezing basement.* MOTHER *sleeps in the upstairs bed, motionless.* HOWARD *stares into space, barely blinking. All are freezing.*

PAT & ELLIOT: *(taunting, teasing)* Lisa . . .

LISA: *(to* PRINCE*)* Maybe the war makes it colder.

PAT: Don't get too close, Lisa!

LISA: Maybe it's just December.

ELLIOT: He'll mount you.

PAT: Mount you.

LISA: Or maybe it's summer and Hell has frozen over.

PAT: Mount you.

ELLIOT: A litter of mutt puppies.

LISA: I need someone to squeeze me.

ELLIOT: *(barely audible sentence fragment)* Half-bitch nieces . . .

LISA: Force some warmth inside of me.
I'm a popsicle.
I can hear the snap and crackle
Of my muscles melting.

My heartbeat so . . .
Slow.

HOWARD, MOTHER, LISA, PAT, & ELLIOT: Our stomachs sing out:
Empty cries.
Like a bear woke suddenly from hibernation,
We lumber along in a hunger daze.

Will tomorrow fill our bellies?
Will tomorrow . . .

    PRINCE *howls, hungrily.* MOTHER *expires.*

PAT: I wish I had a steak.

ELLIOT: But even the grass is gone.

PAT: I'd even eat worms.

ELLIOT: In Africa they eat grubs and things.

PAT: Worms.

ELLIOT: Maybe there are worms in the backyard.
Where do worms go during the winter?

PAT: They dig down.

ELLIOT: How far?

LISA: *(to PRINCE)* Good dog.

PAT: All the way to China, I guess.

ELLIOT: I hear down there in China
People eat . . .

> *Brief moment of silence.* HOWARD, *having heard* PAT *and* ELLIOT, *looks up.*

LISA: Good dog.
Good dog.

> *A brief pause.* LISA *realizes that she's drawn attention to* PRINCE. *She looks terrified . . . and for good reason . . .*

HOWARD: Get me my rifle.

> HOWARD *slowly rises, weak.* PAT *and* ELLIOT *again rush to grab the gun off the wall, struggling in their weakness, but ultimately placing it in* HOWARD's *hands.*

LISA: *(building to a scream)* Dad!
What are you . . . ?
No!
Prince!
No!

ELLIOT: Take care of it this time, Dad!

PAT: Take care of it this time, Dad!

LISA: *(in tears)* Prince!
No!
Dad!
No!
Dad, he's a man!

You can't—
A man!
He's a man!

HOWARD: *(at first with terrifying calm)* He's a dog.
He's an animal!
An animal!

> HOWARD *leaves the house, standing on the porch, taking aim at* PRINCE, *who can tell he means business.* PRINCE *takes off running on all fours.* HOWARD *shoots his first bullet, narrowly missing him.* PRINCE *stands up on two legs running, pawing at the air.* HOWARD *takes aim again. He shoots.* PRINCE *is hit and collapses to the ground without so much as a howl. As if on cue,* ELLIOT, PAT, *and* HOWARD *descend on* PRINCE's *carcass, falling on him snarling, digging in with bestial teeth.*

Epilogue: The Three Ravens

LISA, in shock, seeks solace in her mother, only to discover that she too is gone.

LISA performs an act of ablution, carefully washing her mother's body.

Knowing the men will return, LISA prepares to flee. Adding more layers atop her snowsuit, she leaves the house to the sated men.

She walks and walks and walks and walks . . .

Missing

Libretto by Marie Clements
Composed by Brian Current

A Story of Love Left and Remembered

Paula Danckert, Dramaturge

When Marie Clements was invited to write a libretto for City Opera Vancouver in 2016, the title had already been decided. It was to be called "Missing Women." Inspired by the Truth and Reconciliation Commission final report in 2015 and in preparation for the celebrations of Canada 150, City Opera Vancouver saw an opportunity to create a new chamber opera for their audiences that was unlike anything they had previously experienced. They also wanted to reach out to a population that was not part of their usual subscriber base.

The project was driven by many factors: the call of the Truth and Reconciliation Commission to educate the public about the injustices perpetrated against Indigenous peoples; the monies made available to do so; an ongoing interest in putting urgent and complex matters in opera form; and a drive to develop new relationships with artists from varied backgrounds. These were among the elements that informed the ambitions of the company to make an opera about the brutal and ongoing realities of Missing and Murdered Indigenous Women and Girls. Opera is no stranger to tragedy; it has the scale to take on the most difficult of human concerns. In the face of the size of the subject, the invitation came with an obvious and immediate challenge for Clements: how to find the angle to create an opening through which a story could play out that was not fashioned from the pain and suffering of Indigenous peoples for the benefit and edification of white settlers. That story has been told far too many times. But what is an opera to do with the horrors of such subject matter as "race-based genocide"[*]? What needs to be seen or heard, again, for the story of deep-seated continual colonial violence to be told? How much more needs to be shown or witnessed? And to whom, by whom, for what purpose?

Clements was vivified by the prospect of upending the news version of accounts, the one that reduces and confines an entire life to a headline, a story so commonly repeated it warrants no details or further investigation; yet the same story that contains the entire life of a beautiful girl or an accomplished woman. What is that life, what might it have become? That girl, that woman, that life is still carried, continually carried, by those who continue to love her and miss her. The physical presence may no longer be there: taken, stolen, disappeared, murdered, missing, yet everything otherwise still lingers, still exists.

The space left by the missing is not empty. Clements knew that in that space there is profound grief, because where that life had been now was only love, love left. The long trail of turbulence caused by the violence of a person uprooted from her life affects all matter of humanness. That was the story that Clements wanted to unearth, the story she wanted sung. She wanted the beauty of prospective life, and the deep mourning of loss, to be seen and heard. That is how the name of the opera went from "Missing Women" to "Missing."

Making the opera was a process of collaboration that engaged Indigenous and non-Indigenous artists and administrators, an environment in which Clements is a veteran. I joined the project in the early stages in my capacity as dramaturge and as long-time collaborator with Clements. I am a white settler. The entire producing and administrative staff are white settlers and both the composer, Brian Current, and the director, Peter Hinton, are white settler. The characters in the opera, for the most part, are Gwich'in, and the singers who play them are Indigenous. The conductor is Muscogee Creek and Choctaw, Tim Long. Concerning the spectators, enough was known about the opera public in general and the subscribers in particular, to have a sense of the makeup of the audience.

Because the process would involve a great deal of outreach to the communities and families who were most affected by the ongoing trauma, Clements's

---

[*] From the Lexicon of Terminology in the 2015 Reclaiming Power and Place: Final Report of the National Inquiry into Murdered and Missing Indigenous Women and Girls.

expectation was that there would be a mix of (some) Indigenous and (more) non-Indigenous people in attendance. Presentations of the work at various stages would be made for people in Vancouver's Downtown East Side, and privately to families still suffering devastating loss. With all this in mind, Clements wrote a libretto from the vantage point of those who know the most, have the most wisdom, and carry the most experience on all matters of missing: Indigenous women. But she directed the address to the white settlers of the audience by angling it through a character with whom they could most identify: a white girl.

At first glance it appears Ava is the central figure, but as conductor Tim Long points out, "The white girl is the liaison for the audience into the piece,"* the heart of the story is with the Native Girl's mother. It would be from her perspective that the storylines were to be drawn. Music would help Clements make this polyhedral delivery by centring it in the long sounding voice of the Native Mother who, in a settler world, all too often goes unsung and is, therefore, rarely, if ever, heard. In her libretto for *Missing*, Clements was using opera to invert the more common storytelling perspectives with voices of the otherwise.

The composer, Brian Current, was chosen for the project through a "blind audition"** process. The producing company selected a jury that would hear submissions from four composers who had written an aria from a ten-minute excerpted piece of the libretto. Kwagiulth/Stó:lō mezzo-soprano, Marion Newman, who would eventually be cast as Dr. Wilson, sang each of the submitted pieces for the jury, who then selected the composer. Coming together for the opera would mark the first meeting for Clements and Current. It would be Clements's first time writing for opera and Current's second. She was new to opera and he was new to drama. A great deal was to be learned from each other, both positive and negative. This process would be fascinating, valuable, and often difficult.

The early moments of the score direct attention to the line of a highway, a rainy night . . . driving in a car . . . someone hitchhiking . . . then a crash; a young woman comes to, hanging upside down in a tree. The first notes are sung by Ava, the white girl, coming into consciousness. The line and the upside-down viewpoint

---

* All of the quotations in this article are taken from personal interviews that I conducted with the participants.

** A term used by the producing company, not my term.

in the woods are the opening images of the opera. In many ways, they became the metaphors, for the work we were doing in collaboration as Indigenous and non-Indigenous creators and participants.

As the themes in the libretto played out in the score, they manifested in relationships in the rehearsal hall. Clements was drawing storylines that marked choices made by her characters and which also illuminated ingrained and perpetuated presumptions of what makes a recognizable narrative. As the music was learned and character motivations were made clear, so too were the underpinnings of decades-long biases regarding the relationship between how stories are told and understood, according to who is doing the telling. The shift in perspective challenged the reigning order of affairs, which affected the dramatic structure of the opera, processes in the rehearsal hall, and relations between artists and administration.

Making new performance work is always difficult, but making new opera is like a breach from the imperium of an age-old repertoire that rules the form. I, for one, had entered the early stages of making *Missing* thinking that in terms of form and content the roles were set as follows: form = music = opera = Eurocentric = old; content = libretto = story = Indigenous = new. Clearly something is wrong with this picture. Soon into the project that thinking had to be reorganized; the old form was the Indigenous storytelling into which the new content from western European traditions was introduced.

Rearranging the roles loosened up other predetermined ideas long cemented in the confines of a colonialized hierarchy. For example, one does not have to be an opera buff to know the names Puccini, Mozart, or Verdi, but only a few would know the names of their librettists. Tradition always assigns status and authorship to the composer, first and foremost because opera is all about the music. Yet, to credit Current as the author of *Missing*, who admittedly had just recently begun to understand the realities of the murdered and missing women and girls, would have been preposterous. Current knew, as did everyone else, that the lead credit had to go to the librettist, Clements. Within the strictures of opera tradition, this apparent minor detail signaled a tectonic shift. It also marked a change in relations among the people involved in the project; we were all aware that roles were being rearranged, but we did not know how these new dynamics would affect the process or the production. Though the music is everything, this opera belonged to the librettist because the form—the Indigenous storytelling—and the content—the subject matter of the telling—was the lead player both in shaping the music as well as in its delivery. Everything else followed suit.

Here is how Current describes part of the process of realization that necessitated change:

> The more I understood both the wider ramifications of what this project is and the wider ramifications of this tragedy of the missing and murdered women that is still going on, then it became more and more understood that my role here should become more of a supportive one. And so, the ways that my eyes were open to this tragedy, the same way my eyes and ears were open to the best way that I could be part of this, was just to support Marie's vision rather than to take a leading role.

As in all opera, languages identify time, place, culture, and aesthetic. They are central to the music and the storytelling. *Missing* is sung in English and Gitksan, the language of the people of the Pacific Northwest, including those who live along the Highway of Tears. With the Gitksan language comes Indigenous philosophies, constructs, and belief systems that have long been threatened or silenced, or have disappeared under the brutal tactics of colonialism. But language regenerates culture, keeping it alive, which is the purpose of including the Gitksan; by putting it in the opera, old ways of thinking, living, and being are retrieved and recommunicated in a new form. Learning languages is part of the practice and discipline of opera singers. And so, it was true of *Missing*: the Gitksan needed to be learned, which was a process unto itself.

The teacher and speaker of the language, Vince Gogag, made tapes for the company and was in the rehearsal hall to help with learning the sounds of an ancient language that was new to everyone in the room. This is what Marion Newman had to say about her experience of singing in Gitksan:

> It feels good to be singing that language back into the air. Making those audiences hear it. To try and highlight for them why it is so important to do what we can to save what is almost lost, and to mourn that which is lost, that we won't be getting back. It does feel like it is a very important

part of this kind of storytelling. And whether or not we can understand it or fix it now, our ancestors, who we believe are with us, can, so that matters a lot.

Singing the Gitksan was an act of reclamation. It was a way of giving life back to something else that had been stolen, missing; a way of putting it back into the world. Surtitles were another way of manifesting the language for the audience, by presenting what Gitksan looks like in all its shape and sound. About composing for the Gitksan language, Current had this to say:

It is so beautiful, that language, because, first of all, it is very musical because it has all these sounds . . . kind of popping sounds, like air sounds [makes "whooochooosh" sound with voice and lips] a lot, not just music but really different music, which was really exciting. Another part of that was to make sure that the melodies and the rhythms of the Gitksan informed the melodies and the rhythms of the music. It was really important that everything flowed from the language, [. . .] so the recordings of him [Vince Gogag] became . . . the foundation of the musical material.

Learning the Gitksan was doubly demanding because of the sounds that Current describes, sounds that are unlike any of those in the languages of Western European opera. Here is how Marion Newman describes some of her experience learning the Gitksan:

There is a layer of frustration because it is something you've never heard before. So, I don't have references. Like, what does the X mean? Why is there a *chwwqch*? Where is the vowel? What is that squiggly line? It is not in IPA. It's a different IPA, it is an Indigenous Phonetic Alphabet not an International Phonetic Alphabet [. . .] needing those tapes and listening but asking "How do I sing that?" One of my words is a slide up . . . *hlgulxw* . . . that slide up, "What does that mean? Am I supposed to crescendo that or . . . *hlgulxw* . . . it's all air, except for the gu, everything else is made in air, and there is music, and there is an underlay and I am going, "Is anyone even gonna' hear that? How the hell am I supposed to sing that?" And it means "baby," and I speak it during the language lesson. It ended up working but, man, I had to do a leap of faith there. There is a huge sadness that I have never had access to this before now.

Accessing the knowledge that comes with the Gitksan is a process that roots the relationships between the Indigenous characters and the white characters in the land of origin, an Indigenous world. That process is a part of the reordering of affairs, a "reworlding" of the events. The upside-down meaning in Clements's opera transposes the story of a Native girl in a white world to a repositioning of white people in an Indigenous world.

Tim Long talks about the characteristics of the music and how it transformed as the worlds collided or aligned:

> The music is both simple and difficult because it is tonal, largely tonal. It is influenced from minimalism and I love minimalism . . . Minimalism locks you into tempos and rhythms so there is no flexibility. So, for a lot of the piece you are locked into rhythms until [the] character [Native Girl] starts singing in Gitksan and then he [Current] loses a sense of time, and suddenly . . . it sounds like it is just floating. Even though it is articulated on paper, he loses that sense of time and I think it is amazing. It was almost as if it was improvised, with no metre at all. When Ava and Devon were getting married, that was minimalist. It was repeating rhythms; even though they were doing Native ceremony, they were still within that non-Native kind of rhythm that was happening . . . And my god, when Ava and the Native Girl had that duet about the baby, phew, just breaks your mind . . . That made a huge difference to me to hear the two different worlds.

The music of the two different worlds charts the trajectories of the characters as they move in and out of each other's realities. It also marks a shift in consciousness from the torpor of the status quo to an awakening of responsibility. It is a point clearly noted when Native Mother asks, What are you missing? In making this direct challenge to the audience, she asks them to consider, if not recognize, what this horror is about. Yet as disparate as the Indigenous and non-Indigenous worlds are, neither is far removed from opera in that they both have long standing traditions with it. Marion Newman offers her perspective: "Singing is what we have all done to tell our stories as Kwagiulth people, as Stó:lō people, forever . . . because that is how our hearts hear; that is how our hearts remember."

Tim Long knows about the mixing of worlds and marked his experience of the opera in the following way:

> When I was in Victoria, I bought a Kwagiulth drum from Joan Glendale* and she blessed it every day of its making. And then I asked Carey Newman** to design something for it. So, he designed it and painted it, and the three images on it are my parents' clans. So, there is a racoon for my dad, there is a wolf for my mother, and then the third image is a sparrow—which represents the opera. And I have that hanging prominently in my office at Eastman so everybody who comes in sees it, and it is a one of a kind. That is memory. It is honouring both my parents and the twelve hundred and more missing Indigenous women, so I got so much from that, all of that really.

Perhaps it is not surprising that opera, as an old/new form, became a meeting place for Indigenous collaborators and others to gather together to publicly confront wrongdoing, to attempt redress, to provoke change; to sing in honour of the murdered missing whose love some hearts remember.

---

*   Joan I. Glendale is a drum maker from the Kwakwaka'wakw Nation. She lives on Vancouver Island.

**   Cary Newman is Marion Newman's brother. Like his sister he is Kwagiulth/Stó:lō and he is a renowned visual artist.

Writing Missing

Marie Clements, Librettist

When I was asked to write on Missing and Murdered Indigenous Women and Girls, there was just a stone that laid heavy in my chest. It didn't move and it didn't want to open. It just laid large inside me, threatening gravity. Yet there was an overwhelming insistence that grew in waves—to lean into it—to not back down—because that is what I signed up for when I chose to write, to become an artist.

Missing was not meant to be easy. Not for the producing companies, not for the artists in creation and performance, and not for audiences. It was meant to bring us face to face with the fact that we are all human yet we are all not equal. In *Missing* we see two young women, one non-Indigenous and one Indigenous, and we begin to understand that they have a lot in common. Their future holds beauty and promise—one and the same. They have plans for the future; yet only one gets to fulfill the potential they were born to.

I've written about Missing and Murdered Indigenous Women and Girls before. I've decided I will continue to write about it until I don't have to. In this way, I am not alone. I join other artists, musicians, writers, performers, human rights activists, and Indigenous families in what is now a chorus of voices repeatedly saying: "Enough. Enough." This is not an Indigenous issue. It is a human issue that can only be resolved by recognizing each other.

They say that music brings people together, that it opens hearts because it is a universal language. They say that opera can unfold the greatest of tragedies in the most achingly beautiful way. It is fitting then that *Missing* takes on the most tragic and horrific issue of our time in hopes that we cannot only have the courage to bear witness, but rise to tell a story that can hopefully create change one heart at a time.

Composing Missing

Brian Current, Composer

In 2016, City Opera Vancouver and Pacific Opera Victoria got in touch to ask if I would consider auditioning as a composer for a project they were developing about Missing and Murdered Indigenous Women and Girls. This meant that I would set a scene of the libretto for their jury, who would not know who the composers were. At the time, I had heard of the missing Indigenous women, but it was simply a headline. Like nearly every other non-Indigenous Canadian, I would sigh and simply turn the page. Fortunately, the jury chose my submission, and this started a sequence of events that opened my eyes to Canada's murderously unjust treatment of Indigenous people.

Indigenous people in Canada have known about these crimes all along. They have historically had an unspeakably difficult time in Canada, from outright genocide during colonial years, to an abhorrent state-sanctioned residential school system of forced separation from family, language, and culture (and where many died—many of these schools had graveyards), to forced adoptions during the 1960s, to forced sterilization, to today where, while many Indigenous artists and thinkers (like my colleagues described in these pages) are inspiringly paving the way forward towards an equitable future, many Indigenous families still live in extremely difficult conditions with high rates of suicide and addiction.

And while the 2019 report of the National Inquiry found there was no "reliable estimate of missing and murdered Indigenous women, girls, and 2SLGBTQQIA persons in Canada" unofficial reports list more than 4,200 names. Four thousand, two hundred. Imagine if 4,200 white women vanished from Ottawa or Portland or Victoria or Adelaide—there would be major international outcry. This is not something that happened in the past. During the time I was working on the opera, four Indigenous women were murdered in Winnipeg and two went missing in Ontario north of Toronto.

The libretto was written by the astoundingly gifted Indigenous playwright and filmmaker Marie Clements. It is beautifully authentic and wonderfully musical. She has said that it was important to work with a composer who is not Indigenous, as the story is about the coming together of Indigenous and non-Indigenous worlds. Throughout, it was a priority for me that I did not "manhandle" the libretto in any way, as was the composer's traditional inclination, but rather provide a platform for or amplification of her story. My goal was to take a supporting role, rather than a leading role. The producers were sensitive to this as well: four out of the seven cast members were of Indigenous background, as were half of the designers and crew. Everyone immediately understood the sense of mission surrounding this piece and got to work.

Right from the beginning, it was important that all materials relating to Indigenous language and culture were treated with absolute sensitivity. I was grateful that our producers began the process, before one word or note was written, by consulting widely within the Indigenous community in Vancouver. At every workshop, presentation, or large meeting, there were Indigenous land acknowledgements and cedar brushing and smudging ceremonies, all of which were new to me, and all of which I became more and more grateful to be part of. I can only hope that these ceremonies provided even a small amount of comfort to the communities affected by the tragedy.

There are roughly sixty distinct Indigenous languages in Canada and my understanding is that they are quite different from one another. About one third of the opera is sung in Gitksan, the language spoken by the Indigenous community on the northwest coast of British Columbia. This is the region of the Highway of Tears, where many of the women were kidnapped and where much of the opera takes place. My hero of the project must certainly be Vince Gogag, who provided the translation and pronunciation of the Gitksan, as well as advised on cultural protocols related to the Gitksan community. Gitksan is a wonderfully beautiful language, with popping high consonants and vowels made completely of air sounds. It was a real pleasure to receive recordings of Vince speaking in his first language and spend several weeks painstakingly transcribing them into musical notation. Melodies and rhythms were created to preserve Vince's speech patterns. Also, there is a wedding scene sung in Gitksan where we asked Vince if he might find a traditional wedding song from his community. He believes that these have now been lost, but he was kind enough to share with me a recording of his grandfather singing traditional Gitksan songs. With Vince's permission, the melodies of these folk songs were used as the melodic structure of the wedding scene in the opera, with the rhythms of the language informing the rhythms of the music.

Vince was also open about granting permission for other Gitksan protocols, such as the use of Indigenous drumming. This was something that I was quite nervous about. As a non-Indigenous composer, it presented a minefield of potential appropriation, which would be yet again another instance of a white man stealing from the Indigenous community. After much questioning of Vince, I was convinced that it would not be insulting to have an Indigenous cast member playing a frame drum on stage and that Gitksan drum protocols allowed for this.

One of the workshops took place at the Native Education College in Vancouver, where we presented early scenes of the piece to a college-aged Indigenous audience. These included scenes that incorporated Indigenous drumming. Following the workshop, we asked for feedback. Again, I was anxious about being inadvertently offensive, but the feedback we received from the audience was very thoughtful and insightful. The students said that they found the drumming to be comforting and a positive intersection between operatic culture and Indigenous culture. This gave me some courage that we were on the right track.

Missing is not a work of fiction. It is a tragedy that is not fiction and it is a nightmare that is not fiction. Native women really have been, as Marie's libretto states, the victims of "fists and hammers, screwdrivers and knives," and "cut up and fed to pigs," and, outrageously, "carved up for the courts of law, so you can see better." Can you believe that for the first time in Canada body parts of murdered women were brought into a courtroom as evidence? All of this, combined with scenes like one of a young woman crying for her mother while being stalked in the woods or the Native Mother crying for her lost daughter, wore heavily on the creators, cast, and crew, necessitating breaks and counselling throughout rehearsals. Most importantly, the premiere performance was a closed-door presentation only for the families of the victims, with no tickets or press. This was the most important of all the performances. Their feedback was nothing short of heartbreaking.

Through this piece, I hope that you will learn more about Canada's Missing and Murdered Indigenous Women and Girls, vote based on it, and help ensure that laws are strengthened so that these women are protected and that it never happens again. You can donate to the Native Women's Association of Canada at www.nwac.ca.

Designing Missing

Andy Moro, Designer

In 1608, while Champlain was establishing dominance in the New World by building a fortress at what would become Quebec City, the very first opera was being performed before the court in Mantova, Italy. *L'Orfeo* features an inexplicable descent into hell for the innocent Euridice, an unsuspecting woman bitten by a snake while picking wildflowers. Monteverdi's work, like Champlain's wall, has stood the test of time.

Opera houses would multiply exponentially across Europe through the 1700s and beyond, as would European settlements on Turtle Island. While divas and divos were groomed, Indigenous people were displaced, enslaved, hunted, and enlisted by the occupying forces to cull furs and pelts for the voracious European market. Baroque Europe was flush with an opera-attending elite adorned in the glistening skin of our industrious beaver.

Indigenous women had been a commodity for a century already.

Christopher Columbus famously wrote:

> A hundred castellanoes* are as easily obtained for a woman as for a farm, and it is very general and there are plenty of dealers who go about looking for girls; those from nine to ten are now in demand.**

---

* A Spanish gold coin valued at approximately 435 maravedis in 1492—equivalent to $0.37 CAD today.

** John Boyd Thatcher, *Christopher Columbus His Life, His Work, His Remains as Revealed by Original Printed and Manuscript Records*" (New York: G.P. Putnam's Sons, 1903), 435.

So, it is significant that Marie Clements uses this form to address an ongoing genocide. Like Pontiac's famous lacrosse game at Fort Michilimackinac, Marie Clements has been formally invited to perform inside the fort. She accepts the invitation with a sharp and steely awareness. Once inside, once the gates are closed and the house lights fade, she attacks. Her only weapon is truth. Her language is refined, and her humble power is completely disarming.

The scale and opulence of this form are typically inaccessible to artists outside the mainstream. In this time of mandated "Reconciliation," one must gauge whether an offering is authentic or yet another thin veil for the gentry to dodge accountability and assuage guilt with trinkets.

Missing is an atlas—Indigenous mapping that articulates the experience of getting to a place, in significant contrast to the settler version of mapping that is preoccupied with boundaries of ownership.

Marie digs tirelessly through asphalt, sediment, and bedrock. She offers us each a shovel. With her, we unearth truth.

> From the darkness, the sound of rain falling. Then—a solid white painted line is slowly drawn through the aisle, dividing the audience and stage like the white line of a long highway.

Missing has been waiting to come. It is a sentient story with thousands of eyes and mouths. It has studied us while shining brightly from both blue skies and black. It has collected feathers and bones and shells on our shores. It built shelters and grew wings. It burst from trees and fell to earth.

> The leaves fell like hands over my eyes. Did I tell you? The leaves fell like hands across my face. Their palms reading the curve of a road that is a vein. The curve of a life that doesn't want to end.

Designing for any discipline is a balance of inspiration, talent, craft, and hardline pragmatism. Marie makes the poetic aspect easy. Sparrows, falling leaves, bones, roads, beginnings, and endings. Snow, stars, sun, and moon. Birth wrapped inside death. Fire, flapping wings, fluttering memories. Love.

MISSING BY MARIE CLEMENTS - PAINT UPDATES

Western theatre is historically presented in the proscenium style, like a classroom or a church. The conductor occupies the most prominent position in the picture, the orchestra formidably placed between the storytellers and their audience. Of course, it is logical that the conductor is quite literally front and centre. All players need their cues, but culturally, socially, politically, for this story it is counterintuitive to position a white male in a position of such overt dominance. In a bittersweet twist of circumstance, the premiere was conducted by Timothy Long, of Muscogee Creek and Choctaw descent. To have the opportunity to witness Mr. Long so proudly and confidently leading the work was a gift.

The production process inevitably includes managers, crews, inventories, budgets, truck dimensions, timelines, and technical limitations. It is important to recognize these tangibles as an integral part of the design toolbox in order to steer them towards serving the work. Money and time are absolute. Inspiration and imagery are invited and invented with the tools at hand.

When the work itself addresses oppression, colonization, alienation, and occupation, the degree to which it is influenced or inhibited by mainstream ideology is especially pronounced.

In the Feast Hall there is dance, story, song, and shared experience. Coming of age, marriage, birth, and death are recognized formally and collectively. There is spectacle, celebration, and grief. Time expands. At the Potlatch, the host family showers all in attendance with gifts. It is in giving, rather than having, that one's wealth is measured.

The feast-hall facade in this early scene in *Missing* appears first as a ghostly, black shape. It is both longhouse and the absence of longhouse. The imposing facade of these magnificent shoreline structures welcomes and defends from guests. We the audience, citizens of "Canada," are the guests.

The Potlatch ban was enforced until well within the lifetime of many members of the present-day opera community. The ban was an extension of John A. Macdonald's "Iron hand on the shoulders of the Indian" policy thus criminalizing social gathering, tradition, and ceremony. For this reason, the core architecture of *Missing* is deliberately devoid of image. By covering the longhouse with scrim, projections can recreate and wilfully erase the impressively imposing painted front wall, selectively revealing what is behind the facade. Tradition and truth hiding in plain sight, safe from the enforced and unjust "rule of law."

Traditional Gitksan formline can only be employed with respected protocols and permissions. A collaborating team member graciously offered to *Missing* the formline work of a respected Gitksan ancestor. This was an unexpected and profoundly generous gift. Using this beautiful work, the projections were built, cued, and integrated through the month-long rehearsal process.

On opening day, as the proverbial last minute passed, one relative of the artist expressed discomfort with the use of the work. While that discussion should have occurred several weeks earlier, the fact that permission was not absolute meant the work was no longer available. Family protocol rules and unanimity is critical.

The production had thankfully enlisted Kelli Clifton, renowned Gitga'ata designer and artist to create a formline graphic for the *Missing* marketing campaign.

Kelli says of her design:

> The sparrow is in flight to signify a sense of hope. Although this is a positive trait, as an artist I couldn't ignore the heavy emotional content that is being addressed in *Missing*. I wanted to honour this by portraying a woman in the body of the sparrow to represent all those missing and murdered.

She had, of course, seized upon the central image presented by Clements. The humble sparrow. Blending in. Unassuming and resilient. Overlooked and omnipresent. Surviving against all odds in diverse and often punishing circumstances.

With Kelli's permission, this designer locked himself in the technical booth at noon on the day of our premiere to reconstruct and re-cue the entire projection score, from this single image.

Kelli agreed to me reconfiguring and reconstructing composite imagery from the bones of her brilliant work. This is a trust and generosity I have not experienced before or since in the world of design; true humility, faith, and courage.

With gratitude and perhaps a few new strands of grey, this designer completed an intense, exacting process precisely as our first audience was entering the house.

It seemed this was exactly what the work wanted from us:

THE NATIVE GIRL: Gi'hl nel dzay ya ts'im lachs. Gi'. Kamts'in ksinahlchwi' wihl bahasxw. Nel dzay ya.

AVA *looks at it and under her breath softly—*

AVA: I'm sorry I never picked you up.

THE NATIVE GIRL *smiles.*

THE NATIVE GIRL: G̲ak̲ax hl nel dzay ya ts'axwildi hl s̲kiksxwt.

THE NATIVE GIRL *arches her body upwards and she becomes almost all white in the light.* AVA *watches as her light fades and the sound of a small bird's wings and the spirit light of a bird moves across the dark sky.*

AVA: A broken sparrow still can fly.

THE NATIVE GIRL: Sowii gipaygwin. Sowii gipaygwin.

AVA *looks at her own body and turns to stand upright. A* CT *scan light moves down her body and reveals a positive scan of her body; white fractured veins in her bones where they had been broken in* THE NATIVE GIRL—*a car accident: her ribs, her hip, her arm. The scan moves downwards creating a frame around her that reveals and darkens in movement.*

Lights out.

Missing was co-commissioned and co-produced by Pacific Opera Victoria and City Opera Vancouver and developed over two and a half years. It premiered in Vancouver and Victoria in November 2017 with the following cast:

Ava: Caitlin Wood
Native Girl: Melody Courage
Jess: Heather Molloy
Devon: Kaden Forsberg
Dr. Wilson: Marion Newman
Native Student/Angus Wilds: Clarence Logan
Native Mother: Rose-Ellen Nichols

In 2019, Pacific Opera partnered with the Victoria Native Friendship Centre, Prince George Native Friendship Centre, Regina Treaty/Status Indian Services, Regina Symphony Orchestra, and Prince George Symphony Orchestra to remount *Missing* for performances at the Baumann Centre in Victoria, at the Regina Performing Arts Centre, and at the Uda Dune Baiyoh House of Ancestors Convention Centre in Prince George, with the following cast and creative team:

Ava: Caitlin Wood
Native Girl: Joanna Diindiisikwe Simmons
Jess: Heather Molloy
Devon: Jan van der Hooft
Dr. Wilson: Marion Newman
Native Student/Angus Wilds: Kyle Lehmann
Native Mother: Rose-Ellen Nichols

Librettist: Marie Clements
Composer: Brian Current
Director: Peter Hinton
Conductor: Timothy Long
Scenic and Projection Design: Andy Moro

Costume Design: Carmen Thompson
Lighting Design: John Webber
Assistant Lighting Design: Alia Stephen
Sound Design: Sandy Scofield
Additional Sound Design: Troy Slocum
Dramaturge: Paula Danckert
Gitksan Translations and Diction Coach: Vincent Gogag
Gitksan IPA Transcriptions: Michael David Schwan
Surtitles: Anika Vervecken and Teresa Turgeon
Stage Manager: Chris Porter
Assistant Stage Manager: Bradley Dunn

The sparrow has been able to survive and thrive in spite of its natural predators. It has become a symbol of the idea—nobility of the common person is inherently strong within us.

Characters

Ava
The Native Girl
Jess
Devon
Large Man's Shadow
RCMP Constable
Dr. Wilson
The Native Mother
Angus Wilds
Native Student

Place

Vancouver, Highway 16

Time / K'apk'ohl

Fall. Winter. Spring. Summer. / Kwsit. Maadam. Gwoym. Sint.
Yesterday/Now. / 'Kyoots/Gyo'n

Prelude

Highway 16. Just West of Prince George. Fall.

From the darkness, the sound of rain falling. Then—a solid white painted line is slowly drawn through the aisle, dividing the audience and stage like the white line of a long highway.

There on the side of the highway, THE NATIVE GIRL, *age sixteen, stands hitchhiking on the deserted road.*

There on the other side—lights up on AVA, *age twenty-two, as she drives along the highway. Jagged flashes of light and darkness move across her face.*

THE NATIVE GIRL *suddenly looks up at* AVA*—their eyes meeting and locking—suspended in time.*

AVA *drives past* THE NATIVE GIRL. *Time passes.*

The sound of a car skidding on the wet road, the sound of the car's metal scraping, the sound of AVA *letting out a low scream as the car crashes into the base of a tree.*

The sound transforming—

Lights up on THE NATIVE MOTHER, *age fifty-seven, as she reacts to the sound of the crash—understanding deep within her something is so wrong.*

Act One

Scene 1: Highway 16. In A Gully Off the Side of the Road.

It is still dark except for the car's headlights that reveal AVA's body hanging upside down in a tree.

AVA wakes—her eyes suddenly open in a terror, blinking. Her breath—catching and then slowing as she watches leaves from the tree begin to fall. She follows the movement of falling leaves to the ground where—

Below her, like a shadow of herself, THE NATIVE GIRL lies outstretched on the ground.

AVA: She was lying there. Did I tell you?
She was lying there under the tree. I looked at her. I looked at her until I saw her.

THE NATIVE GIRL: Until I saw you.

AVA: Really until she saw me.

THE NATIVE GIRL: La<u>x</u>la<u>k</u> hl 'yens wihl lii han'un la<u>x</u> 'tse'li'. Mehldi' loona? La<u>x</u>la<u>k</u> hl 'yens g̱adax 'tse'li'.

AVA: Their palms reading the curve of a road that is a vein.

THE NATIVE GIRL: Hle hlek hl gandidils ehl nee dii 'nim hlisxwt.

AVA: I'm hanging in the wind. Who are you, girl?

THE NATIVE GIRL: 'Nii'hl baahasxw. Nda skidim go'ohl baahasxw mi'y? Nda skidim go'ohl baahasxw?

A small sparrow appears on a branch. THE NATIVE GIRL *watches it.*

Gi'hl nel dzay ya ts'im lachs. Gi'. Kamts'in ksinahlchwi' wihl bahasxw. Nel dzay ya.

AVA *looks at it and under her breath softly—*

AVA: I'm sorry I never picked you up.

THE NATIVE GIRL *smiles.*

THE NATIVE GIRL: Gakax hl nel dzay ya ts'axwildi hl skiksxwt.

THE NATIVE GIRL *arches her body upwards and she becomes almost all white in the light.* AVA *watches as her light fades and the sound of a small bird's wings and the spirit light of a bird moves across the dark sky.*

AVA: A broken sparrow still can fly.

THE NATIVE GIRL: Sowii gipaygwin. Sowii gipaygwin.

AVA *looks at her own body and turns to stand upright. A* CT *scan light moves down her body and reveals a positive scan of her body; white*

fractured veins in her bones where they had been broken in THE NATIVE
GIRL—*a car accident: her ribs, her hip, her arm. The scan moves
downwards creating a frame around her that reveals and darkens in
movement.*

Lights out.

Scene 2: Hospital Room.

Lights up on THE NATIVE GIRL *as she sits on a chair beside* AVA *who is
lying on a bed, bruised and battered, recovering from her accident.*

AVA's *best friend,* JESS, *age twenty-three, an ultra-preppy law student,
walks in with* AVA's *handsome ex-boyfriend* DEVON, *age twenty-two.
They stand around her bed as* AVA *opens her sleepy eyes.*

JESS: You don't look like yourself.

AVA: I don't feel like myself.

JESS: What do you feel like?

AVA: Like I am myself but missing a part of myself. Moving across something
but never understanding the beginning, never reaching the end.

JESS: I missed you. I waited for you
each day. I prayed for you each day.
Please let her live. Please let her
breathe. Please let her come back to
us. Every day. Every day. I said these
things. Every day I wished you alive.

DEVON: I waited for you each day.
Each day. Please let her breathe.
Every day. Every day I wished you
alive.

AVA: I was in a deep sleep far from myself. In a dark sky.

JESS: I missed you. I waited for you each night. I prayed for you each night. Please let her live. Please let her breathe. Please let her come back to us. Every night. Every night. I said these things. Every night I wished you alive.

DEVON: I waited for you each night. Each night. Please let her breathe. Every night. Every night. I wished you alive.

AVA: I've lifted from a nightmare. Today is like flying into a dream.

JESS: You're here now.

AVA: Am I?

JESS: I can see you. I can hear you. You are alive.

AVA: You can see me?

JESS: All nightmares come to an end. All darkness meets the light. I can see you. I can hear you. You are alive.

DEVON: All nightmares come to an end. All darkness meets the light. I can see you. I can hear you. You are alive.

AVA: But what about her?

AVA looks over.

JESS: What about who?

JESS looks to see who she is looking at. DEVON does the same. No one is there.

Scene 3: UBC Campus. Lecture Hall Podium.

Guest speaker, Gitksan law professor, DR. WILSON, *age forty-five, walks on the lecture stage and adjusts the mic at the podium.* DR. WILSON *looks out at the audience as* AVA *and* JESS, DEVON *and other students take their seats in the audience.*

DR. WILSON: What do you see when you see me?

There is an uncomfortable silence as DR. WILSON *looks directly at the* UBC *students.*

Anyone?

No one raises their hand. It is deathly silent.

Do you recognize me?

JESS looks around at her fellow classmates and proudly answers.

JESS: Do I recognize you as what?

She looks directly at JESS.

DR. WILSON: As a human being. Do you recognize me as a human being?

JESS is taken aback.

There are three thousand Native women "Missing" in North America. Three. Thousand. Missing.*

The students begin to shift in their seats uncomfortably.

Answer me this— What happens to a society when we can't recognize another human being—as another human being? What happens to a society when we can't recognize a part of ourselves—*as* a part of ourselves? What are *we* missing?

JESS: I don't understand.

She looks at AVA *for support.*

AVA *is looking at* DR. WILSON *intently.*

DR. WILSON: You don't understand.

JESS: I don't understand what you are trying to get at. What are you trying to say?

AVA: Jess . . . just let her . . .

DR. WILSON: What are you missing?

JESS: Just let her what?

AVA: Speak.

DR. WILSON: What does missing mean to you? Does missing mean we lost something? Is it *our* fault?

---

*   Please note these stats are constantly updating.

JESS: Our fault?

AVA: Jess, please.

JESS defiantly.

JESS: No. It's not our fault.

DR. WILSON: Do you think they lost themselves? It's their fault they went missing?

JESS: I'm not saying that.

DR. WILSON: Maybe it's their fault they are Indigenous. First Nations. Indian?

JESS: This is not about race. This is not about the colour of your skin, how much money you have, where you were born.

DR. WILSON: Then what's it about?

JESS looks to AVA.

JESS: Say something. Say anything.

AVA: I saw a Native girl on the highway.

JESS: What are you talking about?

AVA: I saw her . . .

JESS turns her attention to DR. WILSON

DR. WILSON: Hitchhiking on a lone highway. She got into a car.	**NATIVE STUDENT:** Missing and Murdered.

JESS: It's about decisions.

DR. WILSON: Having that drink at the bar. Going to that party with friends.

NATIVE STUDENT: Missing and Murdered.

JESS: It's their decisions. It's their fault. You're not being fair.

DR. WILSON: Now you want to be fair.

JESS: I don't want to be attacked.

DR. WILSON: I am attacking—*you.*

JESS: That's what your people do.

DR. WILSON: That's what my people do.

JESS: You make yourselves victims and then you blame society.

JESS looks at AVA and keeps her gaze throughout. AVA won't meet her gaze.

Why are you letting her attack me? Why aren't you standing with me? What's wrong with you? What's wrong with you?

DR. WILSON: Fists and hammers, screwdrivers and knives.

AVA & NATIVE STUDENT: Missing and Murdered.

JESS: Look at me.

DR. WILSON: Matches lit. Flesh burnt. Seared skin.

AVA & NATIVE STUDENT: Missing and Murdered.

JESS: Why won't you look at me?

DEVON *finally joins in—*

DR. WILSON: Aiming their guns, inserting their knives, loading their cocks—

AVA, NATIVE STUDENT, & DEVON: Missing and Murdered.

JESS: We are the same.

DR. WILSON: Our bodies used. Cut up and fed to pigs. Our bodies used. Carved up for the courts of law. So you can see better.

AVA, NATIVE STUDENT, & DEVON: Missing and Murdered.

JESS: Look at me!

DR. WILSON: Our bodies used. Buried in unmarked graves. Our bodies used. Buried by the side of the road.

AVA, NATIVE STUDENT, & DEVON: Missing and Murdered

JESS *looks at* AVA.

JESS: Look at me!

AVA *doesn't turn.*

You are less than me. I said it. I said what we are all thinking. I said it. I said it. I say it. You are less than me. Less than us. You always have been. I said it.

DR. WILSON: You say it. But I have heard you all my life.

DR. WILSON *looks right into* JESS.

Even when you are not speaking. You say it. I have heard you all my life.

JESS looks down suddenly overcome with emotion.

JESS: I'm sorry. But there is a line. I'm sorry.

Her words catching her.

DR. WILSON: A sorry line between us.

She pauses and then—

First a line on our land. Where you will be. And where we will be allowed to be.

ALL: Missing and Murdered.

DR. WILSON: Then a line around our women. Who you will take. And who you will discard.

ALL: Missing and Murdered.

DR. WILSON: Then a line between ourselves and our children. Residential school. Foster care. Scooping under the line of who will have everything and who will have nothing.

ALL: Missing and Murdered.

DR. WILSON: I am here to tell you there is no line between us on the long road. We didn't come to you. You came to us.

ALL: Missing and Murdered.

DR. WILSON: You came to us on the long road you made. On the long road we now travel together.

She stops and looks directly at JESS.

Native women go missing because they are less in the eyes of those who have lost their humanity.

AVA suddenly speaks up.

AVA: Or never had it.

DR. WILSON looks at her. JESS glares at her.

DR. WILSON: Or never had it. Never understood that humanity has a responsibility. Never understood we have a responsibility to each other.

AVA looks directly at DR. WILSON throughout. JESS is stunned by the turn in the room and begins to cry.

DR. WILSON: If you can cry for yourself, cry now like you have lost your mother.

AVA & NATIVE STUDENT: And no one hears you.

DR. WILSON: Cry now like you have lost your child.

AVA & NATIVE STUDENT: And no one stands with you.

DR. WILSON: Cry now like you have lost your sister.

AVA & NATIVE STUDENT: And no one does anything.

DR. WILSON: Cry now like you keep losing them over, and over, and there is no end. And no one does anything. There is no end, no end, no end, to this sorry line.

ALL: Missing and Murdered Women.

DEVON and students get up quietly and exit. JESS gets up unsteadily as DR. WILSON watches. DR. WILSON moves towards JESS compassionately but JESS turns and moves away almost bumping into AVA.

Scene 4

AVA: Jess?

JESS: Get away from me.

AVA: Jess, please.

She turns.

JESS: Don't look at me. Don't look at me like that
You're the broken one and you pity me? You pity me?

You took their side.

AVA: There are no sides.

JESS: I don't know you anymore. I don't know who you are. We were like sisters. We were like blood. I loved you. I trusted you. We were the same.

AVA: I can't be the same anymore. I have to be more. I have to ask for more. I have to expect more. I can't be . . .

JESS: Me. You can't be me . . .

AVA: Jess . . .

JESS backs away.

JESS: I wish you had died. I wish you were dead. I wish I had gone to your funeral so I could mourn you. Black. So I could cry on green grass. Fresh tears. But look—there are no tears. No tears. I will shed no tears for you.

AVA, taken aback, moves from her as if she has been hit.

Lights fade.

Scene 5: Highway 16. Small Town Cabin. Winter.

In the distance lights fade up on THE NATIVE MOTHER, *age fifty-seven. She sits in front of a flickering fire, her mouth open, almost paralyzed. A low sound comes from her—a keening—so deep it has rooted her to the spot.*

Behind her, a large mountain of a man, her son, ANGUS *Wilds, age twenty-five, turns around with a blanket in his hand, inside the cabin that is their home.*

He looks to the liquid dark sky, and he can see because there is no ceiling, no roof. Snow begins to fall. He moves towards his mother and places the blanket around her shoulders affectionately.

ANGUS: Snow, Mother.

She doesn't look.

Snow. Snow.

ANGUS closes his eyes in a memory and the cabin almost disappears in darkness. He feels his sister's small hand in his. He opens his eyes and looks down and his little sister is there. She is six and he is fifteen. She looks up to him.

Nee dii 'nakwxt gyo'n. Guhl han'un'y. Hla dim bagwi'm.

THE NATIVE GIRL: Gal hlibhlebiksxw hl sise' 'y. Yuk hl sigetxw diit.

ANGUS: Bax pteltxwin.

She climbs up his knee, and then onto his back, and then sits on his shoulders laughing, as he stands and she rises to the sky. ANGUS *twirls her as the snow begins to fall harder.*

Ndahl wilhl sise'en gyo'n?

THE NATIVE GIRL: Hiisolagyaxxw da.

He begins to laugh with her, twirling. He slows—out of breath. He turns and, in the turn, she is gone.

She is gone. The memory is gone.

ANGUS *closes his eyes tight and stretches his hand out in a desperate wish.*

ANGUS: I'm sorry. I should have looked after you. I should have made sure you were safe. Take my hand now. Take my hand. Please. Please. Take my hand now. I am sorry.

Behind him the still cabin is there. Behind ANGUS *his mother's paralyzed keening. Inside him—*

Ga ha'win. Ha'u. Ga ha'win.
Guuhl han'un'y 'min bets'y niin.
Hugyaxet win t'k'ihlxw'm.
See hluxsxw'm tsim maaxs.
T'aan lax noo'ohl'y.
Luhogyax'm hl wii gyet.
Nee diitna hl basx'm.

Nee dii basx agu.
Si 'wii 'nakwdin nii'y.
Gimxdi'y niin.
Gimxdi'y niin.
Ga ha'win. Ha'u. Ga ha'win.
Dim guudi'y hl han'un.
Dim 'min bets di niin.
Hla ha'w'm dim welix'y niin
Ga ha'win. K'e a god'n ga ha'win.

Lights fade.

Scene 6: Downtown Eastside. Vancouver.

AVA *walks on the street close to Main and Hastings. She looks up; sees wires crossing. She looks over; a small bird flying in the sky, its reflection now lower, moving past a plate of glass on a storefront.*

AVA *follows the sparrow's flight across the glass, and then suddenly sees* THE NATIVE GIRL *in her reflection.*

THE NATIVE GIRL: Where are you going, girl?

AVA *closes her eyes spooked.*

DEVON: Ava?

AVA *opens her eyes to the sound of his voice.*

AVA: Devon.

DEVON: Who did you think it was? You okay?

AVA adjusts.

AVA: I don't know what to say. I don't have the words. The right words. I've changed. Everything has changed in me. I don't recognize myself.

DEVON: I see you.   **AVA:** Are you sure?

DEVON: You told me once I had to get serious. I had to make a choice about what was important to me. I said you were. I said . . .

AVA: I wasn't ready. I wanted things.

DEVON: I wanted you.

AVA: I wanted things to be perfect, not knowing perfect is not things. It's in the living. It's in the moment of who we are.

DEVON: I see you. I want you. I want us.

AVA: We'll start this new beginning.   **DEVON:** We'll start this new beginning.

Lights fade.

Scene 7: UBC. Learning Exchange. Downtown Eastside.

AVA sits in her first Gitksan language class as DR. WILSON stands in front of the whiteboard writing down words and pronouncing them in song as AVA repeats them, learning.

DR. WILSON: Wilp

AVA: Wilp

DR. WILSON: No<u>x</u>

AVA: No<u>x</u>

DR. WILSON: Gimxdi

AVA: Gimxdi

DR. WILSON: Kwsit

AVA: Kwsit

DR. WILSON: Maadam

AVA: Maadam

DR. WILSON: Gwoym

AVA: Gwoym

DR. WILSON: Sint

AVA: Sint

DR. WILSON: You speak like you were meant to speak our language.

AVA: I feel like I am remembering it. I feel I know it between my bones.

DR. WILSON: Words come to our voice to connect us to what is broken in us. Now finding the space in us to heal. Here. Blood. Here. Bones. Here. Heart. Here. Voice.

AVA: Here. Here.

She smiles.

Ha'miyaa.

AVA picks up her books and turns to leave class. She stops. One more question . . .

How do you say "baby"?

DR. WILSON: Hlguhlxw.

Rose smiles. Lights fade.

Scene 8: Ava and Devon's House. Bathroom.

AVA looks at herself in the bathroom mirror. She places her hands on her stomach and her attention goes here.

AVA: Hlguhlxw.

AVA struggles with the Gitksan word . . . and then hears—

THE NATIVE GIRL: Hlguhlxw.

AVA looks up and into the mirror as THE NATIVE GIRL smiles back at her.

AVA: What do you want from me? What do you want? I have my life; what do you want from me?

AVA sinks to the floor crying and then looks back up. THE NATIVE GIRL has disappeared and she is now completely alone.

AVA: Don't go. I'm sorry. Where did you go, girl?

THE NATIVE GIRL: Where did you go, girl?

AVA: I am right here.

THE NATIVE GIRL: I am right here.

AVA: Where is here for you?

THE NATIVE GIRL: Right now.

AVA turns and finally sees THE NATIVE GIRL in clear sight. She walks towards her.

AVA: What do I look like to you?

THE NATIVE GIRL: Like you could be me. If I was you.

AVA smiles and moves a strand of hair from THE NATIVE GIRL'*s face.*

AVA touches the scar on her head.

AVA: My head still hurts.

THE NATIVE GIRL: I know.

AVA: And here. A broken wing.

THE NATIVE GIRL: But still a bird.

AVA: But still a bird.

THE NATIVE GIRL: That can see things no one else can.

AVA: That can see things can be beautiful.

THE NATIVE GIRL: Even with these fresh scars.

Lights fade.

Scene 9: Ava and Devon's Backyard.

DEVON *and* AVA *stand together in a small gathering of friends about to get married.* AVA *looks beautiful and pregnant in her white wedding dress and* DEVON *handsome in his black suit.*

The sun shines through the budding cherry tree where they stand under falling white blossoms. THE NATIVE GIRL *stands by* AVA *dressed as if she is getting married.*

DR. WILSON *appears and is going to give them away as husband and wife in a traditional Gitksan wedding tradition.*

End of Act One.

Act Two

Scene 1: Highway 16. Small Town Cabin. Spring.

In the distance lights fade up on THE NATIVE MOTHER. *She sits in her chair with her hands together on her lap, palms open as a small stream of cherry blossoms falls from high above.*

Her mouth open, almost paralyzed. A low sound comes from her—a keening—in a dream of her daughter's wedding she will never attend.

Lights up on ANGUS *as he stands in the kitchen area cleaning a salmon, filleting it and adding it to the salmon that hang in a long line to dry.*

In a house with no ceiling THE NATIVE MOTHER *suddenly shoves the blossoms from her lap and hands, taking her rage to the blue cobalt sky and bright sun that is above the house with no ceiling.*

THE NATIVE MOTHER: Nee dii sgi dim hloxs. Needxw hloxs.

ANGUS stops at her first words in months.

Nee dii sgi dim hloxs. Ax xslaxatxw.

She gets up unsteadily and ANGUS *rushes to help her rise. She talks to the sun, shaming it.*

Hli jima wilax hl neem di goyp'ax̱'n. Hli jima wilax win neem di gabitxw'n. Joog'n. Joog. Da'wihl hlguhl'm hanak̲'y. Nda'm wila goy'pax̱'n ehl nee huxdii wilt go'y?

She eyes the blue. Shame.

X̱slax̱atxw lax̱a. X̱slax̱atxw. Hlen x̱slax̱atxw. Joog'n Neemidii gya'y a? Nee mi dii gya'at a? Nda iist? G̲ahlaux hl ts'ax'm lax̱a'n nda hl ts'ax'm mi'y'y?

ANGUS: Na'? Na'.

THE NATIVE MOTHER: Hlida sgyed'n
Ts'etlxw win gi'nitx hlox̲s
G̲alx̲dil hl x̱slax̱atxwm lax̱a.
G̲alksa gabitxw se, galksa gabitxw hl ax̱xw.

Hlox̲s gan hl bi'lust
Wilax diit hl wen
Wilax diit good'n
Wilax diit ginax̱'n
Dim edigwil
Luuyeltxwt go'o'y.

Hlida sgyed'n
Ts'etlxw win gi'nitx hlox̲s
G̲alx̲dil hl x̱slax̱atxwm lax̱a.
G̲alksa gabitxw se, galksa gabitxw hl ax̱xw.

Hlguhl'm hana'k̲'y 'niin
Hla dim ha'win. Gyo'n.
Wilp. Hla dim ha'win.
Gyo'n. G̲a ha'win.
Dim gud'y hl han'un

Dim 'min betsdi'y 'niin

Dim welix'y niin. Ha'wi'm.

G̲a ha'win. Gyo'n.

K̲e' god'n ga ha'win.

She screams out to the blue.

Aba!

Lights fade.

Scene 2: Ava and Devon's Apartment. Living Room.

AVA sits exhausted from not sleeping. DR. WILSON is holding their newborn baby, rocking her with Gitksan words as DEVON watches them.

AVA: She cries.

DR. WILSON: That's what babies do.

AVA: She cries like there is no end.

DR. WILSON: Maybe she needs to hear her voice to understand she is in this world now. New.

AVA: Where do you think she was before?

DR. WILSON: It's not for me to say. It's for her to know and let go of.

AVA: It's hard to let go.

DR. WILSON: They say that, don't they. We know that, you and I. But still she has come to you. Perfect like this. It makes you think maybe the world she came from was perfect.

AVA: It's hard to let go.

DR. WILSON: If she came from this, maybe this is where we go back to when we die.

AVA stops and looks at her.

AVA: Do you really think this?

DR. WILSON looks down at the now sleeping baby.

DR. WILSON: I think it when I hold her. When I look down on her like this. When I hold her like this. The world gets bigger than all the things we can't make sense of.

DR. WILSON lays the baby in AVA's arms. They both fall asleep. DR. WILSON motions for DEVON to bring a blanket over. He does and she covers the mother and child. Both sleeping now in peace.

Lights fade.

Scene 3: Highway 16. Forest. Dusk. A Nightmare.

The sound of THE NATIVE GIRL *stumbling out of a car that isn't seen. The sound of her footsteps, and behind, the sound of his footsteps . . . just headlights splashed across the darkness to reveal a thick forest.*

AVA *moves frantically, falling and running from the sound of footsteps, then from a large man's shadow that appears above everything, moving above her, stalking.*

AVA *from her darkened living room.*

AVA: I am running
I am running
A scream inside my throat
Rising up to the cool air
He is there. Or there.
He is coming
He is coming

THE NATIVE GIRL: The branches like long hands
Dig into my flesh. Long hands.
Pointing like sharp knives
Into my chest

AVA: Below me a shadowy step
My feet sinking and catching on
Rocks and leaves and parts of trees
Sinking and stumbling, my legs like lead

Out of breath THE NATIVE GIRL *hides behind a giant cedar tree. She looks for the stars. She looks to the trees.* THE NATIVE GIRL *pleads as the dark shadow moves.*

THE NATIVE GIRL: Above, stars above   **AVA:** Please hear me
Please help me   Please hear me
Trees stand with me
Please help me

THE NATIVE GIRL: They are silent
They are stunned
Holding their breath
In a desperate prayer

Please. Please.
Tell my Momma.
Please. Please.
Tell my Momma.
Tell my Momma.
Tell my Momma.
I ran.

AVA: I am running. I am screaming but no one hears me.

THE NATIVE GIRL hears his footsteps moving slowly towards her. She turns and runs in slow motion.

THE NATIVE GIRL: You better not hurt me

AVA: I am running. I am screaming, but no one hears me.

THE NATIVE GIRL: Momma, I ran
Momma, I ran

THE NATIVE GIRL falls and turns around as his shadow approaches.

AVA: You better not hurt me

THE NATIVE GIRL: I want to live
I want to live
I want to live

THE NATIVE GIRL begins to cry.

AVA: I'm sorry, Momma
I'm sorry, Momma

She closes her eyes bracing herself.

THE NATIVE GIRL: Oh Momma. Oh Momma.
Momma. Momma.

THE NATIVE GIRL opens her eyes in a fear that is paralyzing. He isn't there.

A silence with no breath.

And then a sound there. And then there.

THE NATIVE GIRL: I want to go home.   AVA: He is there. He is there.
Home.   He is right there. Right there.
I want to go home.
Home.

The large man's shadow appears suddenly over THE NATIVE GIRL and grows into a real man's body high above her.

THE NATIVE GIRL inches back as his body moves over her.

AVA: He is . . .

Lights out.

Scene 4

AVA screams. DEVON *moves to her in the darkened living room where the trees outside cast long shadows across the room. The baby begins to cry.*

DEVON: Ava, wake up . . . Ava . . .

DEVON gathers her up in his arms.

Ava, please wake up . . . It's just a bad dream.

AVA: It's not a dream. It's not a dream. It's a nightmare.

DEVON: A dream gone bad. A dark night.

AVA: Am I here? Am I really here with you?

DEVON: You're here, Ava. You're safe with me.

AVA: Touch me . . . Am I real? Am I alive? Please tell me I am alive. Tell me I am alive. Tell me I am alive. You are my husband. She is our baby. Tell me. She is our beautiful baby.

DEVON: Ava, you are alive. I am your husband. She is our baby. We are safe here. We have plans. We have our whole lives.

AVA: We have plans. We have our whole lives.

DEVON: We have each other.

They cling together falling back asleep.

Scene 5

DEVON sleeps but the baby fusses, beginning to cry. AVA picks her up trying to sooth her, but instead she begins to cry herself.

AVA: Having you has scared me
Having you has scared me
Having you has made me realize
I have everything to lose.

AVA walks in the space, calming herself down as much as the baby. The baby keeps crying.

Please don't cry. Please don't cry. Everything will be all right. Everything will be all right. Momma's here. Momma's here.

AVA looks over and sees THE NATIVE GIRL watching her.

Please go away. Please don't take her. Please go away. Please go away. Don't look at her. She is not yours. Don't look at her. She's mine. She's mine. Please don't take her. There are so many bad things in the world. So many bad things that can take what we love away.

THE NATIVE GIRL: I just want to hold her. I just want to hold her like I would never let her go. I just hold her in my arms. I want to say I love you. I want to say I will never let anything bad happen to you. You don't have to be scared of me.

AVA moves towards THE NATIVE GIRL. Crying, she places the baby in her arms.

THE NATIVE GIRL & AVA: Hlida sgyed'n
Ts'etlxw win gi'nitx hlo<u>x</u>s
<u>G</u>al<u>x</u>dil hl <u>x</u>sla<u>x</u>atxwm la<u>x</u>a.
<u>G</u>alksa gabitxw se, galksa gabitxw hl a<u>xx</u>w.

Hlo<u>x</u>s gan hl bi'lust
Wilax diit hl wen
Wilax diit good'n
Wilax diit gina<u>x</u>'n
Dim edigwil
Luuyeltxwt go'o'y.

Hlida sgyed'n
Ts'etlxw win gi'nitx hlo<u>x</u>s
<u>G</u>al<u>x</u>dil hl <u>x</u>sla<u>x</u>atxwm la<u>x</u>a.
<u>G</u>alksa gabitxw se, galksa gabitxw hl a<u>xx</u>w.

> THE NATIVE GIRL *walks with the sleeping baby towards* DEVON *and looks at him sleeping.*

THE NATIVE GIRL: You never told me what you called her? What is her name?

> AVA *looks at her and smiles.*

AVA: Sparrow.

THE NATIVE GIRL: Nel dzay ya.

> THE NATIVE GIRL *lays the baby down in* DEVON's *arms and then looks at* AVA *but hearing her own family.*

THE NATIVE GIRL: I need to go back so I can go home. Home. I am your daughter. I am your sister. Home. I will take your hand. You will lift me up. You will carry me home. I want to go home. Home.

THE NATIVE MOTHER & ANGUS: You are my daughter. You are my sister. You will come home. Now. Home. You will come home. Now. Come home. We will take your hand. We will lift you up. We will carry you home. Come home.

The trees outside take over the living room until there is nothing but trees and two women standing.

Scene 6

THE NATIVE GIRL: I wanted to be you so I could live. I had plans like you have plans.

AVA: I know.

THE NATIVE GIRL: My head hurts.

AVA touches THE NATIVE GIRL's temple and blood begins to fall from her own temple.

AVA: I know.

THE NATIVE GIRL: My arm hurts.

AVA touches THE NATIVE GIRL's arm where stab wounds begin to bleed and blood begins to ooze from her own arm.

AVA: I know.

THE NATIVE GIRL: My private parts hurt.

> *AVA touches THE NATIVE GIRL's hips, and blood begins to seep through the cloth in her own clothes.*

AVA: I know.

THE NATIVE GIRL: My heart hurts.

> *AVA touches THE NATIVE GIRL's heart. AVA touches her hand. They look at each other.*

THE NATIVE GIRL & AVA: I know.

> *AVA touches her face. THE NATIVE GIRL touches hers.*

I saw her eyes. Did I tell you? I saw her eyes in me. I saw her face. Did I tell you? I saw her face in mine. Did I tell you? I saw her life. Did I tell you? I saw my life in her.

> *THE NATIVE GIRL lies down. Her breath heavy, and then, barely breathing, she looks up past AVA. THE NATIVE GIRL's gaze looks up at a branch where a small sparrow perches on a limb.*

AVA: Lying here like this. She saw a sparrow in the branches. She whispered her breath like the wind.

THE NATIVE GIRL: Sparrow.

AVA: Fly away.

THE NATIVE GIRL: A broken sparrow still has wings.

AVA: A broken sparrow can still fly—home.

Coloured leaves begin to fall over THE NATIVE GIRL's *body.*

THE NATIVE MOTHER & ANGUS: Ga ha'win. Ha'u. Ga ha'win.

Lights begin to fade as AVA *watches the sparrow take flight.*

Epilogue

Highway 16. Just West of Prince George. Fall.

In the distance the lights fade up on THE NATIVE MOTHER *as she stands at the open door of her cabin—her mouth open, her body shaking.*

Behind her, ANGUS, *barely able to remain standing.*

Before them an RCMP *constable gravely stands. His mouth opens—*

ANGUS *slowly falls—a ground with no floor—he rocks himself in a low keening.* THE NATIVE MOTHER *goes to him and raises his face tenderly.*

ANGUS *looks over at the* RCMP *constable.*

ANGUS: My sister was on her way home from school. She was going to graduate. She was going to learn her language. She was going to go to law school to become a lawyer. She wanted to have a family. She had plans. She had plans. She wanted to live. She wanted to love. She wanted what every human being wants.

THE NATIVE MOTHER *looks up as coloured leaves begin to fall.*

THE NATIVE MOTHER: Where did you go, my girl? Where did you go, my girl? Why did you go, my girl? Why did you go, girl? How can our daughters live? How can our daughters live?

She looks at the audience.

Do you see me? Can you see me? Do you recognize me? I am a mother. If you have had a child. If you have loved a child. I am you.

All members of the cast move forward and begin to stand closely behind
THE NATIVE MOTHER *and* ANGUS.

We are waiting. We are waiting. We are missing. We are missing. We are missing. Them.

Lights begin to fade.

What are you missing?

Slide: AVA *Wilds, age sixteen, found west of Prince George, Highway 16. Last seen hitching home from school. Missing and Murdered.*

Above them a movement. A single sparrow flying into the cabin.

THE NATIVE MOTHER *looks up at the sparrow.* ANGUS *looks up and the rest of the cast look up as sparrows begin to fill the cabin until there are three thousand; their beating wings creating their own orchestration.*

The walls of the house begin to fall from the sound. The space is completely vacant except for the humans standing together watching as the sparrows lift off, swirling across a dark sky; a moving darkness met by light.

Darkness.

Nigredo Hotel

Libretto by Ann-Marie
  MacDonald
Composed by Nic Gotham

The *Alchemy of* Nigredo Hotel

Baṇuta Rubess, Director

In an opera, the libretto is the skeleton; the music is the body and the soul. *Prima la musica,* so the saying goes, and so it feels a little strange to tell you the story of the creation of the opera without the music hovering within reach. I hear it in my ear as I think of the scenes, the lines. There was a time when I could sing the whole damn piece from beginning to end, though completely incorrectly, since Nic Gotham wrote the music in a way that one calls "difficult."

I will try to be straightforward and tell you how it happened.

"The Reunion of the Soul & the Body" by William Blake.

I wasn't married to Nic yet, but we were living together: I was a theatre director, and he was a jazz musician and saxophonist who had discovered a lust for opera. I'd never seen an opera in my life and I was barely interested in this hoity-toity art form. But then Nic introduced me to Stravinsky's operas, to Judith Weir, to Philip Glass, to John Adams. I began to see the potential. He asked me if I knew anyone who would like to write a libretto. I was astonished when my friend Ann-Marie MacDonald volunteered; even more astonished when Nic proposed that they base their creation on an obscure book of philosophy, Edward F. Edinger's *Encounter with the Self*. But Ann-Marie was game and so began this extraordinarily rich project that allowed so many artists to stretch their wings and deepen their knowledge of, dare I say it, the human soul.

Nic and Ann-Marie's ideas invited us to learn about so much: to contemplate the Book of Job and the Song of Solomon; to immerse ourselves in the artwork of William Blake, the English poet and painter whose work is so allusive and alluring. We studied the works of Carl Jung and the notions of alchemy, and no one studied them more than Ann-Marie. She created the story of a neurosurgeon, a man of science, who has lost his soul. One night he thinks he has hit a child on the road and hides out in a decrepit, Hitchcockian motel run by a monstrous concierge called Sophie. The terrifying crone—his anima—locks him in his room and torments him with nightmarish visions, ultimately bursting through the ceiling. He wrestles with her until he understands that she is the inner child he "murdered," the soul that he has ignored, and in a final glorious aria, based on the Song of Solomon, he unites with her.

The opera begins with the neurosurgeon at work, ready with his scalpel; it ends with the successful operation complete. As the surgeon strips off his scrubs, something is stuck in his throat; he coughs and coughs until out comes a feather from Sophie's boa. Ah, the audience sighs (we hope); this visit to the hotel happened in his unconscious, and the white feather is a message from the Holy Spirit, from Sophie, a synonym for Sophia, who, in the Bible, equals Wisdom.

I'm not even sure if Ann-Marie put that ending in the libretto, since it was an idea that came out of a lot of brainstorming just a few days before opening night. The white feather stuck in the throat seemed a perfect conclusion for the string of symbols and imagery that had been developed in fervent collaboration with Wayne Strongman, the conductor, our two lead performers, and the signal contribution made by lighting designer Paul Mathiesen and the set and costume designers Jerrard and Diana Smith, a couple of artists legendary for their work with R. Murray Shafer.

This was the dream design team and one of the best collaborations of my entire career. The four of us were galvanized by the imagery of William Blake and committed to recreating it onstage. We translated the Jungian concept of alchemy into the idea that humans suffer as if trapped in a glass retort and then get heated up by adversity until they suffer through a dark night of the soul: the *nigredo*; that leads to an epiphany and spiritual release, the *albedo* of purification, but the final goal was the ecstasy of *rubedo*, the red and gold of alchemical success. In Ann-Marie's libretto, the neurosurgeon Raymond was literally being cooked in his room as the radiator grew hotter and hotter—just like materials in an alchemist's glass container. Jerrard Smith created a claustrophobic hotel room that was intended to go up in flames, with the world's most disgusting sink and a sickly, dirty green radiator that could shake and emit steam. In the first designs, Jerrard even created an amazing backdrop that would constantly slowly move, like a towel you pull down in a public bathroom; the idea was that as the opera proceeded, the back wall would look increasingly look like it was on fire. I have a vivid memory of Tarragon's Artistic Director Urjo Kareda scratching his chin at this point and asking, "So, how much is this show going to cost me exactly?" The sliding back wall had to be cut. The lighting was going to do the trick instead.

And ah, the lighting. An entire aria could be devoted to Paul Mathiesen's lighting. The libretto has two characters: Raymond and Sophie, and I told Paul that I wanted the lighting to be the third character; that Light had to tell a story and comment on the proceedings. Enlightenment, after all, was the reward one hoped for after the *nigredo* of spiritual suffering. Paul took this brief very seriously and created his own lighting opera, with a lighting cue after every four bars in the music; infinitesimal shifts that kept the audience unsure of what exactly was going on, creating an environment constantly in flux (and lux). I might be exaggerating, but this is how I remember it; I remember being given permission to sit with Paul and his assistant in the Tarragon Theatre way into the wee hours of the night, setting one lighting cue after another, so that the audience would feel the organic, steady heating up of the hotel room. After Sophie fell through the ceiling, the lamp fell down as well and became a swing for her as she sang her one glorious aria. The whole room had to transform into a magical, erotic space of red and blue and black and white, and Paul knew how to make the light dance and shimmer in all the right places. He made an extraordinary contribution to the success of the opera, and I was so very proud when he won a Dora for his work.

(Note that the assistant working for Paul was one brilliant Philip Beesley who is now a renowned installation artist in his own right.)*

The Smiths were nominated for their design work, both for set and costume. Though Raymond's costume was pretty straightforward; Sophie was a special challenge. Her first lines are rough: *Toilet's down the hall, and there's a bathtub two bucks extra . . .* And she's got to look like a slag, like a female monster. However, at the end of the opera, she comes crashing through the ceiling, has an enormous stage fight, and then turns out to be ravishingly beautiful. We wanted to recreate Blake's image of the reunion of the soul and the body for this moment, and Diane came up with a simple, beautiful, flame-like gown.

There was only one little hitch with that gown, we discovered.

Ann-Marie's libretto hinged on a stunt: Raymond hears something caught in the ceiling, is it a bird? Then a finger comes poking through, and when he inspects it, a hand shoots through and grabs him by the hair. Sophie comes crashing through the ceiling and he tries to fling her off until she subdues him.

There weren't many sopranos in Canada who would take on a stunt like that for an independent opera company. In fact, the whole project was rather suspect from the standard soprano's point of view. She would have to sing in an ugly, growly voice at the beginning of the opera—risking her highly trained vocal cords—and was only allowed to really shine in her one major aria after the most physically taxing scene in the show. She would have to learn difficult music in which the tones might shift unexpectedly. She would have to know how to act—a demand, which in the early 1990s, was still pretty radical as far as opera goes—and kudos to Wayne Strongman and his leadership for developing so many singers who are up to the task now.

He and I auditioned a whole slew of singers and fell in love with Shari Saunders's voice. She was a stunningly pretty and salty young woman from Down East who

---

* The whole team was nominated for Doras, except for yours truly, something that rankled then and rankles now and will always rankle as long as female directors continue to be overlooked, forgotten, or outright dismissed—as it continues to happen today, even in the Oscars. And I'm only going to talk about the original team in this preface, though I've had the honour and joy of directing *Nigredo* with other casts, most importantly with Patricia O'Callaghan and Alexander Dobson in the leading roles.

made a big point of telling us that she wasn't an actress, she was a singer, though yes, she had worked with Opera Atelier and so had some experience with ambitious spectacle. Shari was a very quick study and turned into an excellent actress, but above all she was what the theatre calls "a trooper."

In order to execute this stunt, Shari was going to have to climb up to the top of the set and then crawl along a set of pipes. In the near darkness, she would have to punch through the paper ceiling and then rely on her partner, played by Jonathan Whittaker, to guide her hands to his hair, and then she'd hang upside down from a bar before she slid headfirst along his body while he gripped her legs.

The stunt was devised by the fight director John Stead and meeting him for the first time together with Shari is another unforgettable moment. As he walked into the rehearsal studio, he ripped off his shirt with a gesture one might call swashbuckling. There he was in his jeans, undershirt, and single giant bear claw hanging from his neck, a trophy from his hunting days. "Hug me," John demanded, spreading his arms wide. Shari plunged in. John wanted her to be fearless and to trust him implicitly and that's what Shari did. (She won a well-deserved Dora for the role eventually, though, since she was out of town, I had to get on stage to pick it up for her, so I guess I had my moment of glory.)

I'll never forget the very first time Shari tried out the stunt in costume. It was at the Tarragon, and the set wasn't finished yet; all the pipes were deliberately left exposed, so that Shari wouldn't have to try out the drop in darkness. All the technical staff assembled in the theatre, as did Urjo Kareda, the producer, and the marketing staff. All the musicians sat in the audience, including Wayne, the conductor. The room throbbed with anticipation: how was this stunt going to work? "I'm climbing up now," Shari called out from the back, and we could hear her crawling along the pipes. "I'm doing it now," she said, and flipped upside down, hanging from the pipe by her knees. What we saw in that moment was unexpected: a charming derriere in black underwear, belonging to a woman with a dress hanging over her head like a wilted tulip. The whole theatre was gripped by silent laughter, yet nobody laughed out loud, thank goodness. If Shari was humiliated, she might simply refuse to repeat the stunt. Hands clapped over our mouths, we heard her say, "Something's wrong. Can I do it again?" The stage manager helped her get off the pipe and quickly sewed two rubber bands to the dress, so she could pull one onto each ankle and the illusion of dignity and beauty would stay intact. The mishap never happened again, of course.

One of the unusual factors for the premiere version of *Nigredo Hotel* was that the male singer, Raymond, came from the musical theatre, rather than opera. Learning Nic's music was harder than expected. However, since Jonathan's background was theatrical, the questions he asked of the character were the ones asked by any actor: *What's my motivation? Why am I here? What am I playing at this moment, exactly?* These were questions that were of little interest to an opera singer, and I had to tailor my directorial strategies to each of my stars. With time, I hardly rehearsed them together since their needs were so different—and that, in the long run, seemed like the right thing to do for a story that revolved around two entities who were lost to each other.

In general, *Nigredo Hotel* was a crash course in directing opera, and I have directed many pieces involving live music and singers since then. There is no greater privilege than going to work at ten in the morning and having a fantastically gifted and hard-working artist open their mouth and sing for you, only you, the director. *Nigredo* brought me into a very special world uniting word and music and idea and spectacle, and I've relished every single opera I've been allowed to direct, from this first one to my last one at the moment, an opera called *Sweat* produced by Bicycle Opera.

Finally, a few comments regarding the major players: Wayne Strongman and Claire Hopkinson, Nic Gotham and Ann-Marie MacDonald.

My memory is a little fuzzy around the chain of events, but I believe the first thing that happened is that we heard about a guy called Wayne and the company he was leading, a company that was going to focus on making new Canadian chamber operas. Over a lunch, we pitched our idea and he took to it immediately. Claire Hopkinson joined the team pretty soon after that (I think?).

Nic and I had met Claire already with our very first creative venture, a jazz play called *Boom, Baby, Boom!*, which Claire's company produced. Claire had an extraordinary appetite for wild and ambitious theatrical ventures, and she was instrumental in creating a space for our visions.

I basked in Wayne's courage and warmth and love for Nic's music. It was always a pleasure to enter the rehearsal room and encounter his eagerness for exploration. If I made my actors lie on the ground for warm-ups, Wayne stretched out too. In an art form where the conductor can be Maestro and become unapproachable, Wayne was always a partner. His keen intelligence, his hyperawareness of how words and music worked together, made him one of the best collaborators a librettist and composer could ask for.

I had worked with Ann-Marie as a co-creator and an actor, and witnessing her leap into the poetry required for opera was nothing short of exhilarating. I will let her libretto speak for itself.

As for Nic's music: I write about it with no objectivity at all. The year we opened *Nigredo Hotel* is the year we got married. When we went on our tour of Britain, I was very pregnant. We took our baby, Dzintars, with us on the cross-Canada tour. Nic was a super-cool jazz man when I met him, and shortly thereafter he got very interested in music written by such minimalist greats as Morton Feldman and Jim Tenney. This confluence of musical tastes can be felt in *Nigredo*.

This was his very first opera and only the second time that he'd even written for the human voice. He went on to write a second opera with me, and later, many pieces for singers and choirs. I wrote a libretto for his third opera in the year before he died.

I love the music for *Nigredo*: it's witty, and clear, and is mushy as hell when required. A music critic chastised Nic's settings for being too much in "lockstep" with the syllables and decried the lack of hummability. Well, I can hum the opera, and I can also vouch for the fact that Nic was utterly uninterested in creating a tonal piece. The "Wisdom Aria" is the most accessible of all the songs in the opera, and the most performed. But what I hear the loudest is the duet at the end. "For love is stronnnnnnnng as death," the baritone and soprano roar together, "many waters cannot quench love." That's the point where musically, Nic really lets go, and all of Nic's romantic nature gets to rise to the top. I'm going to stop writing these words, and go downstairs to make dinner, but this duet is going to be in my ear now for days to come. If I'm lucky, in my dreams I'll hear a scratching in the ceiling, a fluttering as if a bird is trapped there, and maybe my soul will punch its hand through the ceiling and grab my hair and come sliding down my body in order to enlighten me.

Writing Nigredo Hotel

Ann-Marie MacDonald, Librettist

My collaboration with Nic Gotham on the chamber opera *Nigredo Hotel* remains among the most fruitful and satisfying of my career. From the outset, there was an apt synchronicity, Nic and I both having become fascinated and inspired by the Jungian version of the alchemical model of personal and artistic transformation. We both felt passionately that music and words could "marry" like body and soul—indeed, like all the famous "opposites" that are reconciled and unified when turning lead into gold. Thus, our process mirrored the story we chose to tell, as we committed to creating an opera where words and music would unite as equal partners. At times I would initiate by presenting Nic with words, and sometimes he would start a scene rolling with music to which I would write words. We traded input in a way that is not always the case between composer and librettist, whose respective areas of expertise are traditionally guarded. We welcomed one another to tread freely on each other's "turf" and turned our mutual lack of fluency in one another's creative language to our advantage in an intuitive and uninhibited exchange that enriched both process and product. Throughout this process, Baņuta was there as dramaturge, midwife, and *soror mystica*, guiding us from those early days when the opera was germinating, through workshops, the rehearsal process, and to the glorious realization of a bold, beautiful, and moving theatrical work—a work that saw the dark night of the soul transform with the *rubedo* of dawn, into the gold of a brilliant new day.

Nic Gotham's Nigredo Hotel *Score*

by Baņuta Rubess

Nic was a leader in the Toronto jazz scene when he was suddenly gripped by the desire to write an opera. Ann-Marie MacDonald agreed to write a libretto, but what about? One day, Nic burst through the door, elated. He'd found the perfect material in a second-hand bookstore, and beckoned with a slim volume in his hand. I took one look at the cover and burst into laughter. The title was *Encounter with the Self: A Jungian Commentary on William Blake's Illustrations of the Book of Job*. "Where's the drama in that?" I scoffed. Nic knew where it was: in *Nigredo Hotel*, in the light born from darkness. Over the many years of our marriage and collaborations, I came to treasure Nic's deeply philosophical nature. He took his optimism very seriously. It permeates his music, even the compositions he wrote so furiously in his very last weeks. *Many waters cannot quench love.*

Remembering Light and Shadow for Nigredo Hotel: *Snapshots*

Paul Mathiesen, Lighting Designer

In one of the first design meetings, director Baṇuta Rubess asked me to look into three conceptual references: the dread in the horror film, *Eraserhead* (1977) by David Lynch; *The Cabinet of Dr. Caligari* (1919) a film by Robert Wiene with its warped, hair-raising, anxious imagery; and the sumptuous colour photographic portraits in the *Sittings* series of 1979 and 1980 by artist Lucas Samaras.

I left the meeting with these notes: "aquarium shadows/night-vision goggles/veil of light/red feather/red wine splotch on pristine white napkin/inferno/spectacle." I had an exhilarating sense that the light was to be an uncanny take-no-prisoners character in the piece. Baṇuta had given me carte blanche. I knew virtually nothing about opera. I sought help from my collaborator and principals. One night after rehearsal I was talking with Nic Gotham about his music and Ann-Marie MacDonald's story. He told me, emphatically, "The dark is way more interesting than the light." I was enthralled. Now, this was something I could run with—skiagraphic light as a visual howitzer.

The two-character story takes place in one night. Raymond, a neurosurgeon in crisis, driving his Jaguar home, hits somebody on the highway, pulls into a motel to recover his nerves, and is harassed by a slovenly, rude female host, Sophie/Sophia (wisdom). She is Raymond's anima (feminine/other half); Sophie will guide Raymond through a series of trials, leading him to psychic fulfillment. How's this for a plateful of ideas? The story incorporates arcane references in alchemy as discussed in Edward F. Edinger's commentary on Carl Jung's psychological reading of William Blake's etchings of the biblical story of Job. The essential image for

The Shadow Dance, 1675. Engraving by Samuel Dirksz van Hoogstraten.

Baṇuta was the Jungian metaphor of man reaching enlightenment after a "dark night of the soul" through the alchemical process of turning base metals into gold.

Snap 1: Model and rendering from set designer Jerrard Smith.

Idea: Concept design of corporeal playing space of severely raked walls, floor, and ceiling.

- Low-life motel room ornamented by anxious gloomy shadows and surprising macabre fragments of light
- a jalousie-shuttered window with mercury vapour moonlight
- a filthy glass transom over the door of room seven
- a glowing ceiling light fixture (with an apparent mind of its own)
- a gross, eventually piping hot, steam-spewing radiator

- seven enormous pomegranate-red translucent cloth pillars that fall from the ceiling as a *deus ex machina*

Realization: Arrange multiple spotlights slinging out bars of light from extreme low angles. Express light hurled from acute side angles, projecting shimmering patterns and dank shadows of the performers. Lights placed outside the motel room threshold oftentimes heralds Sophie's entrance and personifies her offstage voice as she torments Raymond. Mount lights in any set piece that would glow for a radiant soft light to be used in the final glorious aria when the male/female personalities are united.

Snap 2: Prologue and overture: lights up on war zone.

Idea: Delirious chaotic Mannerist light—*son et lumière*—piled on from an aphotic and melanoid atmosphere metastasizing to a revealing, saturated splendor.

Realization: At one of the first technical rehearsals, Baṇuta asked me to perform a light show to accompany Nic Gotham's instrumental overture. I had memories of broken slats of light and shadow from the venetian blinds of seedy strip motels and from film noir cinematography. I had decided to use this vocabulary as a visual leitmotif throughout the opera, conceived as multiple automobile headlights in the parking lot outside the motel room windows. The striated light splayed probingly over the set under the quizzical music. The feverish cross-fading flat and front-angled projectors caused a notion of random unsettling foreboding.

Snap 3: Arrival of the spiritually suffering Raymond and introduction of the hideous Sophie, torturer and guide to finding spiritual illumination.

Idea: Van Gogh's *The Potato Eaters* was to be the first look at the "T-minus-zero" countdown to the evening's proceedings. First, crepuscular lucifugal light obscures Raymond's steadily building panic. Then cast and attached shadows ensnare the performers with ineffable darkness and light. He cannot turn away from the tormenting ephialtes/nightmare.

Realization: Smith's set with a raked motel room floor was to be elevated above the orchestra, permitting numerous low-angled locations in the floor to mount miniature projectors affording hyperbolic shifting shadows of the performers.

Snap 4: *Nigredo*—first stage in alchemy equals despair.

Idea: Voluptuous and engorged shadows. The rococo shadow play becomes vigorous and even spastic, capturing the building frenzy as Sophie and Raymond engage in battle.

Realization: Virulent colour manifesting unease is pitched in harsh and dramatic directional light. A fierce blue light, like cerulean-blue pigment, flares up permeating the battlefield. Coruscating bilious yellow light drives away the shadows, eliding Raymond's tortured and disquieted worry of having hit somebody on the road. The light is fidgety. Lambency representing Sophie the harridan is constantly intruding into room seven. My phantasmagoria is a performance of shadows as a metaphor for the soul.

Snap 5: *Albedo*—second stage in alchemy equals insight through experience.

Idea: Light the colour of candy snow cones turns from ice white to acid lemon to aureated orange to cherry red in this cauldron. Harsh light drains from the room, passing into a penumbral state of absence.

Realization: First erase realist light, then magnify the light to the burning point. Finally, the overheated intensity dissipates. States of dread and terror are expressed with chiaroscuro strokes of light and shade. The Hitchcockian gestural shadowing becomes red hot, and then falls away to a wonderous colour field. Tenebrism turns to *sfumato*—a jabbing, piercing light exposed by a rip in the ceiling announces the machine-of-the-gods entrance of Sophie falling from above, and the seven pillars of knowledge arrive heralding enlightenment.

Set and Costume Design by Jerrard and Diana Smith.

Snap 6: *Rubedo*—"Song of Solomon" aria—final alchemical stage equals integration of knowledge.

Idea: Luxuriant colour and a dappled texture. Light turns kaleidoscopic (from the Greek for beautiful). A fertile love nest in a forest of pillars. Gothic tracery in luminous shades of lipstick pink splay voluptuous light, enveloping the singers.

Realization: Grace expressed in a scumbled muted palette of glistering pink and lustrous incandescent light for Sophie's erotic aria. She is resplendent in costume designer Diana Smith's glamorous, enchanting gown—a vision in opalescence. The light flares up, then dissolves into notional high-key portrait lighting revealing her numinous beauty.

Snap 7: Coda.

Idea: Simplicity, rational and spiritual harmony.

Realization: A single pellucid white limelight, focused on the doctor, announces his newfound wisdom and innocence.

And, bang, it's over. What just happened?—I was shattered. Having taken the one-hour plunge of a wild carnival ride, I wanted to get back in line for another ticket for the thrill. I would return to the Tarragon Theatre performance numerous times, soaking up the intensity and glamour and to enjoy the extravagant fun of turning Raymond and Sophie into alchemical gold.

Assistant Lighting Designer Philip Beesley and I challenged each other to get the unembellished look of the light for an unblemished numinous beginning look. We made a battery-operated pomegranate prop with one crimson-red seed, from a miniature grain-of-wheat light bulb. It was for Sophia to secretly turn on during her aria and share with Raymond. Thankfully, it ended up on the cutting room floor. (We used a feather instead.) Perhaps, I never completely fathomed the opera, but stimulated by the set, music, and the dynamic Tapestry Opera company, I did "get" the captivating and bizarre story. With strong direction and influences from art, science, and history, and with the profound genius of Rubess, Gotham, MacDonald, and Smith as guides, my whimsical yet red-blooded light self-consciously helped tell an unforgettable story.

Nigredo Hotel was first produced by Tarragon Theatre and Tapestry Music Theatre at the Tarragon Theatre Mainspace, Toronto, from May 20 to June 14, 1992, with the following cast and creative team:

Sophie: Shari Saunders
Ray: Jonathan Whittaker

Librettist: Ann-Marie MacDonald
Composer: Nic Gotham
Director: Baṇuta Rubess
Musical Director: Wayne Strongman
Assistant Director: Alisa Palmer
Associate Musical Director: Shelley Hanson
Set and Costume Design: Jerrard and Diana Smith
Lighting Design: Paul Mathiesen
Stage Manager: Kevin Bowers

Characters

Ray
Sophie

Prologue

A dimly lit and seedy hotel room. The door opens. SOPHIE *enters and slowly crosses towards the window. Halfway through the room she pauses to shield her eyes with her arm as though against a sudden beam of light, although there is none. She arrives at the window, opens the shutters and peers out. Parallel bars of light, like the headlights of a car, strafe the room. She closes the shutters and crosses back to the door, pausing here and there to lightly touch an object or a fixture of the room including the number on the door: 7.*

Another part of the theatre. A white sink. RAY *enters. He is about forty, dressed in surgical greens. He wears glasses. Throughout the aria he prepares for the operating room, scrubbing his hands and putting on surgical cap, mask, and gloves.*

RAY: Until I was a child of seven years
My work consisted all of miracles.
And I, bewildered and amazed at life,
Made up fantastic stories to explain
What I perceived to be great mysteries:
Why my bathtub emptied clockwise down the drain,
Whereas if I lived with penguins at the pole,
My bath would vanish counter down the hole.
And if God were omnipotent as claimed,
Could he change into a rock, then back again?
If so, he'd never really been a rock.
But then I learned of centrifugal force
—of polar opposites, true north and south;

That theology is not concerned with rocks
—that only fools and geniuses love paradox;
And in my bath I washed instead of wondered.

     RAY *exits.*

Scene

    The empty hotel room. Midnight. Moonlight and car lights enter and
    play about the room through slatted shutters that cover the window.
    Soft nature sounds from the orchestra: crickets, owl hoots, the beating
    of wings. Tired old wallpaper. A single bed, a small table, a telephone
    without a dial, a sink mounted upon one wall, its sweaty piping exposed.
    Below the window, an ancient iron radiator. On the wall, a picture:
    chintzy fake lithograph of a British fox hunt.

    Finally, the door swings open and SOPHIE *enters once more, this time*
    followed by RAY *who wears an immaculate suit and carries no luggage.*
    Everything about the woman is a bit grimy and worn. Red silk dressing
    gown from the forties, a wilted white feather boa, and scuffed high-heeled
    shoes minus stockings. A towel-cum-turban swathed about her head. Too
    much makeup.

SOPHIE: Toilet's down the hall and there's a bathtub, two bucks extra, y' get
your damage deposit back in the morning once I check the room, don't piss in
the sink.

RAY: Is there a telephone?

SOPHIE: Two bucks a call.

RAY: Has anyone else come here tonight?

SOPHIE: Nope.

RAY: Did you hear—

SOPHIE: Uh-uh.

RAY: Was there a knock at your door perhaps, or . . . did anyone call out for help?

SOPHIE: I told ya I didn't hear nuthin'. We were sleepin'.

RAY: What about your husband?

SOPHIE: Ain't got one.

She sidles towards him.

RAY: Oh. What I meant was, didn't anyone else hear or see anything?

SOPHIE: There is no one else.

RAY lets this pass. It's dawning on him that she's not all there.

And I didn't see nuthin'. I was playin' solitaire.

RAY: You said you were asleep.

SOPHIE: I'm that good at it, honey.

SOPHIE exits. RAY tests out the bed: it's hard as rock. He spots the fox hunt picture with distaste. He removes it only to expose a graffiti drawing of a cheerful person with breasts and penis. He replaces the picture on the wall, then goes to the window and opens the shutters. RAY takes a deep breath and peers into the darkness, looking for something.

RAY: Perhaps I merely dozed off at the wheel.

And it was all a dream.

A very rapid dream.

Or maybe just an animal.

They run away to hide when they get hurt.

They like to die in privacy.

A man would have preferred to bleed in company.

Just an animal.

Unless it wasn't anything at all.

He goes to the phone, picks up the receiver, and is about to dial when he sees there is no dial. He speaks into the phone.

Hello? . . . Hello?

SOPHIE's voice comes through the receiver.

SOPHIE: Room service.

RAY: I have to make a call.

SOPHIE: Who is this?

RAY: Your guest, of course.

SOPHIE: I don't got an outside line, honey.

RAY: Look, my wife expects me home tonight, there must be a—

SOPHIE: There's a cop shop up the road a piece. You could call from there.

A beat.

Ya want yer supper now?

RAY: I'm not hungry. Thank you.

RAY hangs up. There is a knock at the door. He is startled. He gets up, approaches the door a little cautiously, and opens it. SOPHIE stands there.

I was just talking to you.

SOPHIE: Yeah, that's why I'm here, ya owe me two bucks.

RAY: What for?

SOPHIE: The phone call.

RAY: But I only talked to *you.*

SOPHIE: Well, who'd ya expect, the Queen a' Sheba?

RAY: You cannot charge two dollars for an in-house call.

SOPHIE: How much do you charge for a house call, doc?

RAY: I don't make house calls.

He digs out the money then hesitates.

How did you know I'm a doctor?

SOPHIE: Yer hands. Dead giveaway.

She snatches the money and turns to leave.

RAY: Excuse me—

SOPHIE: 'Dja fart?

RAY: I'll take the key, thank you.

SOPHIE: You goin' bird watchin' tonight?

RAY: Not that I know of.

SOPHIE: Then you don't need the key unless you plan to skip out on me.

RAY: And you don't need the key unless you plan to imprison me. *(refrain and overlap)*

SOPHIE: You know what the door is for!

RAY: I'm afraid yours is the only place within two hours of here. Now, give me the key, madam.

SOPHIE: Call me Sophie, honey. My "madam" days are over.

RAY: Nice to meet you, Sophie.

SOPHIE: What's your name, mister?

RAY: Just call me Doc.

SOPHIE: I wanna know yer name.

RAY: What for?

SOPHIE: You superstitious? Afraid I'll steal your soul if you tell me your name? Maybe I will.

RAY: I consider that unlikely: I don't believe in the existence of the soul.

SOPHIE: Maybe she don't believe in you either.

She laughs until her laugh turns to a cough. She snorts and spits into her hand then examines the expectoration: a red feather. RAY *stares at it.*

Or maybe the cops are after you.

RAY: What makes you say that?

SOPHIE: I'll give you the key if you tell me your name.

RAY: *(he decides)* My name is Raymond. But you may call me Doctor . . . Jones.

He smiles and puts out his hand for the key. She drops the feather into his palm. He recoils letting the feather drift to the floor.

Now listen!—

SOPHIE: Listen Ray, I get a kind of sharp pain here, *(coy)* you wanna take a look?

SOPHIE pulls her dressing gown aside to reveal part of her left breast.

RAY: I'm a neurosurgeon.

SOPHIE: Just give a little listen.

RAY: Take a nap and two Aspirin.

SOPHIE: Just see if I'm still tickin'.

RAY: I can assure you that you are.

SOPHIE: I got a real bad pain.

RAY: My specialty is the brain.

SOPHIE: I'll give you the key if you cure me, Doc.

RAY: Maybe in the morning.

SOPHIE: I might die tonight. *(terrified)* I might die in my sleep.

RAY: Goodnight.

SOPHIE: You took an oath. Ya hypocrite. You took an oath! You're tryin'a kill me! You want me to die!

He presses her out the door and leans against it while she hammers at it.

Ya hypocrite! You took an oath!

The door pounding stops. Her voice comes from farther off. Terribly sad:

Hey, Ray. Hey, Ray.
Please don't let me die tonight.
'Cause if I die I'll take you with me.

A silent beat. Then:

RAY: Paranoid schizophrenic. Why must they always pick on me?

RAY barricades the door with the bed, rests a bit, then returns to the window.

If it was a man.
And if he's hurt or dead . . .
I'll be charged with hit and run.
No, no, I would have felt the impact.
There was . . . hardly any impact.
He could have walked away.

I wonder if he got my license number.

If so, he might sue.

Of course he got my number, I parked the Jag outside.

That's bad. He'll see the Jag and sue for sure.

Dammit, that's not fair.

I swear. I swear there was nothing there!

I got out and looked, then checked in here.

I'm innocent. Because there isn't any evidence.

Because it was all a dream.

It had to be a dream because:

He was very small.

He looked at me.

Oh God. Oh, not a child!

No, no, it had to be a dream because—

I saw the eyes.

He smiled at me.

And he was wearing sunglasses . . .

For God's sake, a racoon!

A fat racoon is all it was,

Out to steal a midnight meal.

> RAY *kicks off his shoes, removes his jacket, and stretches out on the bed, his head just under the door handle. The handle turns but he's smug.*

I'm afraid you can't come in.

> *The door swings slowly open onto the hallway, opposite to the way it opened before.* SOPHIE *stands there, motionless, wearing sunglasses and holding a tray covered with a white cloth. The cloth has a dark red splotch on it.* RAY *is spooked. He leaps up and crosses away from her. They stare at each other.*

SOPHIE: I brung yer supper.

RAY: I'm not hungry.

SOPHIE: It's your favourite.

RAY: How would you know?

SOPHIE: Woman's intuition.

RAY: What is it?

SOPHIE: Leftovers.

>SOPHIE *places the tray on the bed.*

RAY: Why are you wearing those sunglasses?

SOPHIE: Keep off the ultraviolets.

>SOPHIE *exits, closing the door.* RAY *cautiously approaches the tray. He*
>*carries it to the table and sets it down. He kneels and removes the stained*
>*cloth to reveal a glass of red wine full to the brim and a kaiser roll. He*
>*tests the roll: rock-stale. He sniffs the wine and recoils: pure vinegar.*

RAY: Thank God the world doesn't turn on woman's intuition.

>*The shutters slam shut. The ceiling lamp shorts out.* RAY *hurries to the*
>*window, opens the shutters and looks out: nothing. He closes and secures*
>*the shutters.*

Things are always worse at night.
It'll all look better in the morning light.

>*He crosses to the bed and lies down, worn out.*

I obviously dozed off at the wheel . . .

He sleeps for a moment, then a knock at the door. Resigned:

Come in.

SOPHIE: *(off stage)* It's locked.

RAY gets up, moves the bed and opens the door. SOPHIE staggers in, clutching her heart, gasping. She collapses on the bed, convulses, then lies perfectly still.

RAY: Shit.

He's about to take her pulse when her hand shoots up and fastens round the back of his neck.

SOPHIE: Listen.

She yanks his head down towards her chest.

Listen to my heart!

He resists. She's surprisingly strong.

RAY: No!

SOPHIE: You don't want me on yer conscience.

RAY: You're as healthy as I am.

SOPHIE: Bingo!

She starts laughing and is overcome once again by a coughing fit. She goes to the sink and takes a long, cool drink from the tap.

Gimme two bucks 'n I'll run yer bath.

RAY: Out.

SOPHIE: Two bucks a bath 'n a dollar a dance.

RAY: Now.

SOPHIE: I got a message for ya.

He freezes.

RAY: What is it? . . . The police? My wife?

SOPHIE: It's a singin' telegram:

"Raymond, Raymond in the tub,
Mummy forgot to put in the plug.
Oh, my goodness, oh, my soul,
There goes Raymond down the hole."

RAY: How do you know that song?

SOPHIE: Raymond, Raymond in the tub.
Mummy forgot to put in the plug.

RAY: Oh, my goodness, oh, my soul.

BOTH: There goes Raymond down the hole.

SOPHIE joins thumbs and forefingers to encircle her eyes with a pretend pair of glasses and exits, grinning.

RAY: I swear. I swear there was nothing there.

Sound of running water. In the distance, SOPHIE hums "Row, row, row your boat . . . life is but a dream." RAY listens for a bit.

I hate water.
I hate that stark sensation when I step into a swimming pool or bath.
A hot bath is the worst.
It makes me morbidly aware of every inch of flesh,
I feel as though a knife were waiting there to slice the tendons in my feet, to slice the soles to ribbons.
And when I pull the plug, the clockwise sucking down the drain is like a person drowning.

SOPHIE: *(off stage)* Oh, my goodness.

RAY: Someone whom I can't remember.

SOPHIE: *(off stage)* Oh, my soul.

RAY: Someone whom I used to know . . .

SOPHIE: *(off stage)* And in my bath—

RAY: And so I favour showers.
I don't indulge in idle introspection.
Not since I learned to wash behind my ears at seven.

SOPHIE: *(off stage)* —I washed instead of wondered.

RAY lies down once more to sleep when the radiator bursts into life with a violent knocking and begins to rattle about on its moorings. He approaches the rad but steam shoots out forcing him back. He looks around for something to protect himself. He grabs the bedspread and finally succeeds in closing the valve. He rests for a moment, sweating with the heat and exertion, then tries to open the window, but the shutters are stuck.

RAY: Sophie!

The phone rings. He grabs the receiver.

I demand another room!—

What sounds like a child's VOICE, a long way off, comes through the receiver. The VOICE is lost, heartbreaking.

VOICE: Hello? . . .

RAY: Hello, Sophie—

VOICE: Hello? . . . Hello-o-o.

RAY clicks the button on the phone. The VOICE fades.

Where a-a-are you-ou-ou . . .

The radiator explodes into scorching life once more. RAY springs to it and grabs it with his bare hands in an effort to yank it from the wall. He falls back with a cry of pain as SOPHIE's voice comes loud and clear through the phone.

SOPHIE: Hey, Ray, ya want bubbles 'r no bubbles?

He heads for the sink, yelling over his shoulder towards the phone receiver.

RAY: I'm roasting alive in here, this place is an inferno!

He struggles with the tap.

SOPHIE: Heat's extra.

The faucet is dry.

RAY: I demand another room!

SOPHIE: We don't got more.

RAY: *(tearing off his shirt)* There are six other rooms in this hotel!

SOPHIE: Someone died there.

RAY: That doesn't worry me. Unless it was contagious.

He tears off his undershirt.

SOPHIE: They caught fire.

RAY doesn't answer. He stares at the phone receiver.

Hey. Hey, Ray, y' owe me another two bucks.

RAY slowly hangs up the phone. He collects his things in a panic and opens the door. SOPHIE stands there in red-smeared surgical mask and gloves.

Oh, my goodness.

He slams the door, terrified. He looks around the room. There's no other way out. He forces himself under control and reaches once more for the door handle. He turns it. Pushes. Pulls. The door is locked in both directions. He leans his face against the door . . . he looks about. Trapped.

RAY: *(softly through the crack of the door)* Sophie . . . let me out of here. Please.

No answer.

If you do, I'll listen to your heart.

No answer.

I'd love to take that bath now, Sophie.

Desperate.

Please. I've hurt my hands,
I've got medicine in the car,
There's lots of money in the dash,
I'll listen to your—

SOPHIE: *Medice cura te ipsum.*

RAY: Oh God.
Oh God, please don't let me die in here.
Don't let a crazy lady kill me.

SOPHIE: *Medice cura te ipsum.*

RAY: I've never been a bad man.
I've never hurt a soul.

SOPHIE: Knock and the door shall be opened.

RAY: Let me out.

SOPHIE: Raymond, I have something for you.
Something that you left behind.
I've warmed it up, your sweet leftover;
He's coming round the corner of your mind.

RAY: How do you know that song?

SOPHIE: Suffer the little children. Unless you become as

RAY: *(simultaneously)* Someone
whom I can't remember . . .

SOPHIE: *(simultaneously)* one of—

SOPHIE: Just an animal.

RAY: Someone whom I used to know . . .

SOPHIE: *(whispered)* In the beginning . . .

RAY: When I was small,
My father saw the bright tip of my mind and called it me and loved it.
He never saw the creature in the dark who lurked and loved him in return.
When I was small,
My mother watched me from the corner of her eye and called it me and
loved it.
But when she glimpsed the creature of the dark,
And fixed upon his bright and helpless eyes,
She recoiled in horror,
To see her shadow come around again in me.
To see her shadow come around again in me.

VOICE: Hello-o-o?

This is the VOICE *we heard on the phone but it's clearer now and coming from beneath the floor.*

RAY: Hello. Where are you?

VOICE: Where a-a-are you?

RAY: I'm in the next room.

VOICE: How come you left me here?

RAY: You called me before.

VOICE: I called you and I called you.

RAY: Did Sophie lock you in there?

VOICE: No

RAY: Who did, then?

VOICE: You did.

RAY: I just got here.

VOICE: It's dark in here.

RAY: Don't worry.

VOICE: It's cold in here.

RAY: How long have you been locked in there?

VOICE: I'm seven.

RAY: Oh, my God. I'll get you out of there. I'll get you if I have to tear the place apart!

> *He flings himself at the floor and pounds it savagely. The VOICE cries out in pain. RAY stops pounding and strokes the floor.*

Sh sh sh.

> *The VOICE whimpers and begins to travel behind the walls. RAY follows it.*

Are you hurt?

VOICE: Yes.

RAY: What happened?

VOICE: I saw you.

RAY: Where?

VOICE: In the dark.

RAY: When?

VOICE: On the road.

RAY: No.

VOICE: I looked at you.

RAY: No.

VOICE: I smiled at you.

RAY: Oh God.

VOICE: Hello-o-o.

The VOICE is now just outside the door.

RAY: Who are you?

VOICE: My name is Raymond.

RAY: Stop it!

VOICE: Let me in.

The door handle turns, the door starts to open, RAY flings himself upon it with a cry and grasps the handle for dear life.

RAY: Two plus two is four.
East is east and west is not.
From sea to shining shore,
Wolfe, the dauntless juggernaut—
I before *e* except after *c*,
Every good boy deserves—

VOICE: Help me.

RAY: The square root and hypotenuse,
Calculus and eye of newt
—these are a few of my favourite things—
The right brain giveth and the left brain takes,
East is east and the hemisphere quakes
—these are the things to which I cling—

The delicate central nervous system
Drives you home when you cannot,
It applauds when you forgot,
There is no ghost in the machine

VOICE: Hello-o-o—

RAY: —these are the things that I love best—the
Neural tube, the neural crest,
My head upon a neural plate
Served up by Salome at eight
—ask not for whom the cerebellum tolls,
There is no ghost in the machine—
The central nervous nervous system
Drives you home when you cannot,
I'm innocent 'cause I forgot,
There is no ghost in this machine
No Holy Ghost in this machine!

VOICE: Raymond, Raymond in the dark.

RAY: Just an animal.

VOICE: Ra-a-ymond.

Fingers poke through the ceiling. RAY *slowly reaches up and touches them.*

RAY: *(gently)* Sh sh sh.

The hand shoots down and grabs him by the hair. A violent struggle as SOPHIE *is yanked through a gash in the ceiling. Seven scarlet pillars transform the room.* SOPHIE *lands. They fight.* RAY *attempts to escape through the now unlocked door and window, but he is forced back each*

time by a tide of scarlet fabric. He tries to haul himself back up through
the ceiling, but SOPHIE *pulls him down again. Finally, he collapses.*

Who are you?

SOPHIE: *(à la child* VOICE*)* Hello-o-o . . .

RAY: What do you want?

SOPHIE: *Salva me. (in her own voice from now on)*

RAY: I cannot save you.

SOPHIE: *Medice cura te ipsum.*

RAY: I cannot cure myself.

SOPHIE: Listen to my heart.

RAY: . . . Tell me.

SOPHIE: When I was small, I watched you from the corner of your mind.

RAY: Tell me.

SOPHIE: In the beginning:

    RAY *joins in on words in bold type:*

I was at your side each day,
Your darling and delight,
Until you were **a child of seven years**.
Then **paradox** and **mystery**,

Both banished from your sight,
Fled naked to the wilderness in tears.

And then it came to pass:

A creature strayed into the path,
Of your oncoming mind.
A creature frozen in the light,
The piercing rays that split the night
Like knives cascading from the **bright tip** of your mind.
Just a creature in the dark,
Now you must listen to my heart,
And disregard me at your peril.

RAY: Tell me.

SOPHIE: And here is what the creature says:

The ceiling lamp descends. SOPHIE *sits in the lamp and sings.*

In the darkness all alone,
My rocking chair of skin and bone,
Sealed inside my weary tomb
My shadow dripping like a wound
O, where shall you find Wisdom?

Wisdom is a wandering soul,
A fallen woman in the night,
—blessed are the lost
For theirs is the kingdom of wonder—
Wisdom is the word made flesh,
Condemned to live, condemned to death,
And the greatest of these is Wisdom.

My mind has many mansions,
Seven pillars in my head,
—knock and the door shall be opened,
Knock and awaken the dead—

My house is built upon a tomb,
Knock and let there be light.
Blessed are they, who dwell in the dark,
For they shall inherit the night.
Blessed are the cornered ones
For they shall inherit the fright.

The dark holds riches, wealth untold,
A nursery of fear and gold.
In the dark a lost and found,
But where shall you find Wisdom?

In the darkness, all alone,
Your rocking chair of skin and bone,
The child rocks in Mother night,
Her black embrace against the light,
And there shall you find Wisdom.
And there shall you find Wisdom.

SOPHIE goes to RAY and holds him.

RAY: You are dark and lovely,

SOPHIE: His left arm beneath my head,
His right arm around me.

RAY: A little dark.

SOPHIE: Do not look down on me.

BOTH: A little dark

SOPHIE: I am dark and lovely.

RAY: In dreams you beckoned just behind a veil.
And then in nightmares lurked beyond a door.

SOPHIE: In dreams I whispered to you.
In nightmares I cried out.

BOTH: Raymond!

RAY: From dreams, I awoke in love.

SOPHIE: His left arm beneath my head, his right arm around me.

RAY: From nightmares I awoke in fear.

SOPHIE: By night in bed I sought him whom my soul loveth.

BOTH: Where a-a-are you?

RAY: Your eyes behind your veil like doves.

SOPHIE: I sought him but I found him not.

RAY: Let me see your face, let me hear your voice.

SOPHIE: I'm sleeping but my heart is wakeful.

RAY: I dreamt that I was dreaming.

BOTH: Listen!

SOPHIE opens her gown. RAY rests his head against her heart and listens.

SOPHIE: My beloved knocks upon the door.

RAY: Open to me, oh my sister, oh my dove;
For my head is drenched with dew,
My locks with the moisture of the night.

SOPHIE: When my beloved slipped his hand inside the latch hole—

RAY: Beneath your tongue are milk and honey—

SOPHIE: When I arose to open for my love—

RAY: My hands were dripping—

SOPHIE: With my own hands I opened to my love.

RAY: Your parted lips behind your veil
Are like a pomegranate cut—

SOPHIE goes to the bed. RAY sits in the lamplight. SOPHIE presents a split pomegranate.

SOPHIE: Then I found him whom my soul loveth.

RAY: I did not know myself.

BOTH: Such is my beloved.

RAY: How do you know that song?

BOTH: How do you know that Song of Songs

RAY: How do you

BOTH: Oh!

SOPHIE: My goodness . . .

RAY: Oh, my Soul.

SOPHIE: Call me Sophie, honey . . .

RAY savours the juice of the pomegranate from her hand.

BOTH: For love is strong as death.
It blazes up like blazing fire.
Many waters cannot quench!
Many waters cannot quench love.
Behold, thou art fair.
Behold, thou art fair.

Lights fade on the room, then come back up to reveal SOPHIE, alone, reclining upon the bed, looking at the audience. She lights the lamp with a gesture, crosses to the open window, and leans out for a moment, looking. Then, she closes the window, shields her eyes with her arm and turns away as lights fade to black.

RAY enters the area where he first prepared for surgery. He is in post-op disarray—surgical smock open, mask down. He is arrested by a small cough. He opens his gloved hand—a red feather. He blows gently it from his palm.

Fin.

Ours

Libretto by Robert Chafe
Composed by John Estacio

Directing Ours

Glynis Leyshon, Director

At 8:45 a.m. on July 1, 1916, British Divisional Commander Maj. Gen. Beauvoir de Lisle ordered the First Newfoundland Regiment to move forward and engage directly with German troops defending the area around Beaumont-Hamel. It was the first day of the Battle of the Somme, and this singular event changed forever the history of Newfoundland and Labrador.

Leaving the comparative safety of a support trench ironically called St. John's Road, the Newfoundlanders started their advance at 9:15 a.m. . . . marching into enemy fire "with chins tucked down as if walking into a blizzard." By 9:45, approximately 85% of those who started forward were dead, dying, or wounded . . . with most of the bodies concentrated in a blasted part of no man's land identified by the twisted skeleton of a tree known as "the Danger Tree."*

The devastation to the regiment was shatteringly complete. Of the nearly eight hundred Newfoundlanders engaged at Beaumont-Hamel, only sixty-eight men were able to answer roll call the next day. The enduring scars of this battle run deep in the collective psyche of Newfoundland and the memory of these young men, and their ultimate sacrifice is the pulse that runs through every passionate moment of *Ours*, the opera created by composer John Estacio and playwright Robert Chafe.

---

* For a full account of the battle, and for the source of these statistics, please see "The Opening Day, Battle of the Somme, 1916," https://www.veterans.gc.ca/eng/remembrance/memorials/overseas/first-world-war/france/beaumonthamel/somme.

The Evolution of an Idea—2011 to 2014

Interestingly, the evolution of *Ours* was not a straightforward march towards honouring a seminal moment in the history of Newfoundland and Labrador. Rather, the opera developed its present form only after a long gestation process where a wide and disparate number of story ideas were explored. Even the creative team of composer, writer, and dramaturge changed during the roughly five-year development cycle of the opera.

Early in 2011 Cheryl Hickman, the founder and artistic spirit guiding St. John's small but creatively dynamic opera company Opera on the Avalon (OOTA), reached out to two of Canada's best known and most successful opera creators with an audacious proposal. She wanted to commission composer John Estacio and playwright John Murrell to create a new work that related specifically to Newfoundland and Labrador. This commission was a huge undertaking for a company with the limited resources of OOTA. But Hickman was determined to move beyond the standard "top ten" opera repertoire. And even more, she wanted to bring home a story of genuine and immediate resonance for her audience.

Of course, accepting any opera commission requires great thought, but Murrell and Estacio were intrigued and immediately began to discuss various story ideas. Given the relative nearness to the one hundredth anniversary of Beaumont-Hamel, Hickman suggested something to commemorate the events of 1916. However, Murrell, as Estacio remembers, was already intrigued with writing a more domestic story featuring a Newfoundland family set in 1940s St. John's. There was much personal joy for these two men as they began collaborating for the fourth time on the creation of large-scale opera work. Their enduring creative partnership brought them easily into the initial stages of the creative process, and I know that, as with their earlier libretti, this process involved many intimate and lively meetings in local cafés. I can envision them both huddling over napkin-scribbled notes at Calgary's Diner Deluxe, ideas and laughter flowing as various plot ideas were examined and refined.

Sadly, we will never know how this libretto would have evolved as Murrell was forced to withdraw from the project after he received the difficult diagnosis of leukemia. Like those Newfoundland soldiers, Murrell fought his insidious disease by facing it squarely and with chin down, but Canada lost this great man of the theatre on November 11, 2019. And like the many artists inspired by Murrell in his long career in the arts, I now will always include him, along with the fallen of World War I, in the list of those I remember on the eleventh hour of the eleventh day of the eleventh month.

Losing Murrell was obviously a bitter blow for Estacio, both personally and professionally. He was unsure how or even if the project should move forward without Murrell as the librettist. However, Hickman again proved adamant about the need to proceed with the commission, and she approached one of Newfoundland's most celebrated playwrights, Robert Chafe.

As a winner of the Governor General's Literary Award and the creative force behind the respected St. John's theatre company Artistic Fraud of Newfoundland, Chafe was in many ways an obvious choice as librettist. Yet finding the illusive magic of creative chemistry is not in any way obvious. New creative partnerships can make all kinds of sense on paper, but the reality of working closely together to achieve a cohesive piece of music theatre is not easy. As everyone who has created new work knows, explosive disagreements and competing egos are not just the stuff of soap operas! So, gambling on this new partnership was yet another brave risk by Opera on the Avalon.

While Murrell brought a wealth of opera expertise to all his collaborations with Estacio, including their first, *Filumena*, Chafe was plunging into a very new world. As the librettist, he would be writing both with, and ultimately for, a composer who would select and set the text into its musical form. And while Wagner may have argued convincingly for opera to be a *gesamtkunstwerk* (a complete synthesis of music and words), it should be noted that he was his own poet!

By all accounts, the new Estacio/Chafe partnership weathered any initial disagreements with surprising ease. This creative compatibility was in no small part rooted in the clarity of Chafe's narrative vision. As a passionate Newfoundlander and an avid student of its history, Chafe understood immediately Hickman's suggestion to focus on the events of Beaumont-Hamel . . . but with a dramaturgically critical caveat. Yes, this would be an opera inspired by the events and legacy of July 1, 1916. But it would not dwell on the battle itself. Rather, Chafe had the inspired idea to base the opera on an almost forgotten historical figure of that period. Father Thomas Nangle was a priest who rose to enormous popularity during the whole ww i period, eventually leading the Newfoundland and Labrador contingent in the massive postwar Commonwealth War Graves Commission. Historically, Nangle pursued his work in the trenches and after the war with the repatriation of the fallen at the expense of his relationship with his powerful archbishop, E. P. Roche. By focusing on this man and this complex and volatile relationship, Chafe gave the story its dramatic heart and the real creation work could begin.

Estacio found in Chafe a writer whose lean and imagistic narrative style ideally suited the challenging task of lifting prose into the sphere of musical cadence and rhythm. Instead of providing a text dominated by traditional dialogue sequences, Chafe adapted to the task of crafting a libretto that distilled complex character interaction and sweeping action sequences in spare and tough prose. In even the earliest drafts, his writing gave the music a space not only to exist but to expand our imaginative connection with the narrative.

Instead of grounding the text in dialogue-heavy scenes, Estacio encouraged Chafe to craft a libretto that would avoid the pitfall of overwritten sections of recitative passages, a characteristic failing one finds in many new opera librettos. Instead, Chafe's lean text provided Estacio with rich and unforced possibilities for exploring the many musical forms traditionally employed in the operatic repertoire. Powerful choral sequences were always to play a significant role in the opera, both a male and female chorus were part of the brief provided by the commission. But Nangle's story also allowed Estacio the thrilling freedom to explore a meaningful series of arias, duets, and trios. Perhaps most significantly, Estacio and Chafe began to write an almost Verdian quartet sequence at the end of Act One. Traditional unities of time and space were dissolved as a grieving mother and a heartbroken young woman reach across space to engage with Nangle and the young Edward in the mud-filled trenches. The verismo of earlier scenes elevated into something newer and richer as the libretto pushed the piece into a mythic tale of suffering and redemption.

The Workshop Period—2014 and 2015

At this point, the creative team consisted of Estacio, Chafe, and dramaturge Michael Cavanagh, who now was director/producer-in-residence at Opera on the Avalon. The team started to actively work on the story, no more dreaming in cafés about what might be, but rather working as a team to develop a libretto strong enough to fuel an ambitious large-scale opera project. The first of the *Ours* workshops took place in St. John's in May 2014, and the second took place in Toronto in July 2014. As has become a common practice in the development of new opera in Canada, the first workshops were devoted to the libretto and used actors in the various roles rather than singers.

Even in the early drafts of the libretto, Chafe had a strong grasp of the dynamics of his story. His deep love for and knowledge of Newfoundland were of profound value as the story began to emerge and solidify. As their mutual respect and trust grew, Estacio and Chafe grew increasingly comfortable with challenging each other to explore and deepen every moment of Nangle's story. It is at this point that the *Ours* development story took yet another unexpected turn. Michael Cavanagh left the project and Hickman invited me to join the creative team as stage director and dramaturge.

Of course, I was excited by the all too rare opportunity to work on a new opera, but I was also nervous about adding my voice to a process already well underway. I have had the privilege of working on many new play commissions in theatre and I know first-hand just how delicate and important the relationship between writer and dramaturge can be. And while I knew and deeply admired the work of both Estacio and Chafe, my unease was increased by the knowledge that I had not worked directly with either of the creators. But once again, Hickman's instincts for partnerships proved sound. From the very first telephone conversations, Chafe and Estacio welcomed me wholeheartedly to the project and I quickly realized that this deeply emotional journey would be guided by generosity of spirit and wickedly enlivening Newfoundland humour.

The final workshop took place over a week in Toronto in December 2015. And for the first time, we were able to hear Estacio's musical interpretation of the Nangle story. Singers replaced actors and the piece began to emerge in its final form. Also joining the process at this point was Judith Yan, principal conductor for Opera on the Avalon, and throughout this critical stage she functioned not only as workshop conductor and coach, but also as Estacio's musical dramaturge. And while there were still sections that were yet to be composed, the spirit of *Ours* was finally revealed in all its complexity and emotional power.

In a small and personal aside, it was during this critical workshop that yet another obstacle emerged to challenge the final stages of the opera's development. After two thrilling and energized days of musical and theatre dramaturgy, and after a long debriefing with the creative team, I found myself the victim of a particularly brutal robbery and stabbing just outside the friend's house where I was staying. The next day was lost in a haze of police interviews and pain, but with the amazing and wholehearted support of everyone at the workshop and Estacio, Chafe, and Hickman in particular, I was able to return to the hall for the final three days of the process. It may sound like a cliché, but I am utterly convinced that my healing was sped and enhanced by the spirit of focused artistic creation that filled the small studio room. When those young singers, led by Newfoundlander Aaron Sheppard, sang an anthem to their beloved country contained in the final ensemble scene in Act One, a powerful sense of destiny grew within all of us, and our commitment to the legacy of telling this story became overwhelming.

> "We didn't cross the ocean to fight for England
> or fight for Canada . . . or any other land.
> We may be under British order.
> But Ours . . . are from Newfoundland!"

The Rehearsal and Premier—June to July 1, 2016

This sense of destiny, of the essential rightness of the story, continued to fuel us through the rehearsal process in St. John's in June 2016. While very little changed in terms of the score during the rehearsal process, the libretto itself continued to subtly evolve.

Most significantly, a difficult review of a principal female character was undertaken. This mostly involved the character and function of Nangle's wife, Thelma. From the very beginning of the process, Chafe and Estacio wanted to give Thelma a dynamic central role. They understandably wanted to give their opera a central female voice and Thelma was the obvious choice. Historically, after leaving the priesthood a disillusioned man, Thomas Nangle found love and fulfillment in Zimbabwe (then Rhodesia) with Thelma. However, as the opera solidified around Estacio's explosive score, it became increasingly obvious that the Nangle love story belonged to another time and place. But as soon as the Thelma story was moved to bookend the narrative by including scenes taking place in 1949, essentially framing the opera into the fluidity of memory, the final pieces of the dramaturgical puzzle came together.

Exactly one hundred years after those brave young Newfoundlanders marched to their death at Beaumont-Hamel, *Ours* premiered, on July 1, 2016, at the Arts and Culture Centre in St. John's. Led by Brett Polegato as Nangle and Roger Honeywell as Roche, the company poured their hearts into the story that Chafe and Estacio had prodded and dragged and nursed into vibrant life over the previous five years.

All premieres are special but that unseasonably hot summer evening in St. John's was an especially moving experience. Dripping sweat in their heavy woollen costumes, the St. John's singers playing the fallen soldiers of ww i reached out and grabbed the hearts of the audience from their opening chorus and never let go. Chafe knew his audience, knew their story, and knew how deeply they needed to honour the men and women who shaped today's Newfoundland.

Writing Ours

Robert Chafe, Librettist

Newfoundland and Labrador is a place defined as much by its tragedies as anything else. The battle of Beaumont-Hamel (July 1, 1916) has always held a sacred
place in the hearts and minds of this land, shaping not only our political trajectory but our very self-identity. I have long wanted to write about that fateful day.
Many have done it before me, and for many years I spun my wheels on a lack of
clarity of what I could contribute to the conversation. I knew I didn't want to retell
the story of the battle itself, but somehow deal with the scar it left, its unique and
undeniable contributions to the dissolution of Newfoundland as a nation, and the
eerie coincidence of its anniversary date falling each year on Canada Day. What
I ultimately found myself needing was a potent and as yet untold personal story
on which to hang those topics of investigation.

I wrote my first Newfoundland "bio-play" in 2002 (*Tempting Providence*) and
with its success I found in subsequent years no shortage of people offering up
ideas of the next great Newfoundland hero deserving of a play. Of those many
pitching ideas was my friend John FitzGerald, well-known and respected historian
and passionate authority on all things Newfoundland. He handed me a book one
day and told me to read it, that there was a play about the Royal Newfoundland
Regiment there. I was swamped, wrestling with other projects, and so the book
sat on my shelf untouched. Flash forward a few years and an expected call from
Cheryl Hickman (artistic director of Opera on the Avalon) had me suddenly on
the hunt again for that personal narrative about Beaumont-Hamel, this time for
a libretto. I remembered that book and pulled it. *Soldier Priest in the Killing Fields
of Europe*, by retired police officer and dedicated regiment historian Gary Browne,
was my first introduction to the remarkable story of Thomas Nangle.

Nangle was a name all but lost to the general knowledge of most Newfoundlanders, an outcome I partly deal with in the libretto. I knew as soon as I read that book that I had my long-sought-after personal narrative. Nangle's story of the war and the aftermath is the perfect embodiment of Newfoundland's story: the great sacrifices made, the deep and permanent scars, the almost inevitable and irreparable long-term damage done. I knew the best way to honour this extraordinary man with any piece of art was to ensure above all that it was a good piece of art. And to that end, I necessarily slid away from dogmatic historical accuracy, augmenting finer details to fit the condensed timeline, shaping characters to better tell our story clearly and well. Those with a knowledge of the regiment and the period will have no trouble spotting my work: Edward Patrick Roche didn't become archbishop of Newfoundland until 1915, and on and on.

Everyone on the creative and production teams went to extraordinary lengths to forge this piece with authenticity; from the very beginning of development with a studious research and consultation phase, to a detailed approach to design and execution in the final months. The sacred history we dealt with demanded as much. In the libretto I occasionally borrow from the real freely for effect: from Binyon's "For the Fallen," and from the granite headstones of Beaumont-Hamel. And while the regiment soldiers you will meet in this piece are necessarily my creation, the list of names evoked in the early scene of enlisting, and the names spoken later in epitaph and mourning, are very much real. They were "ours."

My eternal gratitude to Gary Browne for his years of effort in commemorating Nangle's service and legacy; John FitzGerald for introducing me to Gary and his great work; and Hugh Nangle, for trusting us with his father's story.

And, finally, my thanks to the great John Estacio. His music lifted this story to a very special place. I'm eternally grateful to him for sharing his genius and big heart with me.

Designing Ours

Patrick Clark, Set and Costume Designer

When Glynis and I spoke on the phone for the first time, the first things we chatted about were images and how to make them exist on stage. We both loved the idea of wood—the dry and sun-bleached wood of decking, the battle-scarred wood of trench warfare, and the wooden floors of Newfoundland houses and churches. The music informed the tone and style of the piece . . . as well as the script, making transitions critical, especially the farewell in St. John's as the ship set sail to the battlefield in France.

The set was all wood, like an old wharf, aged and distressed with time. It also had several levels, practical in that these allowed for both large-cast and small-cast scenes. Besides this, there were two pieces that actually went out over the orchestra pit, to allow the actors to get as close to the audience as possible, and visually, the set embraced the orchestra. Lighting achieved the opening scene in the 1930s as we flashed back to ww i and the sailing of the regiment. The biggest transition was from St. John's to the battlefield of France. To achieve this, sections of the decking pieces were hinged, which allowed the floor itself to slowly open up and create the trenches and battlefield. We also used sails and sheeting to create projection spaces. Locations shifted quickly, so transitions from the church to the battlefield and back again were accomplished by fly pieces and projections.

As always, with opera, you have the freedom to be much more abstract in your designs, because the music and the voices are the real stars of the show. The set offered a background for the singers, but it also allowed the projection designer the ability to move the show scenically from location to location. Design is a collaboration with all facets. The lighting, the projections, the set, and costumes all have to work as a unit, but particularly when you are the set and costume designer, the more you can create spaces that work for the lighting and projection design the better.

The music was fantastic—so beautiful and evocative. It was such a pleasure to work on the piece.

Ours was commissioned and first produced by Opera on the Avalon on July 1, 2016, at the St. John's Arts and Culture Centre, with the following cast and creative team:

Thomas Nangle: Brett Polegato
Archbishop Roche: Roger Honeywell
May: Lara Ciekiewicz
Field Marshal Haig, Recruiter: Stephen Hegedus
Elizabeth Crowley: Elizabeth Turnbull
Edward: Adam Fisher
Thelma: Cheryl Hickman
Arthur Murray: Calvin Powell
Charlie Whitten: Aaron Sheppard
John: Ryan Downey
George Crowley: Michael Marino
Michael: Ryan Bradford
Timothy Nangle: Liam Bennett
Rory Nangle: Matthew McCarthy
Hugh Nangle: Lucas White
Mavourneen Nangle: Jane Hynes
Supernumerary: Claire MacLeod, Sean Connors, Cameron Bennett

Chorus

Soprano: Amanda Dawe-Ledwell, Ashley Cook, Kelsey Downer, Melanie Jardine, Melissa Reid, and Robin Whiffen
Mezzo: Abra Whitney, Ally Bowes, Cathy Jackman, Janet Lawlor, Janna Rosales, Katherine Bowes, Kathy Skinner, Maggie McCarthy, Ryan McDonald, Sarah Cook, Sarah Mole, and Siobhan Donovan

Tenor: Adam Wicks, Christian Garcia, Darrell Roberts, Ethan Lewis, Liam Robbins, Michael Johnston, Ron Hutton, and Sam Primmer
Baritone: Andrew Williams, Callum McGann, Jason Schilder, Matthew Feener, Michael Rosales, and Simon Alteen

Librettist: Robert Chafe
Composer: John Estacio
Director: Glynis Leyshon
Conductor: Judith Yan
Stage Manager: Jamie Tait
Costume and Set Design: Patrick Clark
Lighting and Sound Design: Brian Kenny
Projection Design: Jamie Nesbitt
Technical Director and Production Manager: Mara Bredovskis
Assistant Conductor and Chorus Master: Kimberley-Ann Bartczak
Assistant Stage Managers: Anna Barry, Timothy Foss
Props Master: Andrea Dunne
Props Assistant: Kevin Woolridge
Répétiteur: Stéphane Mayer
Fight Choreography: Glenn Redmond
Wigs and Hair: Robert Reed
Head of Wardrobe: Deborah Clarke
Wardrobe Assistants: Fionnuala McMahon, Barry Buckle
Makeup: Skye Tostowaryk
Assistant to Composer: Dylan Langan

Characters

Thomas Nangle
Archbishop Roche
May
Field Marshal Haig, Recruiter
Elizabeth Crowley
Edward
Thelma
Arthur Murray
Charlie Whitten
John
George Crowley
Michael
Timothy Nangle
Rory Nangle
Hugh Nangle
Mavourneen Nangle

Act One

Scene I

Rhodesia, 1949.

A field of mud.

THOMAS, with his back to us, is kneeling, working on something.

THELMA enters, in white, an exotic flower in her hair; she looks almost immune to the dirt.

She watches him a moment, worried, and then sings.

THELMA: Thomas?
Thomas, what are you doing?
Can you hear me, are you all right?

I'm going inside, I wish you would follow.
The day is bleeding the last of its light.
It looks like it's set to rain.
And here you are, in the mud again.

He looks at her, says nothing, goes back to his work. Then:

Thomas.

THOMAS: I've seen my share of rain.
I've seen my share of darkness.

THELMA: What are you making?

He shows her, a rough wooden cross.

She stares at it silently.

A cross.

THOMAS: Just one more.

THELMA: Who is it for?
Thomas?
Who is it for?

He looks up at her, then slams it into the ground.

Scene 2

August 1914. The muddy streets of St. John's.

A crowd has gathered, whipped into a joyous frenzy by nationalism, the excitement of war. Throughout the following they eventually line up in front of the recruitment desk.

CHORUS: Out here on the edge of empire
They say we are all but forgotten
New found and long lost, they say
Starvin', wretched, and poor
Known for nuttin' more

Than fish and fog.
And a city that keeps burning like a log.

Out here on the edge of the empire
Part of the empire all the same.
Time to prove our worth, they say
Now England is at war.

MEN'S CHORUS: We'll drag the boats ashore,
And do our part
They will know us by our courage and our heart.

WOMEN'S CHORUS: Our boys, they come from far and wide
Content to finally stand side by side
Catholic and Anglican
They'll never be this peaceful again.
And it only took a war
To bring out our best.

MEN'S CHORUS: They say we'll be heading to Scotland
They say we ship out right away

WOMEN'S CHORUS: War comes, it never comes close.

MEN'S CHORUS: So ye should be thankful.

WOMEN'S CHORUS: Thankful to be left
Starving and poor?
Wretched, starving, and poor

MEN'S CHORUS: But after today . . .
. . . forgotten no more!

RECRUITER: All right, form a sensible line!
You must be eighteen years of age or older
And in good physical health.
The Hun don't need no target practice.
Next!
Name!

CHARLIE: Charlie Whitten.
Twenty-six years old last birthday.
And there's no stronger man here,
I'd put money on it.

RECRUITER: Save your money and save your breath,
But we'll take your signature here and here.

CHORUS: Told the King we'd send him five hundred
Why settle for any old few
Send him the brightest.
And the quickest of wit.
The strong and the fit,
Send nothing less.
We'll give them nothing if not our best.

More men sign up; their names called out.

Severally:

Richard Short
James Maher
Stewart Pinsent
Albert Haines

MEN'S CHORUS: They say that the sun shines in Europe

William Bennett
Joseph King
William Ryan

CHORUS: Lands its light on the new fields of war
Michael Walsh
Nathaniel Croucher
Alfred Taylor
Michael Taylor

WOMEN'S CHORUS: You needn't ask what they're fighting for

MEN'S CHORUS: King and country!

WOMEN'S CHORUS: Half of them don't even know!
A chance to roam,
Maybe nothing more.

ELIZABETH: George Percy Crowley!
You get your arse back here right now.

GEORGE: Mom, go home out of it, I said!

ELIZABETH: What, to an empty house?!
That's what ya wants to leave me with.
Yer father down on the Labrador,
His hands worked raw and the bottle on his breath
Ya needn't think it good enough cause
To go running off to yer own death.

GEORGE: I'm a man meself now.

ELIZABETH: Yes, and you only fifteen years old.
Christ, Georgie ya don't even shave!

She grabs him by the collar and drags him off. The crowd laughs.

CHORUS: *(random cries)* Georgie! Georgie! Georgie! Georgie! Georgie!

A young couple in the crowd, EDWARD and MAY.

EDWARD: Will you make a show of me too?

MAY: You should know me better than that.

EDWARD: Darling May,
Thank you for coming with me.

MAY: Of course.
Together in all things.

EDWARD: Together?
Really?
I asked you to marry me.
And you said no.

MAY: Then you asked me to wait for you.
And I said yes.
Here I am, Edward, here I am.

CHARLIE: Some of them say this war will be over
Before we even set foot on foreign soil.

EDWARD: You see,
I'll be back before the kettle cools.

MAY: Don't tell me you'll come back.
I read enough storybooks to know what's what.
That's what they all say when they go off to war.
I'll come back, they say.
And then they don't.

EDWARD: What should I say then?

MAY: Tell me you're not afraid.
It's the one thing I need to hear.
Tell me you're not afraid.
Don't tell me you'll come back
And don't tell me goodbye.

EDWARD: I'm not afraid.

MAY: Then neither am I.

> *He kisses her. They part and both smile.* EDWARD *sees someone he recognizes pass by.*

EDWARD: Father Nangle.

> THOMAS *is dressed in regular clothes, incognito. He quickly shakes* EDWARD's *hand, but keeps walking on by.*

MAY: Who was that?

EDWARD: Our new parish priest.

MAY: He doesn't look like any priest to me.

> THOMAS *is making his way through the crowd.*

CHARLIE: Tom Nangle!
There's another good St. Bon's boy!
Where's yer collar today, good Father.

    THOMAS puts his finger to lips to silence him, a quick handshake, a slap on the shoulder, and then approaches the recruiter's desk.

RECRUITER: Name?

THOMAS: Thomas Nangle.

RECRUITER: Age?

THOMAS: Twenty-five, and in good health.

RECRUITER: Occupation?

THOMAS: *(lies)* A fisherman, like my father.

RECRUITER: Rather be on the water myself,
Than shooting it up with the Hun.
Father.

    He smiles at THOMAS, who knows he's been caught in the lie.

THOMAS: It's any man's right to serve his country.

RECRUITER: No one would argue you that.

    He offers him the paper to sign, but before he can . . .

ROCHE: Father Nangle!
Show yourself!

ROCHE *storms into the crowd, they part for him. He stares* THOMAS *down.*

THOMAS: Archbishop Roche. I'm sorry, Your Grace, I . . .

ROCHE: You're no more sorry than you are obedient.
Get yourself back to the church.

THOMAS: Is that the Lord's bidding
Or your own?

ROCHE: They are one and the same.

THOMAS: I had no choice.
I asked you to let me go

ROCHE: And I said no.

THOMAS: Our country is at war!

ROCHE: You have given your life to God Almighty,
It's too late to offer it to the Crown.

THOMAS: Your Grace—

ROCHE: Go Nangle!
Now!

The men begin to mobilize and prep for departure. CHARLIE *and* THOMAS *share a quick hug goodbye.*

CHORUS: Go then, do us proud!
—On then, do you proud.
You carry the country before you.

—We carry the country just for you
Heroes in the making
—Out here all but forgotten
Just make sure that you come home.
—After today forgotten no more
The proper soldiers right down to your knees
Nothing below but your blue puttees.
Five hundred of our best and brightest
Marching off to war!
Out here all but forgotten
After today forgotten no more!

The frenzy continues as men continue to sign up. Young GEORGE *picks his way through the crowd again, looking over his shoulder for any sign of his mother.*

Individually:

John Curley
Nathaniel Croucher
George Crowley! Nineteen years old!
Harry Crocker
Larry Corcoran
Ignatius Butler
Sidney Burry
Bert Brown
John Breen
Charlie Bowman

And after today
forgotten no more!

Scene 3

July 13, 1916, almost two years later, and less than two weeks after the battle of Beaumont-Hamel. Official word is just making its way back to St. John's.

Another gathering, a decidedly different mood. A man at the front announces the list of the dead.

RECRUITER: Charles Bowman
Bertram Brown
Ignatius Joseph Butler
Lawrence Joseph Corcoran
Harrison Crocker
George Percy Crowley

Forgotten no more.

Scene 4

THOMAS in his robes on the altar, delivers a sermon. Archbishop ROCHE is at his side.

THOMAS: Almost eight hundred men went up and over the top.
Only sixty-eight answered roll call the next day
Seven hundred and ten wounded, missing, or killed.
Our entire regiment laid out flat.

We take comfort in the hope that one day
We will see our fallen sons again.
Although this congregation will disperse in sorrow,
The mercy of God will gather us together

In the joy of his kingdom.
There, let us console one another
In the faith of Jesus Christ.

Amen.

The congregation breaks up and disperses.

Scene 5

After the service, the crowd is departing. THOMAS *still in his robes is with Archbishop* ROCHE. THOMAS *has a simmering anger that he is attempting to stifle.*

THOMAS: Who among us had ever heard of Beaumont-Hamel?
What did July the first mean to any of us before?
No one will forget it now.
I should have been there!

ROCHE: You'd be nothing now
But another name on that long list.
Look at those grieving mothers,
And think of your own.

THOMAS: My mother left me to the orphanage to raise
After my father's death,
Took my picture off the living room wall
So she could start a family fresh.
Many a mother here will grieve their son,
My mother isn't one.

MAY approaches them.

MAY: Father Nangle.
It was a beautiful service.

THOMAS: Thank you . . .

MAY: My name is May.
My Edward is in your parish on Bell Island.
Edward Burke.
How happy he'll be to hear that we met.

THOMAS: Edward Burke.
Slept his way through most of my sermons.

ROCHE: Have you heard anything?

MAY: There is no long list of the living,
Just the dead.
Names and names,
But thankfully today
Edward is not one of them.

THOMAS: A bit of good news.

ROCHE: Is Edward your husband, my dear?

MAY: No, Your Grace.
He asked me to marry him
But I turned him down.
I said no.

ROCHE: Ah well,
A girl as pretty as you
Should marry no man unless she loves him.

MAY: I love him.
Love is not the problem.
Or maybe it is.
I wanted to marry him,
But I said no all the same.
This war is nothing but cruelty.
I know you feel it too.
Seems that the more that you love
The better your chance to lose.
It might sound foolish,
But part of me thinks it true,
That if Edward has no wife to widow,
Maybe he will somehow see this war through.

She forces a smile, and leaves.

THOMAS: My parishioners have all gone,
Every man of age and able to walk.
All my classmates from St. Bon's, Your Grace!
My lifelong friends!
And for two years I've just sat here.

ROCHE: For two years you've done more than that.
Made your wishes endlessly known
And for two years I've said nothing but no.
And I'm tired Nangle,
At the end of my rope.
I'm the youngest archbishop this country has seen
But you certainly don't make me feel so.

THOMAS: Your Grace—

ROCHE: And with this there is no further you can go
And there is nobody else above me
But the pope and God Almighty.
You are newly ordained,
Not yet three years in,
But that's no excuse for not knowing.
We are supposed to be men of peace.

THOMAS: Peace.
Love.
Loyalty.
That is why they all enlisted.

ROCHE: —You made a vow, Father,
To your church and congregation.
And you talk to me of loyalty!

They are approached by George Crowley's mother, ELIZABETH, *distant,
almost numb.*

ELIZABETH: Archbishop Roche.
Sorry to trouble Your Grace with questions
But no one else can seem to tell me.
I wonder if you can.
Where did they bury my Georgie?

ROCHE and THOMAS look at each other disturbed.

ROCHE: I'm sorry, Mrs. Crowley.
I'm afraid I don't know.

ELIZABETH: Yes, of course.
Forgive me.

She turns to leave.

THOMAS: There was a British chaplain with the regiment.
I'm sure your George was given every proper care.

ELIZABETH: I can't help but wonder if he has a headstone, is all.
I hope so.
I'd like to someday have a picture of it.

She wanders away. THOMAS *watches her.*

THOMAS: Many a mother will grieve her son.
How many women will there be like this?

ROCHE: They are not your sole weight to bear.

THOMAS: It is like you don't even care!

ROCHE: You are the most stubborn, frustrating—!

THOMAS: A mother just asked us where her son is buried,
·One of us should be able to tell her!

ROCHE eyes him a moment, shakes his head, walks away dismayed.

ROCHE: I hate rewarding bad behaviour.
So what I do now, I do against my will.

THOMAS stares at him.

The governor has long wanted to send a Newfoundland chaplain.
I'd hoped he would change his mind.
But he is stubborn, like you.

THOMAS *is silent and wide-eyed in anticipation.*

You have been released to serve in the regiment.
You will be on the front by October.

THOMAS *is dumbstruck with the news.*

I give you what you wanted
and you give me nothing but silence.

THOMAS: Thank you.

ROCHE: Don't thank me.
At least not yet.
Thank me when you get home again.

THOMAS *goes to leave.*

You think that I don't care.
When I was in the seminary, Father Nangle,
We learned a legend from an Eastern religion
Of a man who sought to cure the ills of the world,
One single human torment at a time.
When he looked at the endless line of suffering
His head, it burst from the pain.
They called him Avalokiteshvara,
The one who hears the cries of the world.
Our job is to tend to the flock as a whole.
To try anything else will only do you in.

Scene 6

Musical montage.

THOMAS gets in uniform.

He gets his hat and bag.

THOMAS with his newly packed bag walks through St. John's, sees ELIZABETH, shares a small sad handshake of goodbye.

THOMAS steps down off the boat into the mud, looks at his feet, and up at the sky.

A private comes to greet THOMAS, salutes him, takes his bag.

Two soldiers carrying a stretcher with a badly wounded man pass THOMAS; he spins to watch them go.

Explosions, artillery, mud. THOMAS watches the war.

He is greeted by CHARLIE.

Scene 7

THOMAS in the trenches with the men now. They pass a bottle round and it's clearly not their first. Jovial good times.

CHORUS: A few more days till the weather turns
And ya can see yer breath for sure.
The ponds back home will be ready for hockey
That new snow falling so white and pure.

A few more months here and you'll be too cold to notice
How homesick ya feels or the day of the week
Hockey the furthest thing from yer mind then
Numb fingers fight buttons just to take a leak.

A few more battles, till this is over
Ya gets to sleep in yer bed once more
A woman warm on the pillow beside ya
A grand old life worth living for.

Gueudecourt is what they calls this place
Can barely get yer tongue around it
Every town ya been got the same field of mud,
Not much of a view from down here in the shit.

A few more battles, till this is over
Ya gets to sleep in yer bed once more
A woman warm on the pillow beside ya,
A grand old life worth living for.

A few more bottles to pass the time
To toast and celebrate the little we got
A padre finally that sounds like our own
A layer of ice to keep piss in the pot.

CHARLIE: I don't know what religion is coming to,
What kind of clergyman is this,
A case of whiskey under his head,
And a bag of prayer books at his feet.

THOMAS: What did you expect of me all the way out here, Charlie?
Purple robes and incense holders?

CHARLIE: Are you sure you're even a priest, Tom?
Can I still call you, Tom?

THOMAS: The church makes no exceptions
For old friends.
But I do.

MICHAEL: Awfully good of you, Father Nangle,
To arrange your own welcoming party.

JOHN: Charlie Whitten, pass it this way

CHARLIE: Ah, hogging the whiskey
Forgive me, Father Tom, for I have sinned.
It's been two years since my last . . .
bottle.

MICHAEL: Will you hear his confession, Father?
We're tired of listening to him.

CHARLIE: I say this to you, Father Tom Nangle,
A shocking revelation, it's true.
Save my soul, do your best,
But don't waste your time on the rest.
Nothing but a bunch of Protestants.

The men laugh. EDWARD cuts through it.

EDWARD: Catholic or Protestant,
What does it matter when you are dead.

*The men go silent. EDWARD is a different man than we saw in St. John's.
A pronounced scar on his face. A troubled darkness about him.*

Father Nangle is really here to administer funerals.
Don't let the Lord catch you in a lie, Father.

CHARLIE: Here, Edward,
You needs this more than me.

EDWARD doesn't take the bottle.

EDWARD: I fear you came too late, Father.
So many funerals you missed.

THOMAS: Confession and communion.
That's truly why I'm here.
No more funerals, please God, Edward.
Just confession and communion.

JOHN: Though there's no confessional
Nor either bite of bread.

ARTHUR: Ah, no confessional, sure what do we care?

MICHAEL: What's a secret or two among friends?

CHARLIE: Stuck with ye from Gallipoli to Louvencourt,
Secret? What's a secret at all here?

MICHAEL: A secret's a thing no other man should know.
Like the stink of your feet
Or what you says in your sleep.

CHARLIE: Well, then secrets here are as scarce as the women.

ARTHUR: Scarce as a minute of silence from that.

JOHN: Yes, shut your mouth, Charlie
Like a good Canadian boy.

MICHAEL: In Scotland they called us Canadian, Father.

CHARLIE: I told them to open their ears,
I sounds nothing like a Canadian.

CHORUS: In Scotland they called us Irish too.
American, Australian
Any flavour you choose.

CHARLIE: Called us Canadian,
I'm no more Canadian, b'ys
Than the ones that gave me this.

> *He pulls back the collar of his shirt to reveal a nasty scar, and the men laugh.*

> *They are interrupted by Field Marshal Douglas* HAIG, *who appears at the end of the trench.*

THOMAS: Attention!

> *They jump to attention and hide the bottle.* HAIG *stares at them for a moment. Eventually:*

HAIG: Keep your voices down now, gentlemen,
As well as your heads.
There are snipers everywhere.
You'd do well to remember.

> *And he is gone. The men sit again.*

CHARLIE: Haig himself that was, Tom.

Can you believe it?

Like seeing the king down here in the muck.

THOMAS: Field Marshal Haig.

EDWARD: Field Marshal Haig. The butcher.

CHARLIE: Edward—

EDWARD: If anyone should have taken a bullet at Beaumont-Hamel,

The butcher's your man, right there.

ARTHUR: Be quiet, Edward! Be quiet!

EDWARD: Showing off your scars for a laugh.

He's the reason we got them.

CHARLIE: Shut up, man!

THOMAS: Boys—

EDWARD: It was his stupidity

That sent us up and over the top!

CHARLIE: It will be your own stupidity that sees you court-martialled.

Know who it is you're talking about.

ARTHUR: And what you're talking about too!

Are you here to follow orders or not?

Well, he's the one what gives them.

THOMAS: Come on now, boys.

Come on.

ARTHUR: I'm sorry, Father Nangle.

EDWARD: I'm sorry.

THOMAS: It's a happy night.
A happy night.
Here we are all together.

CHARLIE: Here Edward, have a drink.

EDWARD: I'm sorry, Father.
I am.

He turns away to sleep, leaving the men in heavy silence.

MICHAEL: Don't mind him, Father.
He hasn't been the same.

JOHN: They say Haig himself is haunted by it.

CHARLIE: They says a lot and only half of it's true.

THOMAS: I asked to sign up.
When war was first declared.
I would have been there with you.
But they sent a chaplain from Britain instead.

CHARLIE: In Scotland we told them to open their ears.

CHORUS: We didn't cross the ocean to fight for England,
Or fight for Canada, or any other land.
We may be under British order,
But ours . . .

CHARLIE: . . . are from Newfoundland.

ARTHUR: To the fallen.

CHORUS: May we see you none too soon

CHARLIE: To bed, b'ys. To bed.
Before Haig comes back.

Severally, as the men tuck into sleep:

CHORUS: Goodnight, Father.

Scene 8

THOMAS is left alone in the eerie silence.

Eventually:

THOMAS: How quiet it can be,
When the guns are all still.
The countryside silent now the trees are all gone,
And there are no leaves left to mark the wind.

No one would believe it in St. John's,
The silence.
Or how soundly they all sleep.
This cold night, all this mud,
And I'm the only one awake.

How much does it take
To break a man?
Two long years on the front.
Hundreds gone in half an hour.
Where are all the broken boys I expected?
So heartsick, and yearning for home.
Restless and afraid,
Men undone
By what they've seen.

Not these men.

Not most of them.

He looks across at EDWARD *sleeping.*

Scene 9

A small silence, and then he thinks of something. He reaches into his pocket, extracts a string of prayer beads.

THOMAS: Prayer beads.
A gift given
To so many men here.
Many a mother's parting souvenir

Across time and space ELIZABETH *appears, she holds a set as well.*

THOMAS: A reminder.
To pray every day.
Awake now when I should be sleeping
With this rosary in my pocket.

ELIZABETH: Take these, my dear
Georgie.
They should be with you.
A reminder.
To pray every day.

ELIZABETH: May they send your
thoughts
To a happier place.
Somewhere closer to home.

THOMAS: No mother's gift, just
my own.

ELIZABETH: Somewhere closer
to home.

THOMAS: I can't put her out of my mind.

ELIZABETH: My reckless, stubborn
Georgie.

THOMAS: Asking where her son was
buried.

ELIZABETH: Never heeded a word
I said.

THOMAS: And we with no answer
to give.

Elsewhere, MAY, *thinking of*
EDWARD.

Lara Ciekiewicz. Photo by David Howells.

MAY & ELIZABETH: Some boys dream
Of war.

THOMAS: I should have been here.

EDWARD awake at another end of the trench thinking of MAY.

EDWARD: Some girls dream of
marriage.

> **MAY & ELIZABETH:** You were deter-
> mined to go.

EDWARD: You said you'd wait for me,
Just not as my wife.

> **MAY:** It was all I could do

EDWARD: Did you say no because you knew
Somehow I'd end up like this?

MAY & ELIZABETH: The more that you love

EDWARD & THOMAS: I was warned it would be hard,

MAY & ELIZABETH: The better your chance to lose.

EDWARD & THOMAS: That my courage it might crack,

THOMAS: I said I wouldn't be
changed by it

> **EDWARD:** I promised I would make
> it back.

EDWARD & THOMAS: And here now in the trenches.
I've become a liar, yes, it's true.

THOMAS: I told Edward there would be no more funerals
And now it seems that's all that I do.

He picks up handfuls of dirt.

EDWARD & THOMAS: From Gueudecourt to Sailly-Saillisel

MAY & ELIZABETH: What kind of grass is it grows here in Newfoundland?

EDWARD & THOMAS: From Monchy-le-Preux to Cambrai.

MAY & ELIZABETH: Can a single blade of it be found over there?

EDWARD & THOMAS: Day after dirty day.

MAY & ELIZABETH: What kind of tree is it gives you shade?

THOMAS: Men buried and left behind.
No cross or landmark to be found
And so I mark it on a map.

MAY & ELIZABETH: In case I'm ever asked again.

EDWARD: I'm not right, May

MAY: I'll say it now.

I say, yes, I'll be your wife, Edward.

EDWARD: I'm not well,
And I won't be anymore.

> **MAY:** I will be your wife, Edward.

EDWARD: These thoughts that crowd
my head,
I can barely make room for you.

> **MAY:** Just come back to me.

EDWARD: All I can see.
Bullets and blood.

ELIZABETH: All I can see is you
—All I can see

ELIZABETH & EDWARD: Whether I'm awake or I'm dreaming.

THOMAS, ELIZABETH, MAY, & EDWARD: As this war, it rages on,
No one knows the final cost.
Those buried shallow in the mud
May not be the only lost.

THELMA: Thomas.

Scene 10

As the din of the previous settles, THOMAS *hears her voice, looks about him.*

THELMA: Thomas.

She appears at the top of the trench, in white, the flower in her hair.

THOMAS: I never asked for proof of God's grace.
And yet here you are.
His angel.

EDWARD: Father Nangle?

THOMAS is jolted from his thoughts, looks at EDWARD *at the far side of the trench. He looks back but* THELMA *is gone.*

The others are asleep.
Will you hear my confession?

THOMAS stares at him a moment, gathers himself, and then motions to EDWARD *to come closer.*

THOMAS: Yes.
Of course, Edward.

EDWARD: Forgive me, Father, for I have sinned.
I lied.
I lied to my darling girl
I lied to my May.
She asked me once if I was afraid.
And I told her that I . . .

THOMAS is suddenly distracted, an odd and foreboding feeling. EDWARD notices.

Father?

THOMAS: Sh, Edward.
Be very still.

A distant shot rings out of the night sky and THOMAS is struck. He slumps down, motionless. EDWARD ducks his head in a panic, terrified and confused.

EDWARD: Father Nangle!
Father Nangle!

His cries wake the men still sleeping in the trench. They scramble to THOMAS's side. As they are preoccupied with THOMAS, EDWARD backs away in horror and grief, and unseen by the other men, he quickly bolts off into the night.

End of Act One.

Act Two

Scene 1

THOMAS lies horizontal. His head lit in the darkness. He is wrapped in a blanket. Is he sleeping? Is he dead? Is he still on the battleground wounded?

There is the sound of artillery and men screaming.

Cutting through it we hear EDWARD's *voice:*

EDWARD: Father Nangle!
Father Nangle!

THOMAS twitches at the sound of it.

Father Nangle!

And then another voice:

MAY: Father Nangle.

THOMAS opens his eyes and the lights brighten.

Scene 2

He is in his office at the church. THOMAS *sees* MAY. *He tries to regain his composure.*

THOMAS: Sorry, May.
This cold winter chill.
As a child I'd welcome it
But as a man I've had my fill.

MAY: It's a far cry better than your days in France.
How is your shoulder?

THOMAS: The ghost of the pain,
Nothing more.
A bullet scar the size of a dime.

MAY: They say some of the men returning
Aren't right in the head.
Shell-shocked, they are calling it.

THOMAS: How are you?

MAY: —A bit better than at Christmas.
Still no word. I miss him so.
Have you ever been in love, Father?
Is it wrong for me to ask?

THOMAS: No. I have not.

MAY: You never thought about marriage?
Or having a family?

THOMAS: I always wanted to join the clergy.
Even when I was a boy.
The sisters at the orphanage,
They made me a collar.
Cut from white paper and pinned to my shirt.
I played in the mud and it was the only thing clean.

MAY: Thank you for seeing me.

THOMAS: It's the least I can do.
Edward would have wanted
Me to watch over you.

MAY: Would have?
I'm sorry, Father,
But you talk about him like he was dead.

THOMAS: He ran away.
That's what they say
No one has seen or heard from Edward
Since that night I was shot.
The war is over and done
Those men alive are safely home.

MAY: Some women like me are lucky, then.
Many more are, sadly, not.
With their letters of condolence.
And look at me. What have I got?
There's nothing for me, not good or bad.
No man standing beside me,
But no news of the worst.
So I got no reason yet to fear.
Edward is alive.
I have his last letter here.

He addressed it to "my May."
"His," that's what I am.
Though there's no wedding yet to make it so.
And he's mine, Father.
And so he will be,
When he comes back home.
Hope. Hope lives, Father.
Please don't take it away.
Tell me, is it so wrong
That until I see his name in granite
I won't believe that he's gone?

A knock on the door, ROCHE enters.

THOMAS: Archbishop Roche,
You remember May.

ROCHE: Yes, of course.
I hope I am not interrupting.

MAY: Father Nangle and I were discussing faith.
And I was just about to go.
Thank you, Father Nangle.

THOMAS: Take care of yourself.

MAY: Do not look so worried, Father.
There's really no need at all.

ROCHE: Remember, my dear,
Your faith is a gift.

She smiles, leaves. They watch her go, and once she's gone:

THOMAS: She still has hope that her Edward will return

ROCHE: Love is a powerful force.

THOMAS: So is denial.
If he deserted as they say
He will take a bullet either way,
From our side or from theirs.
May will get no comfort.
She will have no rest.

ROCHE: You'll have plenty of time to rest here.
Your parish on Bell Island
Must be delighted to have you back.
A good place to settle.
A well-earned rest and a gentle life.
You look troubled, Father Nangle.

THOMAS: I look troubled, do I?
I'm sorry to let it show.
I won't be on Bell Island much longer.
I asked you here to let you know.

ROCHE: Let me know what?

THOMAS: I have been asked
To represent Newfoundland
On the Imperial War Graves Commission.
I'm going back to France.

ROCHE: You spend more time in France
Than you ever have in a church!
The war is over, Father Nangle.
The war is over!

THOMAS: Yes, and we must ensure it's not forgotten.
Every man, woman, and child in the country
Should know Newfoundland's future
as a product of her past.

ROCHE: Newfoundland's future?
Does she have one?
The country is on the verge of collapse.
A war we couldn't afford
A debt that we must repay.

THOMAS: The country will persevere.
And you talk about faith!
Newfoundland sent her best
To fight for her future, and now—

ROCHE: Yes, Newfoundland sent her best,
And for that alone we should be proud.

THOMAS: Proud that they all lie rotting
Unnamed and unmarked in France!

ROCHE: I know the work you'll be asked to do.
Finding the dead.
Bodies that have been in the ground for years.
Some of these men were your friends.

THOMAS: I'm not asking your permission this time.
It's not your right to say yes or no.

ROCHE: Thomas—

THOMAS: I have no choice but to go.

Scene 3

An eerie suspense as THOMAS *and his crew walk through a mud field in France. His men carry shovels, a stretcher.*

THOMAS consults his map, checks the surroundings for landmarks. He writes in his book. He sees something and stops the men. He points.

The men look at him, and back at where he is pointing.

THOMAS: The colour of the dirt,
It's darker there.

The men stand and stare for a second, and then slowly put on their breathing masks. They make their way over and begin to shovel.

The noise of shovels scraping earth, dirt thrown.

Adam Fisher and Jean-Philippe Lazure. Photo by David Howells.

THOMAS's eyes over the top of his mask stare into the distance; the rhythmic sound of the shovels and breathing of the men at work.

The men eventually find something, and all stop digging and just stare.

This is clearly the beginning of their work here, none of them are quite prepared for it.

THOMAS steps over and stares down at their discovery.

One man reaches into the hole and pulls out dirtied cloth. The body is obviously wrapped.

He unwraps the cloth further, and is struck by the stench. He composes himself, looks more closely in the hole, searching, and then looks back at THOMAS and shakes his head. THOMAS lowers his mask enough to speak.

Their tags were removed at death,
And sent to administration.
Look for a piece of paper in the pocket.

The man gets closer to look, but he wretches, takes himself further off to be sick.

THOMAS walks to the grave and reaches in. He removes a stained and barely legible piece of paper. Squinting, he is barely able to read.

Arthur Murphy.

The team seems struck by their first identification. They all pause for a second in reverence.

Unseen by the men, ARTHUR rises out of the ground.

ARTHUR: Mother had me a space in the family plot.
Only child, between her and father.
I always thought it morbid,
Asked her what would happen when I got married.
She laughed it off,
Like she knew I'd never get the chance.

Two of the team get in the hole and lift out the cloth-covered body, and put it on the stretcher.

THOMAS is staring at another patch of ground. He lowers his mask enough to speak. He points.

THOMAS: These holes were made by rats.

Another two of the team begin digging there.

GEORGE rises out of the ground.

GEORGE: I didn't think they would let me go.
I thought they'd catch me in the lie
And turn me down.
I was fifteen.
I was fifteen years old.

The team have found his body now. THOMAS reads the paper. Shakes his head, at the recognition of the name.

ARTHUR & GEORGE: So many men were turned down,
And I felt sorry for them.

The team load GEORGE's "body" unto a stretcher. GEORGE and ARTHUR watch them.

ARTHUR: It was all for glory.

GEORGE: It was all for adventure.

ARTHUR & GEORGE: Every man had his reason to go.

The team have found three more bodies, and have hoisted them out of the earth. THOMAS *searches for identification but there is none.*

THOMAS: No note of identification.
His face already long gone.
This one here with no head at all.
Pie Jesu dona eis requiem

CHORUS: A soldier of the Great War.
Known unto God.

The team has found another body. THOMAS *reads the paper and he has to sit down.*

THOMAS: Charlie Whitten.

CHARLIE rises out of the mud.

CHARLIE: All the b'ys from St. Bon's were going.
Twenty of us went down to sign up together.
Send the b'ys from St. Bon's
And watch the German's flee.

CHORUS: If ya lucked into a dry place
Ya gets to sleep like a log.

CHARLIE: Send the b'ys from St. Bon's

CHORUS: Guy next me to lost a finger.
To a rat the size of a dog.

ARTHUR, GEORGE, & CHARLIE: So many men were turned down,
And I felt sorry for them.

CHARLIE & CHORUS: Send the b'ys from St. Bon's

CHORUS: A soldier of the Great War.
Known unto God.

EDWARD rises out of the mud.

EDWARD: I remember being hopeful
And then hope went out like a light.

THOMAS tries to read his paper, but can't.

THOMAS: His head split and mangled.
Nothing left but a body gone soft.
Pie Jesu dona eis requiem.

EDWARD: Made it through Beaumont-Hamel

CHORUS: Made it through the worst.
So few of us still standing
From those five hundred of the first.

CHARLIE: Cambrai.

ARTHUR: And Monchy-le-Peux.

EDWARD: Run away and get back home
Only to face the ones that knew.

CHORUS: The smell of last night's rain in the air
The suck of mud under your boot.
The order up and over the top
Guys falling before they can shoot
The bullets ripping into the ground.
The sound when they hit something softer.

ARTHUR: I took one in the chest

GEORGE: I took one in the gut

CHARLIE: I took one square in the face,
And that was the end of me.

EDWARD: I didn't care anymore.

CHORUS: Send the boys, the blue puttees.

GEORGE: I tried to crawl back home.

EDWARD: I ran as fast as I could.

ARTHUR: I couldn't run at all.

CHORUS: The sky was blue
There was sweat in my eyes.
Or maybe it was blood.
I was tired and so I closed them.

EDWARD: I tried to remember your face.
I wanted to say your name

But I heard voices,
The voices of men
I didn't know if they were ours.
So I ran away from them.
But they could see me,
And they shouted
And then something fast split open my head.

CHORUS: My father's name given to me,
—A soldier of the Great War, known unto God.

A soldier of the Great War
Known unto God

And now by nobody else.

THOMAS: *Pie Jesu.*

The stretchers are lifted and carried out. The muddied men walk away into the darkness.

THOMAS is left alone. He removes his mask.

Everything is silent for a moment.

And then the "Last Post" is played.

Something large moves towards THOMAS through the dark. As it enters the light, we see it's covered in Union Jacks.

Scene 4

The opening and dedication of Newfoundland's National War Memorial in St. John's. The monument looms centre, covered in its Union Jacks.

Archbishop ROCHE *is at the podium. Behind him,* THOMAS *sits silent alongside Field Marshal* HAIG.

ROCHE steps aside and the Union Jacks are removed. There is silence at the sight of it.

HAIG takes his place at the podium. He surveys the crowd silently for a moment.

HAIG: I am proud to honour
Your brave sons
To have this time to thank them.
I offer the sympathy of one who
Knows well
What your boys were asked to do.

I want to thank along with you
Your own Lieutenant Colonel Nangle.
This memorial here in St. John's
Is only one of six,
He fostered, funded, and built.
The others stand proud in Europe.

Throughout the following, six identical caribou monuments slowly move in one by one to flank the war memorial on both sides.

Beaumont-Hamel.
Still battle-scarred and broken
There interred are the valiant dead
Who had been left in graves scattered and unmarked
Their names now etched forever in stone,
Along with the words you sent as epitaph.
Your boys are shaded by the trees of their home,
Imported across the sea
By Father Nangle's decree.

Thank him, Newfoundland.
As you thank your fallen sons.

Scene 5

A line of people, mostly women, line up to shake THOMAS's *hand. The following lines are sung individually.*

CHORISTER: Thank you, Father Nangle

CHORISTER: Thank you.

CHORISTER: Thank you so much, Father Nangle.

ELIZABETH is there. He gives her a photo of GEORGE's *grave.*

ELIZABETH: Thank you, Father Nangle.

ELIZABETH stares at her photo, and reads.

Private George Percy Crowley
Age seventeen.
Rest in peace, my darling son.

CHORUS: Father, in thy gracious keeping
Leave we now thy servant sleeping

Private G. Warford
Age Twenty-two

Thank you, Father
—Gone but not forgotten by his mother.

Thank you, Father Nangle

Give him, O Lord, eternal rest
And may perpetual light shine upon him
A soldier of the Great War
Known unto God.

Private J. Hancock
—Private R. J. Maddigan

Age eighteen
—age nineteen

Private C. F. Taylor
—Private C. S. Hall

Age twenty-three
—Age nineteen

We shall go to him
But he shall not return to us

My son, my son
A crown thou hast won
Of everlasting glory

ROCHE: They shall grow not old, as we that are left grow old:
Age shall not weary them, nor the years condemn.
At the going down of the sun and in the morning,
We will remember them.[*]

CHORUS: Thank you, Father

A soldier of the Great War
Known unto God.

CHORISTER: Thank you, Father

CHORISTER: Thank you, Father.

CHORUS: Private R. J. Maddigan
Age nineteen

CHORISTER: Thank you, Father.

CHORISTER: Thank you.

CHORUS: Private J. Hancock
Age eighteen

CHORISTER: Thank you, Father Nangle.

CHORISTER: Thank you.

CHORUS: Private G. W. Marsland
Never forgotten by his loving mother,
Father, sisters, and brothers.

---

[*] From "For the Fallen" by Robert Laurence Binyon (1869-1943), published in *The Times* newspaper on 21 September, 1914.

As the line of people continues, and they silently offer their thanks, all THOMAS *hears is what the* CHORUS *sings, consuming him, overwhelming him.*

CHORUS: A soldier of the Great War
Known unto God

My son, my son
A crown thou hast won
Of everlasting glory.

    MAY *is there.*

MAY: A soldier of the Great War
Known unto God

CHORUS: Private F. T. Lind
How closely bravery and modesty are entwined

A soldier of the Great War
Known unto God

MAY: A soldier of the Great War
Known unto God

CHORUS: His last words when leaving home were
I only have once to die!
—My son, my son!

My son, my son
A crown thy hast won
Of everlasting glory

MAY, grieving and in despair, is searching for THOMAS.

MAY: A soldier of the Great War
Known unto God

THOMAS is overcome, despondent, at the sight of her, and the line of people that seems never-ending.

Scene 6

THOMAS sits in ROCHE'S *office. He is silent, thinking.* ROCHE *paces, annoyed.*

ROCHE: They are all singing your praises.
They say every man, woman, and child,
Shall remember what he has done!
Every household with your picture on the wall.
You, right next to the pope.

Will they remember
Those that you left behind
All the time spent away from your parish?
No, that shall all go unmentioned, I suppose.
Will you remind them of all of that?
Nangle? I am talking to you.

THOMAS: Faith is a gift.
I heard you say that once.

ROCHE: Did I?

THOMAS: —It's begun to feel more like a test.

ROCHE: Faith is not just a gift
And faith is not just a test
It is both.
Father Nangle, are you listening to me?

THOMAS: No, Your Grace.
I am not.

He reaches up and slowly, decisively, removes his clerical collar.

ROCHE stares at him, shakes his head, annoyed, smiles.

ROCHE: Where do you think you are going?

THOMAS: I am gone.
I'm leaving the country.
Yes, and everything else.

ROCHE: Come back here and sit down.

THOMAS: The country, the church
I am leaving everything that I have left to leave.

ROCHE: Leaving the church!
You can't be serious.
Where can you go that He will not find you?

THOMAS: Give me your blessing.

ROCHE: No!
I will not!
I will not bless weakness and folly!

THOMAS: This is not weakness.

ROCHE: I am no father to one who needs none.

THOMAS: This is not folly

ROCHE: To one who would simply turn, then, and run.

THOMAS: Give me your blessing

ROCHE: I let you go, against my better sense

THOMAS: Nothing is simple.

ROCHE: In favour and faith, I let you go.

THOMAS: You did me no favour! You did nothing for me!

ROCHE: I did, Thomas, and I do.

THOMAS: You did me no favour!

ROCHE: I favour you still! With my time and my patience. And you ask my blessing now! The gall!

THOMAS: I did not ask for myself!

ROCHE: No, you begged! Like a child!

THOMAS: I asked to go for king and country
And, yes, for God, too.

ROCHE: And now you renounce your faith!
Father Thomas Nangle.
Father to none.

THOMAS: Searching those fields of mud
Searching with hope
And dreading what is found
Parts and pieces.
Fragments of men.

ROCHE: Nangle, sit down!

THOMAS: I found a tooth, a soil-covered tooth,
Sitting in the clay, shining in the sun.
I put it in my pocket and I don't know why
I still keep it there, roll it in my fingers,
Like a marble, like a penny.
Some trifle of a thing.
Do you want to see?
No?
No.
A trifle of a thing compared to some things we found
The long dead and lost, rising from the ground.
Some that I buried myself,
Dug up and buried again.
No washing water can strike me clean of it now
I've tried.
I have tried.
But you can smell it on me still. Their blood and their dirt
I knew their names.

I knew their voices.
The sound of their sleeping.

Young May, she still comes to me.
I tell her Edward's passing was peaceful,
And that I trust that he wasn't afraid.
But what do I know about peace?
What I tell her is a lie.
The Edward she knew was long gone
Now buried somewhere in the mud like the rest,
Do I tell her that?
I tell her his passing was peaceful.
While that found tooth sits in my pocket.
Maybe it's his. Maybe her Edward's
The edges still black with somebody's blood
Maybe his. Maybe his.
Bless me, bless me, Your Grace
For I am leaving.
I am already gone.
I can still smell them on my skin.
I am gone.
I am gone.

A long moment as ROCHE *regards the broken man. And then . . .*

ROCHE: You want my blessing,
And my forgiveness.
You can't have it!

A vow broken.
A spoiled priest!

And listen well, for you've never listened before.
All that you've carved in stone
All over Europe and here at home.
It may weather the time
But your name will not.
Do you hear me?
They will forget you, Thomas.

THOMAS: Bless me, Your Grace

ROCHE: They will forget you for this.

THOMAS: For I am leaving, I
am gone.

ROCHE: What you've done, who you are.

THOMAS: I am gone.

ROCHE: Those pictures will all come down
And they will forget
They will forget you
As you have forgotten your vow.
I will make sure of it.
I will make sure of it.

Scene 7

The world dissolves around him, and, as the beginning, THOMAS *is left in the mud alone, staring at the little white cross he's made.*

THELMA is there, watching him.

THELMA: The clouds have all passed over,
And not a drop of rain.
Thomas.
It scares me when you get like this.

THOMAS: Who had ever heard of Beaumont-Hamel?
What did July the first mean to anyone before?
No one will forget it,
I thought, no one will forget it.

He reaches into his pocket and extracts a letter. He gives it to her and she reads it silently.

THELMA: An invitation.
From Mr. Smallwood himself.

THOMAS: My country is a country no more.
Loyalty is why our boys went.
July the first is their day.

THELMA: It's been twenty-five years
Since you left your country.

THOMAS: Rhodesia is my home now.
The only place I could find
Without any Catholics.

He smiles at her.

He goes to her and hugs her.

I saw you when I was in the trenches.
I thought you were an angel
But you, you were my future.

He touches the flower in her hair.

He takes the flower from her hair,

THOMAS *and* THELMA's *four children run and surround them*

The strains of something in the distance:

MEN'S CHORUS: When sun rays crown . . .

THOMAS *slowly lays the flower at the foot of his cross.*

THOMAS: Just one funeral more.
And then it's all done.

The muddied men of the regiment cross time and space, carrying flowers, slowly enter and lay them at the cross.

MEN'S CHORUS: We love thee, smiling land
We love thee, smiling land.

THOMAS: Bury the country
And all the pain along with it.

More voices. The women of St. John's carrying wreaths.

Sarah Loveys, Andrew Love, and the cast of *Ours*. Photo by David Howells.

CHORUS: As loved our fathers, so we love
Where once they stood, we stand.

THOMAS: I can't go back.
I can never go back.

CHORUS: God guard thee
God guard thee

> *They all stand behind the cross, a pile of flowers at its feet. Behind them in the sky a Canadian flag is raised up a flagpole, it blows in the wind.*

THOMAS: I can't go back.
I can never go back.
But I . . .
But I can remember.

> *The music swells and continues as the singers fall silent. They all stare down sombrely at the cross, the pile of flowers. In the air above them, and all around the flag, the boom of incongruous fireworks.*

> *The end.*

Rocking Horse Winner

Based on the short story by
  D. H. Lawrence

Libretto by Anna Chatterton

Composed by Gareth
  Williams

Directing Rocking Horse Winner

Michael Hidetoshi Mori, Director

A dark horse

1. an unexpected winner in a horse race, thought beforehand to have very little chance

2. an almost unknown contestant regarded by few as a likely winner

There is a certain chaos in developing new opera or theatre. In an era that has no popularly acclaimed masterworks, what is a great opera? How does one gauge what kind of impact a show will have on audiences when it has never been seen and, in the case of opera, when it faces the stereotypes of both opera and new music, assumptions that limit those who encounter it:

"There must be more money," "There's never enough"

Tapestry Opera, the Toronto-based company dedicated to developing new works and opera creators, had been pushing to produce *Oksana G.* (composer Aaron Gervais, librettist Colleen Murphy) for eight years. When I took over the role as head of the company, the *Oksana G.* score had already been completed, with a large-scale complement featuring full orchestra, chorus, and a large cast of principals demanding a significant investment. *Oksana G.* was put forward as the flagship for the 2015–2016 season but, so soon after new leadership had taken over, a prudent board of directors rejected the financial risk. Enter the dark horse.

In April of 2014, I had received an email from Gareth Williams, the composer whose *Pub Operas* (a.k.a. *The Sloans Project*) with Canadian librettist David James Brock had debuted at Tapestry Opera in November 2012. Gareth wrote, "I've nearly finished the *Rocking Horse Winner* with Anna (Chatterton)...It's the best thing I've ever done . . . Let me know if you'd like a nosey." I was intrigued! In his excitement, Gareth forwarded me an MP3 of the MIDI. Despite the synthy twang of MIDI, it was exciting!

However, at this time *Rocking Horse Winner* was a forty-five-minute work, composed from 2013 to 2014 while Gareth was in his Scottish Opera residency and intended for young audiences. In my early days at Tapestry, the purse was tight for extra projects, so it sat on the shelf. But when *Oksana G.* was postponed, the time and budget for a world premiere opened up. We would have to expand the show and do some relatively quick turnaround on new material and dramaturgy, but it was possible and pretty exciting. We made the call!

One key change was to shift the role of the "whispering" house from a voiced line for the orchestra to a quartet of four ensemble members who could also bring to life the race scenes. Ava, the mother's character, was another challenge: Anna, Gareth, and I debated whether or not she should have sympathetic qualities. After all, D. H. Lawrence's story begins with:

> There was a woman who was beautiful, who started with all the advantages, yet she had no luck. She married for love, and the love turned to dust. She had bonny children, yet she felt they had been thrust upon her, and she could not love them.

In the end, we agreed she deserved an aria. This would provide an opportunity for the audience to understand her better and, if not love her, at least not outright hate her.

Anna and Gareth did an incredible job of taking the forty-five-minute work and expanding it to just over an hour. To their credit, it never felt as if it was a souped-up kids' show; rather, it went from a first sketch to a work that captured the possibilities of magical realism in a shimmering minimalist score, with deft strokes of vocal lyricism.

Tapestry has been blessed with extraordinary collaborators. From the first workshops, veteran performers Carla Huhtanen as Ava, the mother, Keith Klassen as the charming and secretly broke uncle, and Peter McGillivray as Paul's caretaker brought a lifetime of experience and depth to the workshopping process, rehearsals, and performances. Emerging star conductor Jordan de Souza, not yet

of the Komische Oper, took the reins and ran what I found to be the most effi-
cient and insightful rehearsals I have ever encountered in new opera. But it was
our discovery in young tenor Asitha Tennekoon as Paul that brought everything
together. It is Paul's story. When Asitha sang the first scene in the first workshop
that we did, Jordan looked at me. We smiled at each other: "This is him."

From here forward it was a Cinderella story. Headlined by a not-yet-profes-
sional tenor who was virtually unknown, with little time to build hype, and a
tighter than small budget, designer Camellia Koo helped us put together a stellar
design and production team, including lighting designer Michelle Ramsay, costume designer Ming Wong, and the incredibly resourceful production manager
Shana Miller, all pulling what favours they could to get the most out of the budget.
I should add that it was to be directed by a virtually unknown director (me), who
to that date had only directed showcases and scenes in Toronto.

What followed was intense and ultimately beautiful. The shortness of the
rehearsal time lent everyone a sharp focus, and the piece began to hit its stride.
We were off to the races!

In the intensity of the rehearsal room, you really don't think about what people
are going to think; you are often lost in the music and storytelling. When the show
was ready to open, I was suddenly terrified. I didn't realize how much I had fallen
for this show and really didn't want people to hate it or dismiss it. As a bit of background, I have been performing professionally since I was an eight-year-old child
performer. I know stage fright. However, this kind of fear was new to me, something I had no control over. But, of course, my fears were vain. This production had
an incredible cast of eight experienced singer-actors, five professional musicians,
one of the greatest conducting talents to grow up in Toronto, and an inspired and
veteran design team. Anna's libretto and Gareth's score punched hard, thrillingly.

It was a great relief when the critics were incredibly supportive (if you weren't
bothered by many of them riffing on the word "Winner"). Audiences were slow
to come, but by the end of the run, word had spread and shows were, thankfully,
sold out.

It was over. Joyous, tragic, and a wonderful tribute to all artists involved. It
wasn't until a year later that we found out the show was nominated for nine Dora
Mavor Moore Awards, primarily up against the Canadian Opera Company and
Mirvish's *Come from Away*. We went to the awards with low expectations, but

mostly to have a good time. We were flabbergasted to win in five of the nine catego-ries, including Best Production. The best part of that night was Asitha's last-minute decision to join us for the awards presentation. He was nominated against Russell Braun (*Louis Riel*) and Stefan Vinke (*Siegfried*) among other superstars of the opera world, and wasn't sure if he would come. He did throw together an outfit and show up . . . and then he won! I think we surprised the Toronto theatre scene with how loudly the normally quiet (or absent) opera folk were whooping!

This dark horse had gone from being a show with an indeterminate future, to being featured in our season on short notice, to being nominated side-by-side with million dollar shows, to beating *Come From Away* (in the category they won a Tony for), winning best production, and totalling the most awards of any Toronto show that season.

The work itself is a marvellous example of dark and light: dark magic in the horse, potentially good people tempted by greed, the brilliant light of Paul's spirit and love, and the dark echoing voice of the house, absorbing everything the mother says and doesn't say.

Her obsession with luck rises perhaps from the absence of love. Unlike in the short story, the operatic Ava's husband isn't around anymore. Ava pines for past glory and relevance and sees her awkward son's presence as another reason she is unlucky. He lacks refinement, but searches for love from his mother and sees luck as the way to achieve that. It is a Faustian bargain. He can ride his horse to gain insights into the winners of upcoming horse races, but each ride costs him.

The nature of the house being first heard, then seen, then morphing into ser-vants and hangers-on provides a great device for the advancing of the story. I think this is the genius of the work. They are the voices that propel Paul to ride, that reward him enough to want to do it again, and then ultimately drive him to his death. But who are these voices? I love that the magic of the piece can satisfacto-rily exist as dark fiction, but one can also see how all of the magical things might come from within Paul's head. He hears his mother, and then the echoes of her complaints reverberate in Paul until he infuses them into everything. He obsesses over a rocking horse he is too old to ride and, instead of accepting the shame that his mother dispassionately serves, he makes it his strength and saviour, and the way to win his mother's love. Does he physically ever go to the races? Does it matter?

Like great theatre, this libretto and score has space for these kinds of interpretations and allows for concepts that take into account psychology, imagination, and the tragedy of those who value trappings more than the people around them.

Not for the last time, I am privileged to say, this work is a winner.

Writing Rocking Horse Winner

Anna Chatterton, Librettist

When composer Gareth Williams proposed adapting D. H. Lawrence's "The Rocking Horse Winner," the short story instantly captured my imagination. D. H. Lawrence writes complex characters with a strong story structure. Gareth particularly loved that the house whispers to Paul (the protagonist of the story), a clear singing opportunity. We could both see that the story could be distilled down and yet also expanded to tell a moving tale about greed, entitlement, and a complicated relationship between a mother and son.

I was particularly struck by the plight of the mother character (Ava in our opera), a woman who cannot feel love for her children and is deeply unhappy. It is a brutally honest yet compassionate portrayal of a woman who is frozen in her own life.

The disconnect between Ava and her son Paul creates a deeply complex relationship. Paul is extremely sensitive and feels desperate to fill the void he feels between them. Only he (and the audience) can hear the house that sings to him, but it is no lullaby. Ava and Paul both have very powerful, yet very flawed personalities that burn bright and then ultimately meet their demise by their own follies.

We felt the relationship between the mother and Paul would be stronger and more contemporary if he were in his early twenties, on the spectrum, and still living at home. I made her an upper-class single mother who is dealing with a child with a developmental disability. I was also intrigued by the concept of longing and feeling unlucky. I believe longing is a feeling that can be inherited and is a very powerful motivating factor.

Gareth and I worked closely together to find the right tone in the libretto. I love working with composers who have dramatic instincts and clear heartfelt vision for the opera, as Gareth did for this piece. There is a moodiness about the story, almost a nightmarish quality, which we retained; I would say in many ways the music that Gareth wrote kept the essence of the story intact.

To adapt a short story to a libretto is an intensely pleasurable task. One feels an intimacy with the author while working so closely with their words and characters. This was a deep dive into D. H. Lawrence's world and it felt like a creative collaboration with the late author. It can also feel like a duet, a partnering with a writer from another time, learning their steps, adding new steps, moving together as one. Playwrights have much less time with their audience than prose writers have with their readers, and a libretto must tell the same story in a very spare, minimal language, leaving room for the music, which can evoke emotion and mood much better than text can. And so out comes the chainsaw, to hack away at whatever is superfluous or undramatic for the stage, and in swoops the librettist to write new text, new scenes, and revise characters to create a muscular sprint through the story. Some lines of dialogue are straight from the story. Some are rewritten. Some are entirely original. About a third of the original text from the short story is in the libretto.

It was a delight to get to know Lawrence's incredible imagination. It was a gift to have such a wonderful foundation to start with, and humbling to dare to add, elaborate upon, change, edit, remove, revise, and rewrite his original story. With words, characters, and original story intertwined, our opera races forward with a pounding heart.

Thank you, dear reader, for your interest in libretti. I have been lucky enough to write libretti for opera for the past fifteen years, and have completely fallen in love with the medium. I love the heightened nature of opera and how the audience will accept poetic language if it is sung. However, the libretto, and librettist, are oft-ignored parts of opera, and I am so grateful to Julie Salverson and Playwrights Canada Press for publishing this collection of contemporary libretti to share with the world. It is a wonderful opportunity to give more insight into the collaborative process between composer and librettist, and to shine a light on the words that are created to inspire a composer to write music, which is created to move and compel an audience.

Composing Rocking Horse Winner

Gareth Williams, Composer

Why are they singing? This question is on my mind for the first ten minutes of every opera I've seen and is my main preoccupation during the whole process of making one. That every line is sung, whether it be a comment on the weather, a stranger asking for directions, or a declaration of devotion, seems quite simply preposterous.

That said, it was never in any doubt for Anna and I that "The Rocking Horse Winner" was an eminently singable story. In a world where communication has broken down, where characters are distant from one another, where no one is reaching out to the people around them, singing is the only option. In a world where a little boy hears a house whispering to him through the cracks, doors, ceilings, and floors, it's an easy conceptual jump to make—that we, the audience, might hear that whispering too, and that it might turn into singing.

The glorious task for the librettist/composer duo, then, is to own the artifice of opera. In *Rocking Horse Winner*, a half-remembered chord at the piano seduces a character to hum a simple melody. And slowly, like a spell, the song emerges and seduces others to sing, until everyone is singing. And just like that—we are in an opera. Opera is very like theatre, except it's underwater. There are slightly different rules—mostly about breathing. And, yes, things move a little more slowly, but magical, beautiful things can happen underwater that could never happen on dry land!

The characters in *Rocking Horse Winner* seem, at times, to be aware they are singing; they understand singing as an act of empathy. Paul hears the house sing, and sings to resonate with it. Bassett, his caregiver, sings to soothe Paul's distress. Uncle Oscar sings at the sheer excitement of the horse races—with the convivial charm of a hustler, he sings to ingratiate himself to others. Paul's mother, Ava, hums and sings sadly and inwardly to herself at her old piano.

The whispered demands of the house may be what drive Paul to action and ultimately to his doom, but everything he does is his attempt to silence his mother's sad song. Perhaps he wants the world to be more like the one found in D. H. Lawrence's poem, "Piano":

"A child sitting under the piano, in the boom of the tingling strings
And pressing the small, poised feet of a mother who smiles as she sings."

At every step of the process, in every draft, Paul was always at the heart of Anna's adaptation. An innocent among flawed, but not necessarily wicked, people. When Anna would send me new material, I would find myself worrying about him for days. His combination of openness and vulnerability greatly shaped his own personal musical language and set him apart from the others on stage. I also think we wanted to protect him for as long as possible.

I don't think about the libretto of *Rocking Horse Winner* in the order the audience hears it. It was a living document for such a long time between Anna and me. All the initial ideas, the eureka moments, the discussions and dead ends, the drafts and decisions—they are all buried within the stitching of the work, and it would require some unpicking to clearly see the path taken.

I have no doubt that the librettist is the most generous of all collaborators. The act of creating words for an opera is one of incredible faith. A librettist has to have faith in music that is yet to exist. They leave space for that music, sometimes through sacrifice. Perfectly healthy branches of story get trimmed back to make way for a collection of noises and sounds that won't turn up until day one of rehearsal.

For the process to work, and for the finished piece to blossom, composer and librettist have to trust one another, to be on the same wavelength. They have to cohabit the same make-believe opera world. When Anna and I made *Rocking Horse Winner* it felt like we were in the same space. The connection was akin to a sibling camaraderie. Like a brother and sister making a fort in the back garden on a summer's evening, we put this thing together.

Designing Rocking Horse Winner

Camellia Koo, Designer

In the following conversation, designer Camellia Koo responds to written questions from Bill Penner.

BILL PENNER: Some readers may not be familiar with the designer's process. Could you tell us about your overall approach, and how opera may differ from designing for a play, dance performance, or a television/film project?

CAMELLIA KOO: My job as a set designer is to find a way to support the story through visual dramaturgy—to design the show in a narrative way rather than just designing the room or the location. When I read a script or libretto and listen to the score, I am looking for narrative, psychological, and emotional clues to design to. I'm not interested in accurately replicating a period room or mansion onstage. I'm always looking for something deeper in the world of these characters to show what they are going through over the course of the story. Whether it is theatre, dance, or opera, the storytelling should be the same. I imagine it would be the same with film, though I have never designed for television or film. What differs from those genres of live performance are only the technical requirements, audience expectations, and the tools with which you have to play to convey a narrative.

BP: How does scale, the combination of live orchestration, the emotional strength of song, and the grand themes, affect your design choices? That is to say, within the large ideas of the libretto, the power of the singers' voices, and the score, how do you decide what to show or not show in the elements of your design?

CK: In addition to the libretto, having the music as a simultaneous narrative to design to is particularly unique to opera. In combination, the libretto and score tell me so much about what the world is emotionally and psychologically, and they are my primary source of inspiration for what the design ends up being. The choices that end up being in the opera are also not entirely up to me. I work in collaboration with the director, in this case, Michael Hidetoshi Mori on *Rocking Horse Winner*, and the lighting designer, Michelle Ramsay. Sometimes the director and the performers need practical things that are mentioned in the script, such as the piano. The practical props and elements that characters require have to be integrated into the overall design framework so the look and palette of those objects are always a choice to be made. The primary force driving all choices, though, is to tell the story first—so, what is essential to telling the story psychologically—and less about what period we are in.

For *Rocking Horse Winner*, we needed some sense of a once-prominent and glorious old mansion, so we wanted the design to show this faded glory and skewed, forced perspective to show the tension between the house and the characters inhabiting the space.

BP: I'm curious how you approached the character of "the House." This character, aside from being an inanimate object, sings of possessions, furnishings, carpets, and so on. It's a short piece, what decisions did you and the director make to present the multiple locations within the house, as the physical location, and grasping, demanding nature of the character of "the House."

CK: "The House" definitely is a character in *Rocking Horse Winner*. To us, the walls needed to convey an omnipresence. Sometimes we could see where its voice was coming from, and sometimes we could not. We made the walls transformative, which means we had an image of a wall printed onto a scrim-like material so that when the walls were front-lit, the house looked solid and opaque. When the scrim was backlit, the walls became translucent and sometimes you could see the performers singing the role of house back there like ghosts in the walls, and sometimes you heard their voices but the space behind the walls were clearly empty. Either way, we could always hear the singers' voices through the walls, which added to the atmosphere as a whole.

BP: In the video of the Tapestry production there are chorus members who appear as servants and racegoers. How did these additional cast members come about, and how did they affect your design?

CK: The chorus voices are written into the piece, so we had to include them as important characters. They doubled as the voices in the house walls when we needed them. Because we needed to include them, they actually required a place to go, so they directly influenced the idea of the scrim walls so that we could sometimes hear them through the walls and sometimes we could ghost them in visually, but always through the wall.

BP: I love how the racegoers become the race itself, with chorus members operating tiny horses on rods while they watch from the stands. The horse puppets serve to underline both Paul's inherent childlike nature and the excitement of high stakes betting at the track. How did this idea evolve?

CK: This idea came about mostly out of economy because we come and go from the racetrack very quickly with no time to do a full-on set change.

I was also mostly influenced by the horse race betting games at the CNE (Canadian National Exhibition), where they are sometimes just cut-outs on rotating sticks. And it was a fun way to have him among the horses without having to build six more "live" horses.

BP: You mentioned earlier the collaboration necessary between you, the director, and other members of the creative team. Was there one particular challenge in the libretto that intrigued or challenged the whole team?

CK: Mostly just trying to tell this story, with all its locations, the house, the race track, and so on, in one fluid, visually and dramaturgically economical space. The theatre at Berkeley Street can be quite limiting because of its dimensions and having no wing space and only one door to get on stage from backstage, so the space plays a huge part in how we approach any design.

BP: What does this opera mean to you now? Is there anything from this particular opera experience that has stayed with you?

CK: I remember most shows I work on mostly because of the collaboration of all the artists involved. And it is always exciting to be part of the premiere of a new work. This particular production was planned to be remounted at Crow's Theatre in spring 2020, with the same creative team and I think mostly the same singers. So, it's also exciting to see it have another life so that more people can see it.

Rocking Horse Winner was first produced by Tapestry Opera at the Berkeley Street Theatre, Toronto, from May 16 to June 4, 2016, with the following cast and creative team:

Paul: Asitha Tennekoon
Ava: Carla Huhtanen
Uncle Oscar: Keith Klassen
Bassett: Peter McGillivray

Chorus: Sean Clark, Aaron Durand, Erica Iris Huang, Elaina Moreau

Librettist: Anna Chatterton
Composer: Gareth Williams
Director: Michael Hidetoshi Mori
Music Direction: Jordan de Souza
Set Design: Camellia Koo
Lighting Design: Michelle Ramsey
Costume Design: Ming Wong

Characters

Ava: Paul's mother
Paul: Ava's son
Oscar: Paul's uncle
Bassett: Paul's caregiver
The House

Scene I: Ava at the Piano

AVA: Nothing is as it should be
When I was young, I was called the golden one
All the girls envied me
When I married, they called us flawless
Full of promise
But my husband never found the right ladder
And his failure made him meek
Nothing is as it should be.

But I must keep up!
Our house had the most shine, the most style!
Less isn't more, it's less.

HOUSE: There must be more money! There must be more!

AVA: My son still lives at home
He's always been a difficult one
Insists on things just so

It's a mother's job to love her child
I fuss, they say.
But his eyes they look for more
But I must love him more than anything
For I'm his mother.
Nothing is as it should be.

HOUSE: There must be more money. There must be more.

Scene 2

PAUL enters.

PAUL: Mother! Why don't we have a car? Uncle Oscar has a car! Even Bassett has a car! Why don't we have a car?

AVA: Because we're poor.

PAUL: Mother! Why are we so poor? Uncle Oscar isn't poor. Even Bassett isn't poor. Why are we so poor?

AVA: Because your father had no luck.

PAUL: Why did Father have no luck? Is luck money? What is luck?

AVA: Luck is what causes you to have money. We are not lucky.

PAUL: But what is luck?

AVA: If you're lucky you have money.
It's better to be lucky than rich.
If you're rich you may lose your money.
If you are lucky you can always get more.

PAUL: And Father was not lucky?

AVA: No!

PAUL: And aren't you lucky, Mother?

AVA: No! I thought I was, but I'm not.

PAUL: I am. I'm lucky.

AVA: How?

PAUL: You'll see! Mother, you'll see!

He starts to run out of the room.

OSCAR, BASSETT, & HOUSE: We need more money. We need more money.

AVA: Paul? Paul? Oh, Paul, I worry so for you.

PAUL: Don't worry! I'm lucky, you'll see!

Scene 3

PAUL is riding his rocking horse. AVA moves offstage.

PAUL: *(whisper)* Can you get me there? Get me to luck?
Get me to luck! Yah!!!!
Giddy up! Yah!!!!
Take me to luck! Get me there!
Yah!!!!

HOUSE: Swallow the track! Make him sweat!
Brace him to the max and fly the dust!

PAUL: Yah!!!! Yah!!!!

HOUSE: You can make him sweat! Pound his heart! Brace him to the max!

PAUL: Heyya!

Asitha Tennekoon. Photo by Dahlia Katz.

HOUSE: Slap the reins! Fly the Dust! Gun it to the line!

PAUL: Take me there! Take me there! Take me!

HOUSE: Get him there! Get him there!

PAUL: I must be lucky, oh, I must be lucky.

AVA, OSCAR, BASSETT, & HOUSE: There must be! More!

PAUL: Do it again! Get me there! Ride me to luck. Do it again!

AVA, OSCAR, BASSETT, & HOUSE: Get him to the line. Get him there!
Oh! Fly the Dust! Oh! Slap the reins!
Oh! Pound his heart! Oh! Dig your heels!

PAUL: Yah!!!! Yah!!!! Giddy-up!

AVA, OSCAR, BASSETT, & HOUSE: Gun it to the line!

PAUL: Daffodil!

Scene 4

PAUL slumps over on the rocking horse and breathes heavily. Uncle OSCAR comes in.

PAUL: I got there.

OSCAR: Paul?

PAUL: I got there.

OSCAR: Paul? Where did you get to, Paul?

PAUL: Where I wanted to go.

OSCAR: Good for you! Don't stop till ya get there! Hey! You're a bit big for this toy, aren't you? Paul? What's your horse's name?

PAUL: He has many names.

OSCAR: Poor thing.

PAUL: No! He's not poor. He's a lucky horse. Last week his name was Blue Peter.

OSCAR: Blue Peter won the Lincoln. Say! Could you give me a tip for the Queen's Plate?

PAUL: Honour bright? Pinkie swear? Cross your heart?

OSCAR: Honour bright. Pinkie swear. Cross my heart.

PAUL: Daffodil.

OSCAR: But Daffodil's a dud! What about Mirza?

PAUL: I only know the winners and the winner is Daffodil.

HOUSE: Daffodil.

OSCAR: Honour bright? Pinkie swear? Cross your heart?

PAUL: Honour bright. Pinkie swear. Cross your heart.

OSCAR: Bassett!

    BASSETT enters.

BASSETT: Yes, sir?

OSCAR: How does my nephew know about the horses?

BASSETT: Paul asks me about the horses, sir. About the races and their winners.

OSCAR: You tell him the winners?

BASSETT: No! He tells me, sir.

OSCAR: Let's find out. Bassett, pack the lunch. We're going to the racetrack. Ava. Ava? I'm taking Paul to the races.

AVA: What? Now?

PAUL: Can I, Mother? Can I, Mother? Can I, can I?

AVA stops him.

Please?

AVA: Well . . .

PAUL: Please?

AVA: You might catch a chill.

PAUL: No, I won't! No, I won't! Can I can I? Can I can I? Please?

AVA: Don't race your heart.

PAUL: Please!

AVA: Don't stain your cheeks red.

PAUL: I won't race my! I won't race my heart!

AVA: Calm down.

PAUL: I wanna go! I wanna go! Please!!!

BASSETT: *(to PAUL)* Paul. Remember what we do? Take nice deep breaths. That's it. I'll keep him safe, ma'am.

   Pause.

AVA: Very well.

OSCAR: And we're off!

PAUL: And we're off!

BASSETT: And we're off!

HOUSE: We're off!

They all leave.

Scene 5

PAUL, OSCAR, & BASSETT: So many people! So much noise! Look at all the horses! Horses! Horses! Horses!

OSCAR: Come on, Paul, where's your Daffodil?

BASSETT: *(to PAUL)* Count the horses! Find your beast!

PAUL: Fifth from the inside. Tenth from the outside. Daffodil in red and yellow. There he is in red and yellow.

OSCAR: Right! Right! Right you are! A fiver for me on Mirza and a fiver for Paul on Daffodil! Bassett?

BASSETT: I've got mine on Daffodil. When Paul is sure, it's sure.

   BASSETT kneels down beside PAUL and makes the race come alive for him.

And they're off!!

OSCAR: Come on! That's my girl.

PAUL: Daffodil. Daffodil. Three hundred and fifty lengths to go

BASSETT: In the Queen's Plate! Ocean Swell going for the lead! Mirza second on the outside! Troy gains ground into third! And Daffodil is far, far, far behind!

OSCAR: I knew it! I knew it! Yes! Come on!

BASSETT: Less than a half mile to go and Troy now in the lead with Mirza on the outside. Galileo on the inside on even terms.

OSCAR: Keep it up, girl!

BASSETT: Where's our boy, Paul? Where's our boy, Paul?

PAUL: So loud. Too loud!

BASSETT: Come on, boy . . . don't let me down now . . .

PAUL: There's four brown horses and five black horses. And one dapple mare and one white horse.

PAUL, OSCAR, & BASSETT: Look at all the horses. Horses!

BASSETT: As the field turns for home Troy makes his way through and Ocean Swell is second on the outside, Galileo battles on! Coming hard down the Southern track and Mirza is still there!

OSCAR: Thank the Lord! Thank the Lord!

OSCAR & BASSETT: Come on! Come on! Come on!

PAUL, OSCAR, BASSETT, & HOUSE: Horses! Horses! Horses! Horses!

OSCAR: She's slipping, she's slipping!

PAUL: My Daffodil!

BASSETT: Troy has the lead. But here comes Daffodil! And she wins it! Spectacular win! Impossible upset!!

OSCAR: I can't believe your dark horse won!

BASSETT: When Paul is sure, it's sure as eggs!

OSCAR: And is he always sure? Do you always win? Paul?

PAUL: When we're sure, we're sure, but when we're not, we lose . . .

OSCAR: So . . . Where's the money?

BASSETT: I keep it safe and locked up, sir.

OSCAR: Mmmm . . . I do like a gamble. Let's be partners.

He shakes hands with PAUL.

BASSETT: A mile is made of eight furlongs.
A fifth of a second equals a length
Bloodlines make a speedy horse.
Racing makes order in an unruly world!

OSCAR: I'll patch up my holes and rise again,
No one need know I was fraying at the edge
Sunk to the worms, ready to slither and scram.
So, breathe in the manure, breathe out the money.

BASSETT: I love this boy like he's my own. More and more.

AVA & HOUSE: More!

PAUL: The house will hush

AVA & HOUSE: 'Cause we'll be flush.

BASSETT: But the lady of the house is ice and glass.

OSCAR: A new car for me, all leather and chrome.

PAUL: Mother will say I'm lucky and she'll laugh!

BASSETT: I'll help Paul to keep up the luck!

PAUL: She'll laugh.

OSCAR: I'll laugh.

BASSETT: We'll laugh.

OSCAR: So! Who's our boy for the Prince??

PAUL: Lively Spark!!

BASSETT: Are you sure?

PAUL: One thousand on Lively Spark!

OSCAR & BASSETT: He's sure!

OSCAR: Two hundred on Lively Spark!

BASSETT: Five hundred on Lively Spark!

(*as commentator*) Betting ten to one! And they're off! At the Prince of Wales! Lively Spark moving on the outside, going for

The guns! He's on his own as he crosses the line!

They cheer.

OSCAR: Two thousand!

BASSETT: Five thousand!

PAUL: Ten thousand! You see! I was sure!

BASSETT: You sure were, Paul.

OSCAR: *(to BASSETT)* That'll be all, Bassett.

BASSETT leaves.

Scene 6

OSCAR: Paul? How will you spend the money, Paul? You could buy a real horse.

PAUL: It's all for Mother. 'Cause Mother is unlucky, and if I'm lucky, then maybe she'll stop singing.

OSCAR: Don't you like your mother's singing?

PAUL: No, not her, the house. I hate our house for singing.

OSCAR: Not the house, Paul! Surely your mum?

PAUL: No, not her, the house, the walls, the ceilings.

OSCAR: What does she sing about? Cobwebs and paint?

Peter McGillivray, Asitha Tennekoon, and Keith Klassen. Photo by Dahlia Katz.

PAUL: She's always short of money.

OSCAR: Aren't we all.

PAUL: She sings when the mail drops,

HOUSE: Sing

OSCAR: What do you mean, Paul?

PAUL: She sings when the telephone rings,

HOUSE: Sing

PAUL: She sings when Mother is carrying parcels in.

HOUSE: Sing.

PAUL: She never stops, never stops, never stops.

OSCAR: Can't you make it stop?

HOUSE: Never stops, never stops, never stops.

PAUL: Hurts my head.

OSCAR: You say it never stops, never stops, never stops? Is it inside your head?

PAUL: No, outside my head . . . Listen . . .

HOUSE: We need more. More.

OSCAR: I can't hear a thing.

HOUSE: I never stop, I never stop.
Sings. Cries. Calls.

PAUL: She sings from the walls,
She cries from the floor
She calls from the cracks.
She whispers at the door.

She won't stop, she won't stop, but I thought if I was lucky then she might stop.

OSCAR: Drown it out. Plug your ears.

PAUL: I thought if I give the money to Mother, then there'll be enough and it might stop?

OSCAR: Stop listening, just stop listening.

PAUL: But Mother can't know of our lucky streak. It might end our luck.

OSCAR: It might end our luck . . . and we can't have that! Keep riding, keep winning, and never stop.

PAUL: I won't stop.

HOUSE: Never stop, I never stop.

PAUL: I'll never stop.

OSCAR: Good boy!

Scene 7

AVA at the piano with Paul.

PAUL: Mother, why do you only sing those sad songs?

AVA: Do I? No, I don't! Do I? No, I don't. Not really . . .

PAUL: Mother, why? Mother, why? Why do you seem so sad?

AVA: Shush, Paul! No, I don't. Shush, Paul. No, I don't. You're too young to know of such things.

PAUL: Mother. Mother. Do you know any happy songs?

AVA: No. Well, maybe . . .

PAUL: Mother, will you sing me a happy song?

AVA: Stop! Stop asking, Paul! . . . I'm sorry. I shouldn't have . . .

PAUL: I just want you to smile, Mother.

AVA: It's easy to smile when you're young
The world smiles so wide with you when you're young.
When I was young, I thought the world would always shine.
I was stupid and vain.

HOUSE: You were stupid and vain.

AVA: And when you get old you find deep lines.
The world frowns and snaps shut. Everything is dust!

HOUSE: Everything is dust!

AVA *gets up from the piano.*

PAUL: Mother! I will fetch a broom and dust all the corners for you. Then you'll smile?

AVA: The world smiles for the young.

PAUL: But Mother, I am young. Is the world smiling for me?

AVA: Paul, you will always stay so young.

PAUL: I wish it were tomorrow! Tomorrow is your birthday! Maybe you'll smile tomorrow?

AVA: Perhaps. Perhaps. Perhaps.

AVA *leaves.*

PAUL: Maybe she'll smile tomorrow? Maybe she'll smile tomorrow!

Scene 8

OSCAR and PAUL bring a birthday cake and present to AVA.

OSCAR: Happy Birthday, Ava!

AVA: What's happy about it?

OSCAR: This year is your lucky year!

AVA: Everything is aging around me.

OSCAR & PAUL: Today is your lucky day!

AVA: Luck left me many birthdays ago.

OSCAR: A present for you. Your share from the stocks. You'll like this . . .

Hands her a small gift box, she looks in it.

PAUL: Wow, what luck! Mother?

MOTHER: Eat your cake, Paul. You're too thin.
(to OSCAR) This isn't enough.
Paul? Paul? Why do you stare at me so?

PAUL: Why aren't you laughing?

AVA: Nothing is funny.

PAUL: But why aren't you happy?

AVA: What does it matter if I am happy, if I'm happy or not? Eat your cake.

AVA leaves.

Scene 9

Time passes. Servants come in with boxes and parcels. PAUL anxiously listens to the HOUSE.

HOUSE: Ching ching ring ring the register
Charge it, keep the change.
She's spending it, draining it all . . .
Flowers in winter, fox furs, soft dresses, silk drapes.

BASSETT: Two hundred!

OSCAR: Five hundred!

BASSETT: *(as commentator)* And they're at the last corner! And Little Wonder comes
in second!

AVA walks by humming.

HOUSE: There must be more.

PAUL: I'll know for the National. I'm sure to be sure.

HOUSE: Sprays of mimosa. This handsome chair. That plush chaise longue.
Piles of shiny pillows, a care home for Paul.

The cast and orchestra of *Rocking Horse Winner*. Photo by Dahlia Katz.

BASSETT: *(as commentator)* And we're at the National! Trigio is lagging behind! And he
falls!! He's down!

OSCAR: *(angry with PAUL)* Six hundred short!

BASSETT: *(disappointed)* Two hundred down!

HOUSE: There must be more.

PAUL: I'll know the next one. I'll have to know for sure.

HOUSE: New Persian rugs.

AVA, OSCAR, BASSETT, & HOUSE: There must be more!

HOUSE: Pearls and silk

AVA, OSCAR, BASSETT, & HOUSE: There must be more!

HOUSE: Fur and flowers

AVA, OSCAR, BASSETT, & HOUSE: There must be more!

HOUSE: Champagne and cars.

AVA, OSCAR, BASSETT, & HOUSE: There must be more!

Scene 10

PAUL is talking to the rocking horse.

PAUL: Please! I have to know! I need to know for the Derby.

AVA enters.

AVA: Paul?

PAUL: What if I don't know? I have to know for the Derby.

AVA: Paul?

PAUL: I need to know. Take me to luck. Tell me.

AVA: Paul? You need a trip to the country. You're so frail.

PAUL: I won't. I can't!

AVA: I'll send Bassett away! He's overstepped his role.

PAUL: No, Mother, no.

AVA: I'll tell Oscar to stop all this talk of the races and we'll go.

PAUL: I won't leave the house before the Derby.

AVA: How about I send you to the country? We'll forget all about it.
Look at you, your eyes too bright, your cheeks too flush. You're all nerves.

PAUL: I won't leave the house till the Derby.

AVA: I didn't know you loved this house so much. Just promise me you'll calm
your nerves.

PAUL: Don't worry, Mother. If I were you, I wouldn't worry.

AVA: If I were you and you were me . . . I wonder what we'd do . . .

PAUL: You know you don't have to worry, don't you?

AVA: Time for bed! Dream of the sun, the lake, the sky. Goodnight, Paul.

> *AVA goes to kiss him, he pulls away, she looks at him anxiously, but
> leaves.*

Now I'm all nerves!
But I must dress for the party. I'll have a glass of bubbles to smooth my shakes.

How does that child crawl into my thoughts so?
He is always with me, even when he's not.
He doesn't know woes like I know woes.
All I want to do is primp for the party.
I deserve a little primp now and then.
He gnaws at me. I'm bitten to the bone.

He won't let me be. I'm tired and worn.
He doesn't know woes like I know woes.

She hears the rocking horse.

That noise! It pounds my head!
That wilful boy!
On and on and on and on and on! I'm sick of it!
Paul!! Paul!!

OSCAR, BASSETT, & HOUSE: Come on, Come on Come on Come on!

AVA goes to PAUL. He is madly rocking on the horse.

PAUL: Yah!!!! Giddy-up! Yah!!!
Get me there!! Get me there!!
Take me to luck. Take me to luck. Get me there!!

AVA: Paul!! STOP!

OSCAR, BASSETT, & HOUSE: Come on, Come on Come on Come on!

PAUL: It's Malabar!!!! Tell Bassett it's Malabar!

PAUL falls from the horse. AVA catches PAUL and helps him to bed. AVA leaves.

Scene II

OSCAR and BASSETT visit PAUL who is in his bed, critically ill.

OSCAR & BASSETT: *(whisper)* Paul! We're rich, we're rich!

OSCAR: You did it, Paul! We put it all on! Malabar came in first! We're going to be all right now.

BASSETT: Paul? Can you hear me? You'll never need to get in the saddle again. Rest easy.

OSCAR & BASSETT: We're rich. We're rich!

BASSETT: No more worries.

OSCAR: No more voices.
We'll chuck this old horse and get you a real one!

PAUL: Do you think I'm lucky, Mother? Do you think I'm lucky?

AVA: Maybe.

OSCAR: Maybe?! Ava, we're rich.

OSCAR & BASSETT: We're rich, we're rich. We're finally rich!

PAUL: Do you feel happy, Mother? Do you feel happy? Is it enough?

AVA: We'll see.

OSCAR & BASSETT: We're rich.

PAUL: Uncle Oscar is smiling. Bassett is smiling. Mother, won't you smile?

AVA: Maybe, we'll see.

OSCAR & BASSETT: We're rich, we're rich, we're rich!

PAUL: Mother, be happy? Mother . . .

AVA: Maybe . . .

PAUL: Mother, won't you smile?

AVA smiles and PAUL smiles back.

OSCAR breaks the spell.

OSCAR: Ava! Bring out the bubbly. I know you'll have some around! Bassett, let's go find Ava's bubbly.

AVA, OSCAR, and BASSETT leave.

HOUSE: We're rich, we're rich! We're rich, we're rich?

OSCAR, BASSETT, & HOUSE: There must be more money. There must be more.

PAUL: Bassett?

PAUL crawls from his bed towards the rocking horse.

OSCAR, BASSETT, & HOUSE: There must be more money. There must be more.

PAUL: Uncle Oscar!

OSCAR, BASSETT, & HOUSE: There must be more money. There must be more.

PAUL: Mother!

OSCAR, BASSETT, & HOUSE: There must be more money. There's never enough . . .

PAUL: Mother!

PAUL crawls up onto the rocking horse. He dies, alone.

End.

Shelter

Libretto by Julie Salverson
Composed by Juliet Palmer

Directing and Conducting Shelter

Keith Turnbull, Director, and Wayne Strongman, Artistic Director/Conductor

KEITH TURNBULL: Imaginative leaps in time, space, POV, and much more have existed, they say, for millions of years since the beginning of storytelling. The explosive emergence of film and particularly film editing in our times has radically liberated—technically and aesthetically—the performing and literary arts. Film is often shot completely out of sequence, consecutive scenes recorded sometimes months apart with performers, as in real life, not knowing what comes next or what really came before. Film has acclimatized both creators and audiences to make surprising, unexpected leaps with little if any psychological or other preparation. While making these leaps each viewer fills in the vacuum of "missing" narrative and context and thus each becomes a creative collaborator in imagining narrative, character, context, and much else but most importantly—meaning. This is audience participation in the very core creation of the work.

Shelter embraces the postmodernism of film as well as the ancient form and techniques of parable. Before parables were adopted as fodder for moralists, they were stimulants for deep and caring reflection on choices made or choices to be made.

When you first read the story of the prodigal son, didn't you think the brother had a point?

Shelter is a parable without a moral, without judgment. It's a parable of the birth of the atomic age and of the elements that contributed to that birth. Any "judgment" is the domain of the audience member, of us—the interpreters. The creators do not tell us what to think, or subtly manipulate our feelings and thoughts. They do direct our eyes and ears to the bigger, more global aspects of our atomic age. Their "judgment" is in choosing the subject matter and then in presenting it in ways that bring into focus the major issues that they consider warrant our deep reflection.

Shelter's extremely varied development process over many years allowed the creators to examine a very wide range of interpretive options. However, rather than taking a more traditional approach of finally selecting one or two of these options, they accumulated an expansive, eclectic range of choices. From the sophisticated nineteenth-century romance of German lieder to '40s big band to Hollywood cartoon to circus clown to late-twentieth-century chamber music to Japanese punk, the inspirational sources cover the time span of the nuclear story. The opera is bookmarked by two flights: one bringing the science of nuclear physics to North America and the other taking the resulting nuclear bombs to Asia—over the Japanese sea. Air flight, as indispensable to the nuclear bomb, is further strengthened when the heroic pilot flies in on his mission to find, to woo, and to fly away with Hope, the atomic "bomb." The completion of his mission to drop the bomb is all the more difficult as he has fallen in love with Hope: "*They forgot to say she'd be beautiful.*"

Flight connects European science, philosophy, art, and history to North American vigour, can-do self-obsession, and unfettered ambition; together they create the atomic age.

WAYNE STRONGMAN: Julie Salverson and Juliet Palmer met at Tapestry Opera's Composer-Librettist Laboratory in August 2002. For their maiden voyage at the LIBLAB the pair created a short scene, "Seven Sheets of White," for soprano and mezzo. Two female characters meet at the office photocopier; the mundane, repetitive process allows lonely internal introspection that blossoms into a connection with each other and a sudden glimmer of hope.

Around that time, Julie began collaborating with her Concordia University colleague, Peter C. van Wyck. Their research took them along the route of uranium ore that was mined near Délı̨nę, Northwest Territories, refined in Ontario, tested in New Mexico, and used for the atomic bombs dropped on Japan in August 1945. Tapestry's mandate to develop and produce original operas by Canadian artists was a natural fit for such an "explosive" story. Discovering how to bring such monumental history to the stage became a parallel journey for all of us and for the many public funders who supported the creation of this genre-breaking work of art.

Julie and Juliet were intrigued by the clown genre as a possible way of confronting the tragedy of this story. How to blend opera "high art" with clown "low art" was a key research challenge. In 2004, we embarked on a series of workshops with the guidance of Steven Hill from Leaky Heaven Circus in Vancouver. Clown actors Lisa Marie DiLiberto, Adam Lazarus, Martha Ross, and Claire Calnan improvised scenes in the Ernest Balmer Studio beside singers Tamara Hummel, Deborah Overes, and Ian Funk. The revelations of this experiment were astonishing. Juliet was so fired up she produced the first draft of the score in the following five months.

Hill returned to direct the next workshop at Queen's University in March 2005. With a new score to work through but still improvising many of the moments, it was a brave cast of actors and singers (Charlotte Gowdy, Adam Lazarus, Tamara Hummel, Steven Pitkanen, all wearing red noses) who agreed to perform for an audience of students and the public. The risk was worth it. The gravity of the subject matter juxtaposed against the hapless clown brought laughter, tears, and a standing ovation.

Tapestry had learned over many years to delay commissioning a work until all parties were convinced of the strength of the story and the capacity of the creative team to collaborate. To arrive at that critical decision, our process was consistent: we conducted workshops of specific scenes with our growing roster of experienced performers, and we invited our faithful audience to a presentation, welcoming their feedback in careful exchanges with the creative team and performers.

After the Kingston workshop/performance *Shelter* was ready to be commissioned.

First in the door was the Canada Council commissioning jury in January 2006; this was the "Good Housekeeping seal of approval" we needed to get started. The Ontario Arts Council followed on, one year later. Julie and Juliet were also proactive in finding funding opportunities outside of the government commissioning bodies.

It was time to bring in a director/dramaturge with the broadest possible range of experience to help guide the next stages of the process. I had worked with Keith Turnbull over several winter sessions in the '90s at the Banff Centre when he was artistic director of the theatre arts programs. With its international connections and a new television studio, the Banff Contemporary Opera and Song programs were leading the rest of Canada in creating new possibilities for the art form.

Keith readily accepted the challenge. With the commission contract in place, Julie completed another draft of the libretto and Juliet completed her second draft of the score. Juliet's process was to set the vocal parts simultaneously with the full instrumentation, rather than sketch a piano score and orchestrate later. She chose to augment the piano with clarinet/bass clarinet, a battery of percussion, violin, electric guitar, and acoustic bass/electric bass.

To further investigate the use of clown in a music genre, we brought in an experienced Toronto team: Martha Ross, founder of Theatre Columbus (now Common Boots Theatre), and Dean Gilmour of Theatre Smith-Gilmour, both graduates of the famous École Internationale de Théâtre de Jacques LeCoq in France. The goal was to find a way to pair the improvised genius of the clown with the artful expression of the opera singer. Dean and Martha participated in the February 2007 workshop at Equity Showcase Theatre on Dufferin Street under Keith's direction. It was a great venue for testing out the latest development of our "nuclear family," which now included a teenage daughter, Hope, and a major figure outside the family, the real-life nuclear physicist Lise Meitner. The integration of sung and spoken word and physical theatre came under scrutiny as did the role of the orchestra in the storytelling. Working in a different venue and presenting to an audience outside of the "safe zone" of our own studio was a healthy incentive to critical thinking.

Two major decisions emerged from this workshop that shaped the final development stage:

1) *Shelter* was an opera, after all, and it needed to be through-sung, with the clown element embraced in the articulation of the singing actors;

2) the primary story of our clown nuclear family needed a set-up for context, and a denouement that could include the character of the pilot, where the team's exploration first began.

Lise Meitner became the unifying figure and connecting link that provided the context for this atomic age story. In 1944, Meitner had barely escaped the Third Reich to Sweden from her Berlin laboratory where her team had discovered the secret of nuclear fission—"the secret to penetration is to slow down"—a discovery for which she was overlooked when her research partner Otto Hahn won the 1944 Nobel Prize in Chemistry, which he received in 1945.

Julie decided that the baby bomb would not be "Little Boy" as the United States Air Force named it, but a girl. Meitner is midwife to the birth on stage, which parallels this scientist's rightful place in history, even though she had refused to be part of the Manhattan Project. In *Shelter*, when the baby finally arrives, the fretful Thomas is so relieved, he explodes with pride: "We *did* it," he shouts. Claire immediately erases his male ego with my favourite line in the scene: "*I* did it!" Every mother in the audience applauds.

Conflict is ratcheted up as Hope springs full-grown from her crib—a luminous, libidinous teenager, backed by a Japanese-inspired punk-rock band. All the clown physicality, speech rhythms, and vocal registers drawn out by the extensive clown-based improvisations rise in Thomas's frantic attempt to keep Hope protected, his house locked up. Into this melee comes the pilot with a Geiger counter, providing a swaggering male energy of assured practicality—"I can solve any problem in the air"—and surprised wonder: "They forgot to say she'd be beautiful."

The seduction scene, with Claire enraptured by the sexiness of a "man in uniform," Thomas praying for a happy marriage for his daughter, both parents listening intently from the room below, builds to the ultimate challenge for the opera composer: the ensemble where each character's lines overlap. Meitner, opposed to this union, of course, accuses the pilot of "turning tricks for generals."

The ensemble in the penultimate scene, "Trinity," anticipates the fiery apocalypse to come. From this cacophonous lament emerges the eerie stillness and terrifying beauty of that moment "Over the Japanese Sea": "Ten thousand miles of sky, brilliant blue, red, gold." We are left suspended but falling with Hope over *The Seven Streams of the River Ota.*[*]

The casting of *Shelter* was finalized in the 2008 workshop. Baritone Peter McGillivray's robust presence and comic flair as Thomas balanced the extraordinary Christine Duncan in her debut operatic role, playing Claire. Keith Klassen, a Tapestry stalwart, became the handsome pilot; Andrea Ludwig became Meitner; and Maghan McPhee was Hope.

---

[*] Robert Lepage and Ex Machina, *The Seven Streams of the River Ota* (London: A&C Black, 2014).

The workshop process continued right up until production. By the time the opera premiered, over fifty performers, including instrumentalists, had participated in the process. The final orchestra roster included regular Tapestry orchestra colleagues Ryan Scott, percussion, and Bob Stevenson on clarinet/bass clarinet (specializing in extended techniques). They were joined by new faces to us but seasoned contemporary and classically trained music personalities: Gregory Oh, piano; Jesse Dietschi, acoustic/electric bass; Rob MacDonald, electric guitar; and Sharon Lee, violin.

The production, built for touring, was designed by Sue LePage with magnificent projections by Ben Chaisson and lighting by Beth Kates, all managed by JST Productions (Aidan Cosgrave, another Tapestry veteran). Isolde Pleasants-Faulkner, who has mirrored my baton for the stage cues to most of Tapestry's premieres during my time and after, was stage manager.

The world premiere took place on November 12, 2012, as part of Edmonton Opera's new ATB (Alberta Treasury Branches) Canadian series. My friend Sandra Gajic was the company's new CEO who bravely launched the series with Tapestry's *Shelter* and Queen of Puddings's production of Ana Sokolović's *Svadba*. It was the first time that an opera company in Canada collaborated on a new Tapestry work, including the premiere, although we had already partnered internationally in New York and Glasgow. This premiere caught the attention of the *Wall Street Journal*, who described *Shelter* as an "intriguing, darkly comic fable."

Sandra arranged a visit and colloquium with Danny Gaudet and Walter Bayha, elders from Déline, Northwest Territories, who spoke of how moved they were to see an opera emerging from a story that was part of their history. After all, it was members of their community who, after they discovered that the uranium mined in Déline found its way into the bombs dropped on Japan, made a ceremonial trip to Japan to apologize to survivors.

Shelter will always hold a special place in my heart, not only because of the pleasure of working and learning with the Julie/Juliet team over a decade of development, but because the premiere was the last production of my thirty-five years at Tapestry. Michael Hidetoshi Mori was billed as assistant music director on this show, on his way to becoming my successor as Tapestry's artistic director.

How do you develop new opera? With *Shelter,* as with all Tapestry projects, we learned: "Chemistry isn't enough. You need form, elegance, physics, to release this fire, this hidden energy."

Writing Shelter

Julie Salverson, Librettist

I've always been attracted to catastrophic events. Joseph Campbell says to "follow your bliss," and while most people go after love or fulfillment, I'm drawn to tragedy and the fault lines in the psyche of a culture, the secrets that fester in families, leak quietly into communities, and eventually—sometimes—explode. Such is the story of *Shelter*.

In 2002 I entered Tapestry New Opera Works's intensive Composer-Librettist Laboratory with a story about how, during World War Two, a group of Dene from Canada's Northwest Territories had worked at a uranium mine on their land. The Sahtúgot'ine—Bear Lake People—from Délı̨nę slept in tents made from empty sacks that once held yellowcake, a form of impure uranium. They discovered—sixty years later—that the product of their labour had made its way eventually, if indirectly, into the atomic bomb dropped on Hiroshima. Their response to this news was to fly to Japan in 1998 and apologize to the *hibakusha*, the survivors. I heard this story from scholar Peter C. van Wyck, with whom I eventually travelled for several years exploring the Highway of the Atom. Peter, in turn, had learned of this part of Canadian history from filmmaker Peter Blow's documentary *Village of Widows*.

In the around-the-clock immersion of Tapestry Opera's LIBLAB I met composer Juliet Palmer. She'd grown up in New Zealand, a part of the world with its own relationship to the nuclear industry. Juliet was wickedly adventurous and ready to dive into the wackiness of this project with all her compositional chutzpah. What followed was a ten-year adventure. We worked incredibly, sometimes impossibly, collaboratively. We researched every angle on the atomic story, from the lives of the scientists, to the structure of the atom, and eventually shifted from a historical and sociological focus into the world of fable.

In 2003 Tapestry gave us our opera "audition": a fifteen-minute piece for the opening of the company's new studio theatre. *Over the Japanese Sea* was staged partly in Tapestry offices—with the audience on their feet among the singers, in promenade style familiar to community play projects but new to opera—and partly in the studio with the audience seated. The response encouraged us. Instead of sitting back immobilized by the idea of the bomb, audience members chatted about their connections to the atomic story: a cousin who was an engineer, an uncle who was a miner, a neighbour who worked in a physics lab. We wanted this engagement from people, this energy, and the reaction confirmed our desire to make the opera about the effects of the atomic age on ordinary people, not a creation of iconic figures, heroic or tragic.

Early workshops involved courageous singers and actors—even students in my acting class—willing to explore together the world of clown, which provided the opportunity for a story of both immense magnitude and ordinary humanity. This was helped considerably by the direction of Vancouver's Steven Hill, artistic director of Leaky Heaven Circus. In riffing the heightened precision of opera and the low-brow improvisation of red-nosed clown, we found the world of our story.

Clown evolved for us into a vocabulary that, with the suggestion of the director Keith Turnbull, drew from the world of the contemporary cartoon. But the roots of red-nosed clown are important to how *Shelter* was written. Inspired by the work of French teacher Philippe Gaulier, the clown begins with nothing, is in fact ridiculous but is innocent of this fact, innocent of the impossibility of hope. Ridicule, loss, and suffering are part of life; flopping, messing up, is inevitable: "In the face of this, let us begin," says this clown. It is frightening. There is a nakedness in this kind of contact. The clown is not a hero but is heroic in courage, in being available to the possible, no matter how absurd and unlikely. Pleasure, joy, and fun in this context are not spectacle or escape, but rather the deadly game of living with loss, living despite failure, despite the humiliation of trying endlessly. As Steven Hill says: "Always stay in the shit; that is where the humanity and the possibilities lie."

A Closet in my Brain

Juliet Palmer, Composer

Where do words and music come from? Wading through the multiple drafts and rewrites of *Shelter*, the answer might well be a very large closet—a closet that Julie and I shared. Like the phrase my then-four-year-old spun one day, apropos of who knows what:

> I keep my secrets in a closet in my brain,
> just in an alleyway in my bones,
> an alleyway in my skeleton.

I've lost track of how the seepage between daily life and operatic life occurred, but in a draft from the same year, Hope, the daughter in our opera, is gripped by an uncanny vision of the journey of the uranium along the Highway of the Atom:

> My bones hold secrets, blind alleys,
> A jumble of paths
> From the mine to the lake
> Through burial grounds
> Thick with bones to the desert.

Creating an opera and raising a child: from conception and the pangs of labour, to the years of patient parenting, the parallels seem clear. My adult daughter now holds nested within her many daughters: spidery fingered newborn, raucous toddler, sassy ten-year-old, and thoughtful teenage activist. So, when I think about our opera *Shelter*, I'm not surprised to glimpse within it the shadows of many different possible operas, memories of workshops and rewrites, discarded and almost forgotten fragments. In the footsteps of the physicist Lise Meitner, mid-wife of the atomic age, Julie and I followed "Wege und Irrwege," our journey to the final opera "a jumble of paths, blind alleys."

Opera usually begins with a story that is fleshed out as a libretto and then given voice through music. Eager to bite off more than we could chew with our first opera, Julie and I decided to take the maverick's path, developing words and music in tandem. We were both drawn to clown and its mix of the deeply serious and the absurd. It was the perfect lens through which to bring our atomic fable into focus.

> In our work with the performers, we aim to unearth the essential vocal language of the characters. The physicality, speech rhythms, and vocal registers drawn out by clown form the musical and textual kernel of the opera. When the performer truly embodies the text, we hear how words can sing. In the freedom of clown, the singer uncovers the character's voice. *What* they say is as vital as *how* they say it. —proposal for *Shelter* workshop, 2004

Over two workshops, the director Steven Hill challenged the performers to unearth story and character through fearless play. For the actors, this was nothing new—all had trained in Paris at the École Internationale de Théâtre de Jacques LeCoq. Their open spirit and playful connectedness drew the singers into a creative circle of listening, risking, and learning. Together we encountered the characters who would inhabit our story.

Between workshops, I researched musical sources that would connect the imaginary with the historic and everyday. Lyrics from songs I stumbled upon wound their way into Julie's libretto, while transfigured versions of the music insinuated themselves throughout the score. Inspired by both the wondrous beauty and terrible danger of science, I drew upon music from along the Highway of the Atom. Scientists at Los Alamos listened to big band music on the radio as they waited for the weather to clear before detonating the first atomic bomb in the desert. This prompted me to underpin Thomas and Claire's love-at-first-sight meeting with a distorted version of Duke Ellington's "I'm Beginning to See the Light," a song that topped the charts in 1945.

The physicist Lise Meitner was an ardent lover of Brahmsian lieder: much of her musical language inhabits this world. Three songs form the bedrock of her character: "Nein es ist nicht auszukommen mit den Leuten" ("No, There's No Getting Along With Other People"); "Flammenauge, dunkles Haar" ("Flaming Eyes, Dark Hair"); and "Sind es Schmerzen, sind es Freuden" ("Are They Sorrows, Are They Joys?"). Thomas and Claire fall in love while Lise hovers on the verge of the discovery of fission. Harmonies and rhythmic pulses from Ellington's song shimmer in the shadows as Thomas sings of the angel of history and the irresistible lure of progress:

A storm just blew in from Paradise

Hope's character sings in the spirit of the post-atomic age—from rock and roll to Japanese punk. In Julie's story, Hope grows from a baby into a teenager in the blink of an eye, climbing out of her cradle into adulthood. Inspired by this speed-of-light shift, her vocalizations evolve from prelinguistic babbling into dismantled speech and explode into a rock/punk-hybrid rant infused with "grrrl power." Hope's words and song are rooted in the parallel evolution of both language and melody.

The Cold War hovered over my childhood, threatening imminent catastrophe and planetary doom. Growing up in New Zealand was no guarantee of safety—the governments of France, the UK, and the USA all conducted nuclear tests in the Pacific Ocean. This was brought home in 1985 when I heard the explosive boom as the French government bombed the Greenpeace vessel *The Rainbow Warrior* in Auckland Harbour. Skip ahead fifteen years and I became a citizen of Canada, a country with a strikingly different atomic history. The lights in my house are powered by nuclear power and my neighbourhood in Toronto hosts a uranium fuel pellet processing plant. At night I lie in bed listening to the haunting sound of train whistles and wonder if another shipment of uranium has arrived from the west.

In some sense we all live along the Highway of the Atom and everywhere is downwind. Tripping over tailings and bogged down in radioactive mud, perhaps laughter and beauty will cause us to linger a moment and consider which path leads us out of this mess.

Working with Julie was a deeply collaborative process of shared stories, histories, and songs. In our early workshops, free-wheeling play and improvisation led to simultaneous discoveries of character, story, and music. In subsequent iterations, we time-travelled our way to vocal music linked to historical moments and characters, a network of roots from which the libretto and score grew. Trust, humour, and mutual respect kept *Shelter* moving forward along its jumble of paths.

Designing Shelter

Sue LePage, Set and Costume Design

Big ideas, little lives. For our visual research for *Shelter,* Keith Turnbull and I looked at the work of some brilliant contemporary animators and illustrators who deftly combine whimsey and tragedy. We found photos of hundreds of "modern bomb shelters," which look absurd and archaic today. In the end, the design needed to be playful but leave room for the power of the music and the big ideas to take over.

I played with scale. Only Hope's bed was realistic in size. A huge moon overhead made the singers appear tiny and fragile at times, something we have all felt stepping out into a starry night. This moon also flickered with projections, memories, and mathematical equations that put the inner lives of the characters out into timeless space. The domestic world of the story was scaled very small. The performance area was ringed around by a neighbourhood of little suburban houses only a couple of feet tall. The orchestra seated behind them were giants in the shadows, and the singers could enter like Gulliver striding through Lilliput. Our nuclear family home was a doll house, with a tiny light appearing in the window that was Hope's bedroom. This scale helped the tenderness of childhood and family life seem real and yet a fantasy, like child's play.

I'd like to think that the designs for *Shelter* expressed visually the human condition and the deep values embedded in the story: that we are small specks in the universe, but that every life and every small act is important. It is the libretto that is my guide when I am searching for the visual world of the opera. It is the music that often tells me when I get it right. Together their power is unique. I love to design for opera and be swept along for the ride.

Shelter was first produced by Tapestry Opera and Edmonton Opera at the Jubilee Auditorium, Edmonton, from November 15 to November 18, 2012, with the following cast and creative team:

Lise Meitner: Andrea Ludwig
Thomas: Peter McGillivray
Claire: Christine Duncan
Hope: Maghan McPhee
Pilot: Keith Klassen
Supernumerary: Connor Lafarga

Librettist: Julie Salverson
Composer: Juliet Palmer
Director: Keith Turnbull
Music Director: Wayne Strongman
Set and Costume Design: Sue LePage
Lighting Design: Beth Kates
Video Design: Ben Chaisson
Movement Director: Jo Leslie
Assistant Music Director: Michael Hidetoshi Mori
Production Director: Aidan Cosgrave
Production Stage Manager: Isolde Pleasants-Faulkner
Assistant Stage Manager: Anna Davidson
Lighting Assistant: Jennifer Lennon

Characters

Claire: mother
Thomas: father
Hope: daughter
Pilot: air force pilot
Lise Meitner: physicist

Note

Lines of text by different characters without a separating line space indicates the lines are sung in unison.

Scene I: Love and Science

We hear the sound of a plane. At first, we could be anywhere.

Stage opens to reveal the landscape. It is vast and empty, suggestive of the several landscapes of the story, the world below the plane: a desert, a frozen lake, a wasteland. It is night—there is a brilliant full moon.

We see LISE, *a physicist, in her sixties, dressed as a professional and reserved woman. She is stepping off a plane in New York, 1946, and is overwhelmed by flashbulbs and journalists. She steps back from the bombardment, to recover herself.*

LISE: The atom hides a nucleus
Electrons in an atom like raisins in a pound cake!
Alpha beta gamma
Alpha beta gamma
"*Wege und Irrwege:*
The journey to fission is a
Jumble of paths, blind alleys."[*]
The indivisible can be divided—divided!

The moon goes behind a cloud, lights down on LISE. *She watches.*

Sounds of aimless party chatter, the clinking of glasses. THOMAS *enters. He is awkwardly but nicely dressed. He adjusts his jacket and strikes a casual pose. He surveys the room. He is on a mission, looking for*

---

[*]   Lise Meitner, qtd. in *Lise Meitner: A Life in Physics*, by Ruth Lewin Sime (Berkeley, University of California Press, 1996), 161.

*something. THOMAS's attempts at ease are undermined by an obsessive
orderliness. He is constantly brushing the lint off his jacket, combing
his hair furtively, picking his teeth, straightening the crease in his pants.
He practices party conversation. Nothing coherent comes out until,
finally . . .*

THOMAS: I must make an effort.
How do people ha-ha how—how do people chat?
I have made up my mind:
Find a wife, get a life.

THOMAS begins to survey the room.

A life a wife a life

CLAIRE enters with martini.

CLAIRE: This fundraising party is the perfect plan
THOMAS: A wife if I if I if I

CLAIRE: To catch myself a gentleman—
THOMAS: If I if I if I I I

CLAIRE: A man who likes girls strong. Strong!
THOMAS: If I I I if I I if I I

CLAIRE: With a heart and a bank account.
THOMAS: If I I I I I I I

CLAIRE: A woman can't waste time.
THOMAS: I—

CLAIRE: The clock is ticking, t-t-t-t-t-t-tickin'
The clock is tickin', t-t-t-t-t-t-tickin', tickin'

CLAIRE spots THOMAS.

Brrrrrrring!!!!!
He looks like someone who could use a little fun,
A little fun, a little fun, a little fun, fun, fun.

THOMAS spots CLAIRE winking at him from across the room.

THOMAS: A storm just blew in from Paradise, Paradise!*

CLAIRE: Dance? Dance?

THOMAS: Uh, I don't dance, don't dance, don't don't dance, but . . .
Would you like another drink?
Vodka, whiskey, wine?
Just tell me what you want!

CLAIRE: Let's try-yai-yai
Let's try-ah!
Let's try everything. You do drink?

THOMAS: Yes—

CLAIRE: Me too!

THOMAS: But never to excess.

CLAIRE: No! Never to excess.
No—oh, oh, I have something in my eye.

She grabs him and leans back, blinking rapidly.

___

* Thanks to Walter Benjamin.

THOMAS: *(peering into her eyes)* Just let me help!
(to himself) This is the woman I dream of ev'ry night—

He begins to shake.

Ev'ry, ev'ry night.

CLAIRE: Sit still. You're shaking, you're shaka-shaka-shaka-shaka-shaking.
Are you cold? Ill?

THOMAS: No, I'm never sick:
I try to stay on top of things.

She feels his forehead, leaves her hand there suggestively.

CLAIRE: You aren't well. Can I take you—taka-taka-taka-taka-take you home?

THOMAS: What? What?!

CLAIRE: You, you, you feel like a man
With too, too much time on his hands, hands, hands
On his gentle hands
On his soft, soft hands.

THOMAS *and* CLAIRE *fall in love.*

THOMAS: Your touch, touch, touch:

CLAIRE: Your skin like paper,
Rrrrrrrrr Rrrrrrrrr
THOMAS: Electricity

CLAIRE: Rrrrrripping, rrrrrripping, rrrrrripping, ripping
THOMAS: Electric, electric, electricity

Like brilliant electricity, lights up on LISE. *She is here to make sure* THOMAS *and* CLAIRE *get it right. There are no dark corners while this stage is set.*

LISE: Chemistry isn't enough.
You need form, elegance, physics
To release this fire, fire,
This hidden energy.
To shatter, to split,
You need physics.

THOMAS: *(determined)* I must control myself.

CLAIRE: I must get this right.
    LISE: I must get this right.
        THOMAS: I must get this right.

We'll give the world an amazing child!

LISE: To give the world a strong and pure science,
I take my place in this family.
With Fermi, Curie, Bohr, Einstein,
Thorium, radium, uranium, radioactivity,
Defying the impossible.

THOMAS: We'll give the world an amazing child.

LISE: "Burning eyes, black hair,"
THOMAS: "Burning eyes, black hair,"
CLAIRE: "Burning eyes, black hair,"

Andrea Ludwig. Photo by Catherine Szabo.

THOMAS: Our child—child, child, you
CLAIRE: "Sweet, so sweet"
LISE: "Sweet, so sweet and audacious"[*]

THOMAS: Make me feel brave.
CLAIRE: Hold me.
LISE: . . . brave.

CLAIRE and THOMAS kiss.

Scene 2: The Birth of Hope

The hospital. LISE *dresses herself in hospital garb, puts on rubber gloves, prepares for the birth.*

LISE: Hitler takes Austria.
I am Jewish so leave, leave Berlin with no goodbyes.
Everything I leave.

CLAIRE begins labour.

CLAIRE: Everything I leave. Everything!
LISE: Everything!

Escape across the border to exile in Sweden. Escape—

CLAIRE: Everything I have, everything!
LISE: Everything, everything

CLAIRE: I promise you, child.

---

[*]   Georg Friedrich Daumer, "Flammenauge, dunkles Haar," *Neue Liebeslieder No. 14*, by Johannes Brahms, trans. Michael Palmer, 1874.

LISE: Thirty years of work!
After thirty years shall I be left without even a few books?
"I'm as free as a bird, of use to no one."

CLAIRE breathes; THOMAS holds her.

THOMAS: Tell me what you need—
Water, ice? A back rub?
Just tell me what you need!

CLAIRE: Don't touch me!

CLAIRE ad libs intense focused breathing.

Christine Duncan, Andrea Ludwig, Connor Lafarga, and Andrew Love.

LISE: "A beautiful discovery is so close, close, close, so close."*
The nucleus is a liquid drop
Ready to split

THOMAS: You, you can, you can scream!
LISE: . . . split.

> *CLAIRE screams.*

THOMAS & LISE: So close, so close, close, close coming
Almost there, almost, so close, so close, so very very close.

> *CLAIRE gives birth.*

THOMAS: A girl, a girl! We did it!

CLAIRE: I did it.

> *There is something strange about the baby.* THOMAS *takes it from* CLAIRE, *covers it.*

LISE: "Are they sorrows? Are they joys?"
CLAIRE: Where is she?

LISE: "Tugging at my breast—"
THOMAS: Nurses are washing her.

LISE: "At my, my breast"
THOMAS: Nurses are washing her.
Nurses are washing her, washing her . . .

LISE: *"Sorrows? Sorrows, joys."*

---

*   Meitner, 40.

THOMAS: . . . her

CLAIRE: Thomas! Nurse! Thomas! Where is our baby?

THOMAS brings the baby to CLAIRE.

She looks so bright! Glowing . . .

LISE: "All the old desires"

THOMAS: She's new,

CLAIRE: Like nothing I've ever seen before.

LISE: "*Leave a thousand, thousand*"

THOMAS: Brand new.

CLAIRE: Do we need to know anything?

LISE: "New flowers bloom a thousand thousand"

THOMAS: We just need to wash her.

CLAIRE: What?

LISE: "New flowers bloom."*

THOMAS: Just need to wash her . . . wash her.

LISE: Wash her, wash her, wash her and cover her.

THOMAS: Wash her, wash her, wash her and cover her.

---

*   Johan Ludwig Tieck, "Sind es Schmerzen, sind es Freuden," *Romanzen aus Ludwig Tieck's Magelone no. 3*, by Johannes Brahms, trans. Michael Palmer, 1865.

Scene 3: Bringing Hope Home

THOMAS *and* CLAIRE *stand staring at their house.* LISE *writes up experiment results. The solid is not stable.*

THOMAS: Home sweet home, sweet home. Shelter.
CLAIRE: Sweet—

THOMAS: Mother, father, child
CLAIRE: Mother, father, child

THOMAS: Lullabies, fairy tales, promises
CLAIRE: We're— We are— We're home, baby . . .

THOMAS: Hope. She should get to know her name. I'll lock the door.
CLAIRE: . . . baby.

Hope. My little glow-worm! A ball of fire with lungs of steel.

THOMAS: Hush . . . Hush 'n' bye

CLAIRE: I'll feed you, feed you, I'll feed you.
THOMAS: Don't you cry.

No. I'll do it.

CLAIRE: What what what do do what do what what do what do you
THOMAS: I'll do it, do it, do it. I'll do it!

CLAIRE: . . . know about being a mother?

THOMAS: You can't be trusted. Smoking, drinking, everything to excess.

CLAIRE: How-ow-ow-ow how dare you!
She needs me. She needs me. She needs me. She needs me—

Me! Me me me me me me me me me me me me me me me!
THOMAS: You you you you you you you you you you you you you!

You got us into this. Let me fix what I can. You can't just think of yourself,
Think of yourself.

LISE prepares and tastes formulas.

LISE: Elements decay, change shape.
CLAIRE: Myself my my

LISE: Alpha beta gamma
CLAIRE: My my my
THOMAS: "Oh, you pretty little baby"

CLAIRE: At the hospital they said hold her head!

LISE: Elements decay, change shape.
THOMAS: "When you wake, you'll have sweet cake"

CLAIRE: We need to shop!

THOMAS: "And all the pretty little roses"

CLAIRE: We need to shop, shop sho-op
(mutters) Shop, shop, p-p-p-p. Shhhhh
Oh oh oh oh

Crying.

THOMAS: "Red and blue"

LISE: Alpha beta gamma
THOMAS: "Pink and gold"
"And all the pretty little roses."

LISE: Alpha beta gamma. Radioactivity

THOMAS holds a pillow over the baby.

THOMAS: "Hush 'n' bye . . . Hush 'n' bye"*

CLAIRE goes to the door. THOMAS stops her.

I'll lock the door, shut the windows tight.
CLAIRE: *(improv)* Shh shut up up-tight I'd if I'd hide

THOMAS makes a decision. He puts the pillow down.

LISE: Radioactivity . . .

THOMAS puts makeup on the child in the cradle; we do not see her yet.

THOMAS: Some blush, a bit of paint. When Mommy sees you, she'll feel better.

CLAIRE: At the hospital they said, *(whispers)* "Don't touch her."

---

*   Ruth Crawford Seeger, adaptation of traditional folk song "Hush 'n' Bye," *American Folk Songs for Children.*

Scene 4: Hope Grows Up

HOPE climbs out of the cradle—a young woman of twenty-one. It is
her birthday. She seems very pure. Beautiful. Glowing. The one bright
light. Not macabre. She is, however, very made up, like a Barbie doll,
but something underneath glows. She is not a plastic girl. She is alone in
her room.

HOPE: This—this is, this is this ow! This ow! This is
ha ha ha ha, ha ha ha ha, ow! Ow! Ha ha ow! Ow! Ow!
Our house, this is our house.
She b-b-b-b-b-b-b-b-b-b-b butter butter butter butter butters bread,
He cleans, she busies, he hurries, he cleans, she busies, he hurries
He cleans, she busies, he hurries
Ha ha ha ha ha
A piece of toast, a comb, a toy, a shoe, a mistake, a mistake
Ache
This is our house. Ow!
She butters bread.
He cleans. She busies. He cleans. She busies. He cleans.
She busies, busies, busies, busy busies, busy busies!
A piece of toast, a comb, a toy, a shoe, a mistake!
Sand in the basement.
I play in the basement.
Never leave this house.
A secret in this house.
Stuck within this house.
Stuck! Stu-stu-stuck! Sss-ta! Ssssss! S
Stu-stu-stu-stu
Stuck in this boring little town, mother drinking, father fussing.
Get me out! Ow ow! Out! Out!
I want some fun! I want I want I want I want I want I want to see the world!

CLAIRE: Hope, dear, what are you doing? In your room all day?

HOPE: You d-d-d-d-d-d-d-d-d-d-d-d-d-d-d-d-d-d-d-d-d don't!
Understand me
Understand me, understand me, understand me
Understand me, understand me!
A summer's day.
The light is sweet.
When can I go out?
When can I get out? Out?
It's hot! Hot hot! Hot!

CLAIRE: She's hard to reach. Difficult. Different.

HOPE: Out! Ow, ow! Out!

CLAIRE: Difficult. Different. Difficult!

    LISE, returning from afar, enters house.

THOMAS: *(to LISE)* Willkommen! Welcome!
(calls to HOPE) Hope! I'd like to introduce to you your new tutor.
A lady scientist, European, with credentials.

CLAIRE: Thomas, we never discussed, discussed—

THOMAS: A scientist—meticulous—persistent.
She'll find a way to stop the girl from blowing up!

LISE: I should be glad—
If I still have the capacity to be glad—
To serve this family.

HOPE: *(coming out of her room)* Who are you?

Andrea Ludwig, Maghan McPhee, Peter McGillivray, and Christine Duncan.
Photo by Catherine Szabo.

CLAIRE: *(to LISE)* She hasn't turned out the way we'd planned.

THOMAS: Nonsense! Nonsense!
Our special girl deserves special attention—

Special, special, special!
CLAIRE: Thomas, we never, never— Thomas!

LISE: Leave us alone. I work better alone.

CLAIRE and THOMAS leave.

A secret, a secret in my hand.
An invitation, sealed, official:
Join us in this most exciting project,
This Manhattan Project.
But if I cross this thin line nothing will remain of beauty.

This child has more to give the world
Than turning tricks for generals.

(to HOPE*)* What do you want to be, when you grow up? Grow up?

HOPE: I am grown up—twenty-one today.
I want to dance, love, fly in the light of a summer's day.

LISE: But how quickly the light can slip into darkness.
In 1915 I almost lost my love—

HOPE: Love?

LISE: Of physics—
Forty kilometres from the Russian front.
Ev'ry day more wounded men more wounded
HOPE: Wounded men

LISE: While I made X-rays of their broken bodies.
HOPE: Wound broken bodies

LISE: So . . .
HOPE: So?

LISE: Hope, be on guard,
You listen, listen to me.
Choose how you love.
Don't give away your beauty.
We must refuse this Manhattan Project.
Let me tell you how it all began.
You're old enough to know your history.

Can you see me
Walking in the snow with a young man?

HOPE: Snow. A man?

LISE: The woods are dark
But our voices set the cold air a-crackling.

HOPE: Your lover?

LISE: Physics warmed us both—
Our voices rising to a fever pitch
As we talked our way to fission.
Now I am sixty—
As thin, as thin, as a line.
HOPE: Watch me . . .

LISE: Who sees me? Who?
HOPE: Watch me in this house.

LISE: Waiting, all my life is waiting.
HOPE: Watch me.

Watch me in this house,
I'm the girl at the window looking out.

LISE: Who sees me? Who?
HOPE: Who sees me? Who?

LISE: Now I am sixty—as thin as a line. Who sees me? Who?
HOPE: Who? Who sees me? Who?

LISE: Waiting, all my life is waiting. Waiting, all my life is waiting. Waiting.

HOPE: Waiting, all my life is waiting. Waiting, all my life is waiting.

Scene 5: The Pilot

We hear the sound of a plane. At first, we could be anywhere. It is vast and empty, the world below the plane: a desert, a frozen lake, or a wasteland. It is night. There is a brilliant full moon.

PILOT: I fly, I fly the plane.
I check the instruments, follow the curve of the earth.
The nose of the plane heads west, banking, climbing.
Under her belly, the shadow of the sun, rushing over the water's surface.
I fly the plane. She carves up the sky.
Exquisitely arching curves . . .
I can navigate at night.
I look below: a lake river, a mine that glows in the dark . . . glows in the dark.
I hope for a moon.
I'll try anything they throw at me and get the boys home when it's done.
I can solve any problem in the air, air.
Other than that, it's a drink, deal the cards, and choose a girl.

The PILOT appears outside the house. Takes out his Geiger counter, turns it on. It begins to click. He makes notes.

HOPE: I I I I I I I I I

PILOT: Damnedest noise I ever heard.

HOPE looks at herself in a mirror.

HOPE: Ai-ai-ai-ai-ai-ai I ffffffffffffeellllllllllll I feel something
somethingngng-ong-ong

CLAIRE looks out the window, sees the PILOT, likes what she sees.

CLAIRE: A traveller with dirt on his boots and time on his hands . . .
Well-worn hands, strong, strong well well well well well well
I I I I I I I I I I I I I a-a-a-a-ah

PILOT comes closer. CLAIRE hides, listening.

*HOPE takes off her makeup until barefaced, removes her child's dress,
stands revealed.*

Ah . . .

HOPE: Oo, oo, oo
Ten thousand miles,
He's come to find me.
Will he see me? Will he see me?

The PILOT throws a stone at the window. HOPE steps closer.

PILOT: Can life be so complex
When all I want to do is stand here and watch her undress?

The PILOT climbs to the balcony.

HOPE: The desert wind blows hot across my skin.

PILOT: All I want to do is watch her undress?
Can life be so complex when

CLAIRE opens the window.

All I want to do, all I want to do, all I want to do, to do

PILOT climbs through the window.

Even a physicist—a physicist knows
The secret to penetration is to slow down.

HOPE: Who are you talking to?

PILOT: Myself.

HOPE: Talk to me—talk to me. Talk—talk to me.
Talk to me. Talk to me.

PILOT: I am—listen: "In the sky, a moon . . . a moon.
On your face, a mouth . . . a mouth.
In the sky, countless stars. In your face, two eyes . . . two eyes . . . two eyes
. . . two eyes.
Brilliant light, desperate heat—heat—heat—"*

HOPE: Falling, falling, falling.

PILOT: Heat, heat.

Scene 6: Trinity

Post coitus. The house is decorated for HOPE's *twenty-first birthday.*
CLAIRE *knows that* HOPE *and the* PILOT *are lovers.* HOPE *knows that*
CLAIRE *knows.* CLAIRE *counts place settings.* HOPE *joins her.*

CLAIRE: One, two, three, four, one, two, one, two, three, four . . .

HOPE: Thee, four, one, two, three, four . . .

---

* Otomí song, *Pre-Columbian Literatures of Mexico*, by Miguel León-Portilla (Norman: University of Oklahoma Press, 1969), 95.

PILOT formally knocks on door. CLAIRE *lets him in.*

CLAIRE: A man in uniform.
I'm so happy you came.

HOPE: I'm so happy.

CLAIRE: She's so happy. We're so . . . *(yells)* Thomas!!

THOMAS enters looking puzzled.

CLAIRE *glares at* THOMAS.

We're so happy.
THOMAS: happy.

CLAIRE: Ha ha ha ha, ha ha ha ha, ha ha ha ha, ha ha, ha ha, ha ha ha ha happy
THOMAS: Ha ha ha ha, ha ha ha ha, ha ha ha ha, ha ha, ha ha, ha ha ha ha happy
HOPE: Ha ha ha ha, ha ha ha ha, ha ha ha ha, ha ha, ha ha, ha ha ha ha happy
PILOT: Ha ha ha ha, ha ha ha ha, ha ha ha ha, ha ha, ha ha, ha ha ha ha happy

HOPE: To meet you.

THOMAS: What brings you to this part of the world?

PILOT: Orders. A special directive.

CLAIRE: The man we've been waiting for.

THOMAS: *(to CLAIRE)* Hush.

CLAIRE: *(to THOMAS)* A woman can't waste time. Brrrrring!!!!
(to PILOT) You look like a man who takes chances.
Up for anything life throws in your path.
PILOT: Sounds like more fun than I have time for today.

CLAIRE: Something's burning. Burning, burning, burning . . .
THOMAS: You're upsetting the calm, lifting the lid:
Stop poking your nose where it doesn't belong!
HOPE: Lifting, opening . . .

CLAIRE: Burning!

> *CLAIRE grabs the PILOT.*

HOPE: *(to CLAIRE)* No!

> *CLAIRE pushes the PILOT to HOPE.*

(to PILOT) Talk to me, talk to me.

PILOT: Today the sun rose like any day. Just like any day.
Now ev'rything, ev'rything . . . Now, now, ev'rything has changed.
They forgot to say she'd be beautiful.

Your eyes— Your eyes, your eyes
HOPE: I feel

PILOT: Are brighter than a thousand suns
Your eyes.
HOPE: I've always, always known you.
I feel I've always known you.

THOMAS: Don't touch her.
It's time for you to leave.

PILOT: You're right, sir.
(to CLAIRE) I would like to stay, yes ma'am, but I have my orders.
Every job has its price.
(to THOMAS) I think we understand each other.

    LISE enters.

LISE: *(to PILOT)* I recognize you! You!

PILOT: *(to HOPE)* Now that I've found you, I must take you away.

LISE: You!

THOMAS: No! No, no! No!

LISE: You pimp, pimp! Turning tricks, tricks for generals.

HOPE: *(to PILOT)* I'm going with you.

CLAIRE: I always knew she'd set the world on fire.
LISE: No! You've no idea of the consequences.

THOMAS: A family is only safe together. Outside—outside—
The world is full of danger! Danger! Danger!
Danger! Danger! Danger! Danger! Danger!
What? What! What have I brought into this house?

HOPE: Take me, t-t-take me, t-t-t-t-take me away! Away, away!

THOMAS: The sky turns black, thunder:
Tornado warning.
Lock it up, lock it down.
Shut this house up tight.
Lock it up, lock it down.
Shut this house up tight.

> THOMAS *hammers.* HOPE *is overcome with memory, singing as though in a trance as the others circle her.*

HOPE: Oh-oh-oh-oh
Oh-oh-oh-oh-oh
Open my eyes,
Open my mouth,
Spread my wings, my wings:
A storm, storm is blowing.
My bones hold secrets, blind alleys,
A jumble of paths
From the mine to the lake through burial grounds
Thick with bones to the desert.
Men carried me.
Science handled me.
My bones hold secrets from the mine to the lake
To the desert's burning heat, heat.

PILOT: The physicist told me: "Turn one hundred and forty-nine degrees as fast as you can
Then get the hell out of there."
I'm here to get the job done. Do not cross me.

LISE: If you—if, if you, if you, you cross this thin line,
Nothing will remain of beauty.
Do not cross me. Do not cross.

PILOT: I'm here to get the job done.
Do not cross me. Do not cross me.

LISE: Do not cross me, do not cross me

HOPE starts to go with PILOT.

THOMAS: Lise, please. Lise, go with Hope!

LISE: I refuse, refuse—I refuse! I refuse!

THOMAS: Lise, please. Look after her. Lise, go with Hope!

LISE: Smoke, smoke rising three miles over Hamburg,

HOPE: Smoke

THOMAS: Please!

LISE: Water boiling in the canals.

HOPE: Water. Water

THOMAS: Lise!

LISE: In London burning sparks fly like snowflakes,

HOPE: In London burning sparks fly like snow,

THOMAS: Fly

LISE: But still I refuse the invitation,
This Manhattan Project.
I refuse to answer death with death, death

HOPE: death death—death

LISE: Death death death

HOPE: Death death death

PILOT: *(to LISE)* Don't act so pure.
You and me, we love our jobs. We love the thrill.

LISE: Dangerous tricks.

PILOT: Don't pretend you aren't excited, excited, excited.

LISE: I refuse, refuse, refuse.

PILOT: Whether you refuse or not,
She's leaving with me.

CLAIRE kisses PILOT.

THOMAS: Fallout is a gradual thing. Many years of waiting and finally it comes.

LISE: Fallout is a gradual thing. Many years of waiting and finally it comes

CLAIRE: Fallout is a gradual thing. Many years of waiting and finally it comes.

PILOT: Stations. Start engines. Taxi!
Come, little girl. It's time to go.
Time to go.

HOPE: Smoke steals my—smoke
steals my—breath.

THOMAS agonizes, singing a lullaby to CLAIRE.

THOMAS: "Hush. Hush, don't you cry.
Oh, you pretty little baby.
When you wake, you'll have
sweet cake
And all the pretty little roses."

CLAIRE: "Pretty pretty pretty little
roses.
Blue and red. Blue, re re re re-red
red red"

Maghan McPhee, Keith Klassen, Christine
Duncan, and Peter McGillivray.
Photo by Catherine Szabo.

THOMAS: "Blue and red, Hush Hush, Hush hush."

HOPE: A sleepless sun in a perfect sky.
THOMAS: "Hush, hush, don't cry."
CLAIRE: Cry!

HOPE: Chokes me. Black rain n n n n n sti-sti-sti-sticks to my skin.
White ash chokes me!
THOMAS: "You hush, hush"
HOPE: Black rain, white ash
The angels are blowing up paradise.
THOMAS: "You pretty little baby, hush. Hush 'n' bye."*
CLAIRE: The angels are blowing up paradise.

   PILOT and HOPE exit.

   Fire. Black rain falls.

LISE: "I see
Shining . . .
Two suns
I feel heat on my face
Another sun
Burning"
CLAIRE: I feel heat on my face
Your kiss
THOMAS: Two suns.

LISE: "Through the dusk of tears"
THOMAS: "Through the dusk of tears"**

---

* Seeger.

** Tieck.

CLAIRE: I see two suns burning, burning, burning.
THOMAS: I see . . . black rain sticks to my skin
White ash chokes me.

CLAIRE: Burning, burning, burning, burning.
THOMAS: Burning, burning, burning, burning.
LISE: Burning, burning, burning, burning.

Scene 7: Over the Japanese Sea

The PILOT and HOPE are in the plane. HOPE is a young woman, beautiful, with her whole life ahead of her. The PILOT is handsome, with a scarf over his shoulder, goggles. He is proud. This is his big day.

PILOT: Two-twenty-seven a.m. Eighteen minutes late. Takeoff.
Weather conditions fair. Light winds. Skies clearing.
Climbing, climbing, climbing, climbing to thirty-one thousand feet.

HOPE: A beautiful morning—
Ten thousand miles of sky,
Brilliant blue, red, gold.

PILOT: Look! You can see the whole city!

Look! You can see the whole city!
HOPE: Ten thousand miles of sky.
Brilliant blue, red, gold.

PILOT: Coming, almost there, so very close. My God!

HOPE: A sleepless sun in a perfect sky. Seven rivers run.
PILOT: No turning back. I see it—see it. I see it.

HOPE: Seven rivers run.

PILOT: All clear!

HOPE: Heaven and earth falling, falling, falling
Over the Japanese Sea.

End.

About the Contributors

Robert Chafe has worked in theatre, dance, opera, radio, fiction, and film. His stage plays have been seen in Canada, the United Kingdom, Australia, and the United States, and include *Oil and Water*, *Tempting Providence*, *Afterimage*, *Under Wraps*, *Between Breaths*, and *The Colony of Unrequited Dreams* (adapted from the novel by Wayne Johnston.) He has been shortlisted twice for the Governor General's Literary Award for Drama and he won the award for *Afterimage* in 2010. He has been guest instructor at Memorial University of Newfoundland, Grenfell Campus, and the National Theatre School of Canada. In 2018 he was awarded an honorary doctorate from Memorial University of Newfoundland. He is the playwright and artistic director of Artistic Fraud of Newfoundland.

Anna Chatterton is a librettist, playwright, and performer based in Hamilton, Ontario. She is a two-time finalist for the Governor General's Literary Award for Drama: in 2017 for *Within the Glass*; and 2018 for *Gertrude and Alice*, co-written with Evalyn Parry. Anna's other plays include her solo play *Quiver*, which was produced by Nightwood Theatre and was a finalist for the 2019 Hamilton Literary Awards in Fiction. She was commissioned by the Shaw Festival to adapt the C. S. Lewis novel *The Horse and His Boy*, which premiered in 2019, and her play *Cowgirl Up* premiered as an audio play for CBC podcasts in 2020. With the Independent Aunties, Anna has co-written and performed six plays with Evalyn Parry, created with director Karin Randoja. Anna's work as a librettist has been nominated for a JUNO Award for Classical Composition of the Year, and she has been nominated for five Dora Mavor Moore Awards, including Outstanding New Play and Outstanding New Opera, winning the 2017 Outstanding Production of an Opera. She won the 2020 Gilded Hammer National Impact Award, the 2017 Hamilton Arts Award for Theatre, the 2016 Toronto Theatre Critics Award for Best Supporting Actress, and was named a top-ten Toronto Theatre Artist of 2016 by *NOW Magazine*. As a librettist, Anna has created multidisciplinary works and operas with composers Juliet Palmer, Abigail Richardson-Schulte, James Rolfe, Andrew Staniland, and Gareth Williams, which have been produced in Dublin, Brooklyn, Boston, Saratoga Springs, California, Banff, Victoria, Vancouver, Newfoundland, Hamilton, and Toronto. Anna has been a playwright-in-residence at Tarragon Theatre, Nightwood Theatre, Tapestry Opera, and at the National Theatre School of Canada. She is a graduate of the MFA program in Creative Writing at the University of Guelph.

New Brunswick-based set and costume designer **Patrick Clark** has worked in theatres and taught in schools across Canada for the past thirty years. His designs have been seen on stage at the Stratford Festival, Shaw Festival, Guthrie Theatre, Chicago Shakespeare Theatre, Theatre New Brunswick, Neptune Theatre, Soulpepper Theatre Company, and Theatre Aquarius. He is one of the most sought-after set and costume designers in Canada. He has also worked extensively in the US and in Europe. Patrick received the 2011 New Brunswick Lieutenant-Governor's Award for High Achievement in the Arts. He has also won five Robert Merritt Awards for outstanding set and costume design. The J. Patrick Clark Award for design, stage management, or technical production has recently been established in his name by Theatre New Brunswick, to be given to a promising student training in production or design. He is a member of the Associated Designers of Canada and the Royal Canadian Academy of Arts.

The fourth Poet Laureate of Toronto (2012 to 2015) and the seventh Parliamentary/Canadian Poet Laureate (2016 to 2017), **George Elliott Clarke** was born in Windsor, Nova Scotia, in 1960. Educated at the University of Waterloo, Dalhousie University, and Queen's University, Clarke is also a pioneering scholar of African Canadian literature. A professor of English at the University of Toronto, Clarke has taught at Duke, McGill, the University of British Columbia, and Harvard. He holds eight honorary doctorates, plus appointments to the Order of Nova Scotia and the Order of Canada at the rank of Officer. He is also a Fellow of the Royal Canadian Geographical Society. His recognitions include the Rockefeller Foundation Bellagio Center Fellowship (US), the Pierre Elliott Trudeau Foundation Fellows Prize, the Governor General's Literary

Award for Poetry, the National Magazine Gold Award for Poetry, the Premiul Poesis (Romania), the Dartmouth Book Award for Fiction, the Eric Hoffer Book Award for Poetry (US), the Encyclopedic Poetry School International Fellow Trophy (China), and the Dr. Martin Luther King Jr. Achievement Award. Three of his titles are available in Chinese, Romanian, and Italian.

Marie Clements is an award-winning Métis/Dene writer, director, and producer who ignited her brand of artistry in a variety of media including theatre, film, television, and radio. Of late, Marie's play *The Unnatural and Accidental Women* opened the first national Indigenous theatre at the National Arts Centre in Ottawa, her opera *Missing* produced by Pacific Opera toured nationally, her play *Burning Vision* was produced by the National Theatre School in Montreal, and her commissioned play *Iron Peggy* premiered at the Vancouver International Children's Festival. Marie's fifteen plays have been presented on some of the most prestigious stages, garnering numerous awards and publications including the Canada-Japan Literary Award, and two Governor General's Literary Award nominations. Marie's multi-award-winning films have screened internationally at Cannes, MOMA, the Toronto International, Vancouver International, Central Alberta, and ImagineNATIVE film festivals. Her recent film credits include the dramatic feature *Red Snow,* music documentary *The Road Forward,* and doc series *Looking at Edward Curtis.* Marie is the founder of Urban Ink Productions and artistic director of Red Diva Projects and the president of her media production company MCM.

Brian Current studied music at McGill University and UC Berkeley (Ph.D.). His music, lauded and broadcast in over thirty-five countries, has been awarded a Guggenheim Fellowship, the Barlow Prize for Orchestral Music (US), the Premio Fedora (Italy) for Chamber Opera, and a Selected Work (under thirty) at the International Rostrum of Composers in Paris. Current's pieces have been programmed by all major symphony orchestras in Canada and by dozens of professional orchestras, ensembles, and opera companies worldwide including his Carnegie Hall debut with the American Composers Orchestra in 2005. His music appears on ten commercial recordings, including three albums devoted exclusively to his works. The Naxos recording of his opera *Airline Icarus* earned him a 2015 JUNO Award for Classical Composition of the Year. Current is also an in-demand guest conductor and regularly leads orchestral programs of contemporary music. He has championed nearly one hundred works by Canadian composers. Current has been the main conductor of the Continuum Ensemble since 2011 and has guest-conducted with symphony orchestras and ensembles in Canada, the US and Italy. Starting in 2019–2020 he began as co-director of New Music Concerts (NMC) of Toronto. Since 2007 Current has been director of the New Music Ensemble of the Glenn School at the Royal Conservatory of Music. In 2016 he won the inaugural Azrieli Commissioning Competition, at fifty thousand dollars the largest of its kind in Canada and one of the largest in the world, and in 2018 his *Shout, Sisyphus, Flock* won the Jules-Leger Prize for New Chamber Music.

Paula Danckert is a dramaturge, producer, Foley artist, and teacher. She is the dramaturge on the opera, *Missing*, by librettist Marie Clements and composer Brian Current. She has worked on two films written and directed by Clements, the feature *Red Snow* and the documentary *The Road Forward*. From 2012 to 2014 she was the Foley artist and assistant director on an adaptation of Dylan Thomas's *Under Milk Wood,* a new opera written and composed by John Metcalf, which toured Wales and the UK. For five years she was company dramaturge and artistic associate at Canada's National Arts Centre. Before joining the NAC, Paula was the artistic and executive director of Playwrights' Workshop Montréal for nearly ten years. In Halifax, Nova Scotia, she was president of Playwrights Atlantic Resource Centre, and a drama producer at the CBC. She was also associate producer for Live Art Productions: New Dance Series, foley artist for Salter Street Films, and host of *Artspeak* on CKDU-FM. She has been the associate dramaturge at the New Play Centre in Vancouver, at the Banff Playwrights Lab and at the Stratford Festival. She has developed new works with playwrights all over Canada and in many other countries. Her career in the fields of production and performance span more than three decades. Paula graduated from Canada's National Theatre School where she taught for many years. She is currently a doctoral candidate at the Centre for Drama, Theatre and Performance Studies at the University of Toronto.

Juno-nominated composer **John Estacio** is a recipient of the 2017 Lieutenant Governor of Alberta Arts Award. He has served as the composer-in-residence for the Edmonton Symphony Orchestra, Pro Coro Canada, the Calgary

Philharmonic Orchestra, and the Calgary Opera. He is a recipient of the prestigious NAC Award for composers. His compositions are programed by orchestras throughout North American and his frequent performances and broadcasts have earned him several SOCAN Awards for concert music. His works have been performed at Carnegie Hall, including performances by the Toronto Symphony Orchestra, as well as a performance of his *Triple Concerto* for violin, cello, and piano in May 2012 by the Edmonton Symphony Orchestra. The Toronto Symphony also toured the US with his composition *Wondrous Light*. His orchestral works have been performed by all the major Canadian orchestras, as well as the Houston Symphony, St. Louis Symphony Orchestra, Rochester Philharmonic Orchestra, Fort Wayne Philharmonic, and orchestras in Europe, South America, and Asia.

Born in England in 1959, **Nic Gotham** was a saxophonist and composer. His professional life began in Toronto with the jazz-funk ensemble Gotham City. Studying with James Tenney at York University, he became interested in composition. He led the improvising chamber orchestra, Hemispheres, and the saxophone quartet, Forty Fingers. In 1997, he won the Fred Stone Award for innovation and integrity. He met theatre artist Baṇuta Rubess in 1988 and over the years they created many staged works, as well as two children. They moved to Latvia in 1998, where Nic was a celebrated performer. He taught at the Latvian Academy of Music, and in 2012, received a Ph.D. in Music from Brunel University London. Nic composed some fifty works for various ensembles including Tapestry Opera, the Vancouver Chamber Choir, Arraymusic, Riga Saxophone Quartet, the Latvian Radio Choir, Evergreen Club Gamelan, Sinfonietta Rīga, and the Latvian National Symphony Orchestra. He collaborated with DJ Monsta on a program of jazz 'n' beats. Nic's first opera *Nigredo Hotel* (1992) was a tremendous success with tours across Canada and Great Britain and was later produced in Australia and Vancouver. A second chamber opera, *Oh Pilot* (2004), a collaboration with Rubess, was produced in Rīga and Kaunas, Lithuania. Nic's symphony *Nightscapes* was commissioned by Sinfonietta Rīga and premiered in 2012. He recorded his final piece of miniatures, based on the novel by Martha Baillie, *The Search for Heinrich Schlögel*, a week before he died on July 25, 2013, in Toronto.

Canadian soprano and conductor **Barbara Hannigan** is an artist at the forefront of creation. Her artistic colleagues include Simon Rattle, Sasha Waltz, Kent Nagano, Vladimir Jurowski, John Zorn, Andreas Kriegenburg, Andris Nelsons, Esa-Pekka Salonen, Christoph Marthaler, Antonio Pappano, Katie Mitchell, Kirill Petrenko, and Krzysztof Warlikowski. Both a singer and conductor, she has shown a profound commitment to the music of our time and has given over eighty-five world premiere performances. Hannigan has collaborated extensively with composers including Pierre Boulez, Henri Dutilleux, György Ligeti, Karlheinz Stockhausen, Salvatore Sciarrino, John Barry, Pascal Dusapin, Brett Dean, George Benjamin, and Hans Abrahamsen. Since 2020 she has been Principal Guest Conductor with Gothenburg Symphony Orchestra. She also had conducting and singing engagements with the London Symphony Orchestra, Toronto Symphony Orchestra, Swedish Radio Symphony Orchestra, Münchner Philharmoniker, and was artist-in-residence at L'Orchestre Philharmonique de Radio France. Her major opera roles include Lulu (*Lulu*), Mélisande (*Pelléas et Mélisande*), and Marie (*Die Soldaten*). Hannigan's album as both singer and conductor, *Crazy Girl Crazy* (2017), won a Grammy Award for Best Classical Solo Vocal album, and she was also a Juno Award winner in 2018 and 2019. In 2020 Barbara launched Momentum: Our Future, Now, a major international initiative driven by leading artists supporting younger colleagues. She also continues her acclaimed work with Equilibrium Young Artists mentoring initiative, which she launched in 2017.

Linda Hutcheon holds the rank of University Professor Emeritus in the Department of English and the Centre for Comparative Literature at the University of Toronto. She is author of nine books on contemporary postmodern culture in Canada and around the world. She has edited five other books on cultural topics, and is associate editor of the *University of Toronto Quarterly*. **Michael Hutcheon** is Professor of Medicine at the University of Toronto. A respiratory physician specializing in lung transplantation, his extensive scientific research publications encompass a number of areas: pulmonary physiology; bone marrow transplantation; and AIDS. He has also published in the fields of medical education and the semiotics of both cigarette and pharmaceutical advertising. They have done collaborative, interdisciplinary work on the cultural construction of sexuality, gender, and disease in opera (*Opera: Desire, Disease, Death*, 1996), both the real and the represented operatic body (*Bodily*

Charm: Living Opera, 2000), the lessons opera teaches about mortality (*Opera: The Art of Dying*, 2004), and the later creative life and "late style" of opera composers (*Four Last Songs: Aging and Creativity in Verdi, Strauss, Messiaen, and Britten*, 2015).

Camellia Koo is a Toronto-based set and costume designer for theatre, opera, dance, and site-specific performance installations. Recent designs for opera and ballet include new costume designs for *Jacqueline* (Tapestry Opera), *La Bohème* (Santa Fe Opera); sets and costume designs for *Turandot* (Helikon-Opera, Moscow), *Shanawdithit*, *Rocking Horse Winner*, and *The Shadow* (Tapestry Opera), *Macbeth* (Minnesota Opera), *Candide, Rigoletto, Hansel and Gretel, Carmen*, and *The Tales of Hoffman* (Edmonton Opera), *Simon Boccanegra* and *Maria Stuarda* (Pacific Opera Victoria), *The Lighthouse* (Boston Lyric Opera), *Bremen Town Musicians*, *Second Nature*, and *The Magic Victrola* (Canadian Opera Company's Opera for Young Audiences), *Marilyn Forever* (Aventa Ensemble), *Pelléas et Mélisande*, *Turn of the Screw*, and *La Bohéme* (Against the Grain Theatre), and sets and costumes for *Sleeping Beauty* (Ballet Jörgen). Recent designs for theatre include collaborations with Cahoots Theatre, Factory Theatre, the National Arts Centre, Soulpepper Theatre Company, the Shaw Festival, the Stratford Festival, Tarragon Theatre, and Why Not Theatre among many others. She is a graduate of Ryerson Theatre School (technical production), and completed her MA in Scenography at Central Saint Martins College of Art and Design (UK) and the Hogeschool voor de Kunsten (Utrecht, the Netherlands). Camellia has received six Dora Mavor Moor Awards (Toronto), a Sterling Award (Edmonton), a Chalmers Award, shared the 2006 Siminovitch Protégé Prize, and most recently received the 2016 Virginia and Myrtle Cooper Award in Costume Design. In 2018, she was shortlisted for the Siminovitch Prize for Excellence in Theatre.

Sue LePage has been designing award-winning productions for theatre, dance, and opera for more than forty years. Her designs for *Anne of Green Gables—The Ballet*, the premiere production from Canada's Ballet Jörgen, are now touring Canada and the United States. Recently she designed costumes for *Brigadoon* at the Shaw Festival, where her credits include *Me and My Girl, Ragtime, Guys and Dolls, Arcadia, Saint Joan, Born Yesterday*, and many others. In the world of opera, her designs include premiere productions of new work such as John Estacio and John Murrell's *Filumena*, *Frobisher*, and *Lillian Alling*. In her hometown Toronto recent designs include *Disgraced* (Mirvish/Hope in Hell), *Beauty and the Beast* (YPT), *Innocence Lost* (Soulpepper), and many shows over the years at Canadian Stage, Tarragon, and Factory Theatre. Her work has been seen at most major theatres across the country including the Citadel, Banff Centre, Manitoba Theatre Centre, National Arts Centre, Charlottetown Festival, Neptune, and the Stratford Festival. Sue has been lucky to work with great artists and some of Canada's finest playwrights including James Reaney, David French, Mavis Gallant, Judith Thompson, Tomson Highway, John Murrell, and Ann-Marie MacDonald.

One of Canada's most respected stage directors, **Glynis Leyshon** has worked over the past four decades staging numerous theatre and opera productions. She served as artistic director for two of Canada's most honoured companies—Victoria's Belfry Theatre and the Vancouver Playhouse. At the Belfry Theatre, she was responsible for premiering many acclaimed productions including Sally Clark's *Moo* for the Calgary Olympic Festival. During her time at the Vancouver Playhouse, she again championed a diverse range of work including Morris Panych's *The Overcoat*. She served as director/dramaturge for Kevin Loring's Governor General's Literary Award–winning play *Where The Blood Mixes*, which premiered at the Luminato Festival. She has directed for theatres across the country, including many seasons at the Shaw Festival and at Alberta Theatre Projects, most recently directing award-winning productions of Kate Hennig's *The Last Wife* and *The Virgin Trial*. Other notable productions include the Chalmers Award-winning *The Hope Slide* by Joan MacLeod at Tarragon Theatre and *For the Pleasure of Seeing Her Again* by Michel Tremblay at the National Arts Centre. Her work in opera includes critically acclaimed productions for Pacific Opera Victoria, Calgary Opera, Opera on the Avalon, and Vancouver Opera. Most recently she has acted as dramaturge for a new John Estacio/Clem Martini opera commissioned by Calgary Opera, and is the director/dramaturge for *The Flight of the Hummingbird* by Haida artist Michael Nicoll Yahgulanaas and Maxime Goulet, a co-commission by Pacific Opera Victoria and Vancouver Opera that is set to tour both nationally and internationally.

David T. Little is "one of the most imaginative young composers" on the scene (*New Yorker*), with "a knack for overturning musical conventions" (*New York Times*). His operas *Dog Days*, *JFK*, and *Vinkensport* (librettos by Royce Vavrek), and *Soldier Songs* have been widely acclaimed and performed around the globe, "prov[ing] beyond any doubt that opera has both a relevant present and a bright future" (*New York Times*). Little has been commissioned by the world's most prestigious institutions and performers, including recent projects for the Metropolitan Opera/Lincoln Center Theater new works program, the Kennedy Center, Baltimore Symphony Orchestra, New World Symphony, London Sinfonietta, the Crossing, Kronos Quartet, and Beth Morrison Projects. His music has been presented by Carnegie Hall, Holland Festival, LA Opera, Houston Grand Opera, Opera Philadelphia, Opéra de Montréal, the Chicago Symphony Orchestra, and the LA Philharmonic. From 2014 to 2017, Little was composer-in-residence with Opera Philadelphia and Music-Theatre Group. He has previously served as Executive Director of the MATA Festival and on the board of directors at Chamber Music America, and currently chairs the composition department at Mannes School of Music—the New School. The founding artistic director of the ensemble Newspeak, his music can be heard on New Amsterdam, Innova, Sono Luminus, and National Sawdust Tracks labels. He is published by Boosey & Hawkes.

Ann-Marie MacDonald is an author, playwright, and actor. She is best known for her novels, *Adult Onset*, *Fall On Your Knees*, and *The Way the Crow Flies*, as well as her plays, *Goodnight Desdemona (Good Morning Juliet)* and *Belle Moral: A Natural History*. Her work as an actor on stage and screen has earned her a Gemini Award and a Genie nomination. Ms. MacDonald's writing has been honoured with numerous awards including the Chalmers, the Dora Mavor Moore, the Governor General's Literary, and the Commonwealth Prize. She hosted CBC Television's *Life and Times* for seven seasons and *Doc Zone* for eight seasons. She was the inaugural Mordecai Richler Reading Room Writer in Residence at Concordia University, and she continues to coach students in the Acting and Playwriting Programs at the National Theatre School. In December 2018, she was named an Officer of the Order of Canada, in recognition of her contributions to the arts in Canada and for her advocacy of LGBTQ+ and women's rights. Ms. MacDonald lives in Montreal with her family.

Paul Mathiesen, Lighting Designer, has spent forty-five years in the culture sector, in the US, Europe, and Canada, creating a distinctive body of lighting designs and installations: architecture (Saudi Arabia's National Museum of Riyad; Atlantic Theatre Festival, Nova Scotia; Salter Street Films, Halifax), museums (ten years of lighting exhibits at the Art Gallery of Ontario; the S. R. Perren Gem and Gold Room [GE Edison award of Merit and the IES Design Award of Excellence] at the Royal Ontario Museum), interiors (Harry's New York Bar, Toronto; Susur Restaurant, Toronto), theatre (*You Never Can Tell* for the Shaw Festival, *7 Stories* for Tarragon Theatre; *La Ronde* for Soulpepper Theatre), opera (*Nigredo Hotel* for Tapestry Opera, Tarragon Theatre, and tour to Amsterdam and Brighton; *The Rape of Lucretia* for Canadian Opera Company; *Beatrice Chancy* for Queen of Puddings Opera; *The Magic Flute*, *Orfeo*, and *The Putnu Opera* for the Latvian National Opera), special events (World Leaders: A Celebration of Creative Genius and the Toronto International Festival of Authors for Harbourfront), fashion shows (Perry Ellis, NYC), art exhibits and performances (*Magnetic Fields* for Phillip Barker), and teaching (Professor, Lighting Design at Carnegie Mellon, School of Drama, 2001). In 1977, for Studio 54 disco, New York City, he was the original flyman/rigger and created the position of stage manager. Hallmarks of his work are the production of light events incorporating a dramatic interpretation of light (heightened manipulation of time, space, colour, and movement). Employing new and traditional technologies, he has realized an extensive scope of luminous strategies.

Michael Hidetoshi Mori is a leading international voice in socially and artistically progressive opera and music theatre. An award-winning Canadian/American stage director and the general director of Tapestry Opera in Toronto, he works regularly as a director, dramaturge, producer, and speaker in Canada and the US. Michael specializes in bringing new works from concept to full realization, having commissioned and/or developed more than fifteen new operas over the past five years. As of 2020, Michael is the chair of the Association for Opera in Canada, Canada's association of professional opera companies, and a co-founder of Indie Opera Toronto, a collection of over twelve independent companies in Toronto. Michael's leadership at Tapestry Opera has led to the *Globe and Mail* naming Tapestry as the "leader of the Canadian opera pack" in 2019. Since taking over the company in 2014, Michael has more than doubled its annual commissions and productions, spearheading projects and partnerships with Scottish Opera, Vancouver Opera, the Luminato Festival, the Art Gallery of Ontario, Canadian Stage Company, and Pride Toronto. A highlight among Michael's most innovative creations is Tapestry Explorations (TAP:EX), an annual concert experience that combines opera with other artistic forms. The series has experimented with mixed reality, physical theatre, turn-tablism with film fandom, punk rock, and Persian classical music over its five-year history. In addition to directing and dramaturgy at Tapestry Opera, Michael works in both traditional and contemporary operatic repertoire in Canada and the United States.

Andy Moro is a mixed-blood multidisciplinary artist. His practice began in studio visual arts, foundry-based sculpture, blown glass, large-scale public installation, and pyrotechnics. He has worked in automobile assembly; production film graphics and animation; typography and print design; darkroom and digital photography; 3D display technology; construction and installation; and set construction, projection, set, lighting, sound, and property design. Presently, Moro co-directs the Indigenous activism arts organization ARTICLE 11 with partner Tara Beagan. ARTICLE 11 recently premiered Beagan's *Deer Woman*, designed and directed by Moro, at the Kia Mau Festival in Wellington, Aotearoa (NZ). Moro most recently designed Beagan's *Ministry of Grace* for the Belfry Theatre in Victoria, Ian Ross's *The Third Colour* for Prarie Theatre Exchange, Natalie Sappier's *Finding Wolastoq Voice*, the Dancers of Damelahamid's *Mínowin*, and Marie Clements's *Unnatural and Accidental Women* at the National Arts Centre Indigenous Theatre's inaugural festival. He has collaborated extensively with Santee Smith's Kaha:wi Dance Theatre. Upcoming work includes *Sky Dancers* for Montreal's A'nó:wara Dance Theatre, honouring steelworkers from Kahnawake lost in the Quebec bridge disaster. He is currently developing a series of autobiographical performance/video sculptural installations. The ROOM series has been installed site-specifically at the Arts Commons in Calgary and the historic Auditorium Hotel in rural Nanton, Alberta. Currently, Moro and Beagan are preparing to shoot *Deer Woman* as a solo-performer film in Calgary.

Noted as a "contemporary opera mastermind" (LA Times) and "a powerhouse leading the industry to new heights" (WQXR), **Beth Morrison** is an opera-theatre producer and president and creative producer of Beth Morrison Projects. Named the 2021 Artist of the Year by Musical America, Beth created Beth Morrison

Projects (BMP) in 2006 to identify and support the work of emerging and established living composers. BMP is celebrated as an industry disruptor and tastemaker
at the forefront of musical and theatrical innovation by commissioning, developing,
producing, and touring the groundbreaking new works of these living composers
and their collaborators, which take the form of opera-theatre, music-theatre, and
vocal-theatre. BMP encourages risk-taking and the result is provocative works that
represent a dynamic and lasting legacy for a new American canon. *Opera News*
has noted: "More than any other figure in the opera industry, Beth Morrison has
helped propel the art form into the twenty-first century." In 2013 Beth co-founded
the PROTOTYPE Festival with HERE, which has become "essential to the evolution
of American opera." (*New Yorker*). Beth served a founding tenure as producer for
the Yale Institute for Music Theatre, as well as producer for New York City Opera's
VOX Contemporary American Opera Lab. She first honed her management skills
as the administrative director for the Boston University Tanglewood Institute.
She is currently an advisory board member of National Sawdust and Brooklyn
Youth Chorus, as well as a board member of Opera America, the international
competition, Music Theatre Now, and Voices 21C, a social justice choir. Morrison
is frequently asked to give lectures at conservatories across the country, including Mannes School of Music, NYU, Manhattan School of Music, Arizona State
University, University of Illinois at Urbana-Champaign, and more. Morrison is
also in demand as a speaker both nationally and internationally and has delivered
keynote speeches for Classical:NEXT and Opera Europa among others. Morrison is
a lecturer at Yale School of Drama and Beth Morrison Projects began a multiyear
residency with Music Academy of the West in 2020. Morrison holds a Bachelor of
Music from Boston University, a Master of Music from Arizona State University,
and an MFA from Yale School of Drama.

New Zealand Canadian composer **Juliet Palmer** is known as a "post-modernist
with a conscience" (*The Listener*) whose work "crosses so many genres as to be in
a category of its own" (*Toronto Star*). Juliet is the artistic director of Urbanvessel,
a platform for interdisciplinary collaboration. Recent works: *Choreography of
Trauma*, The Element Choir and Continuum; *Every Word Was Once An Animal*
with artist Carla Bengtson, Jordan Schnitzer Museum of Art, Oregon; *fire break*,
Hamilton Philharmonic Orchestra; *Oil & Water*, Detroit Symphony Orchestra;

Ukiyo, floating world, Urbanvessel and Thin Edge New Music Collective; *rivers*, solo album (Barnyard Records); and the opera *Sweat* (CalArts, Los Angeles; Bicycle Opera, Canada; National Sawdust, New York). Juliet was composer-in-residence at Orchestra Wellington and the New Zealand School of Music (2011/12), and an OAC artist-in-residence at Sunnybrook Research Institute (2018). She is the winner of the Detroit Symphony Orchestra's 2018 Elaine Lebenbom Memorial Award, a Chalmers Arts Fellow (2018/19), and a finalist for the Johanna Metcalf Performing Arts Prize (2019). Juliet holds a Ph.D. in composition from Princeton University and an MMus in performance, composition, and time-based art from Auckland University. www.julietpalmer.ca.

Bill Penner has worked in technical production and theatre management for more than forty years. His experience includes work in the production and presentation of dance, theatre, music, circus, and opera.

Toronto composer **James Rolfe** has been commissioned and performed by ensembles, orchestras, choirs, theatres, and opera companies in Canada, the US, Europe, Asia, Australia, and New Zealand. His work has been recognized with a Guggenheim Fellowship, the K. M. Hunter Artist Award, the Louis Applebaum Composers Award, the Jules Léger Prize for New Chamber Music, SOCAN's Jan V. Matejcek Concert Music Award, a Chalmers Arts Fellowship, an Outstanding Choral Work Award from Choral Canada, and a 2019 Johanna Metcalf Performing Arts Prize. Mr. Rolfe's operas have been performed in Toronto, Halifax, Vancouver, Banff, Edmonton, and New York. *Beatrice Chancy*, his first opera, played to sold-out houses and rave reviews in 1999; his most recent opera, *The Overcoat*, was premiered by Tapestry Opera with Canadian Stage and Vancouver Opera in 2018, and was nominated for ten Dora Mavor Moore Awards. Two solo CDs (*raW*, 2011, and *Breathe*, 2018, nominated for a JUNO Award) are available on Centrediscs. Mr. Rolfe is a composition instructor at the University of Toronto, and frequently acts as a mentor in master classes and workshops. Upcoming projects include new works for: Canadian Children's Opera Chorus (with writer Anna Chatterton); Soundstreams (with writer André Alexis); pianists Simon Docking and Barbara Pritchard; and Halifax's Vocalypse with Janice Jackson, as well as a song cycle with British poet and artist Sophie Herxheimer and a choral song cycle with poet Amanda Jernigan.

Baṇuta Rubess is a director and writer with a string of innovative productions to her credit in Europe and Canada. She made her mark in Canadian chamber opera with *Nigredo Hotel*. She wrote and directed a second chamber opera with Nic Gotham, *Oh Pilot,* presented in workshop by Tapestry New Opera Works, and produced by Latvijas Koncerti at the Latvian National Opera. Other music-based achievements include Gluck's *Orfeo* and an acclaimed children's opera, *The Birds' Opera,* at the Latvian National Opera; an oratorio about cooking and childbirth for the Latvian Radio Choir; and many musicals—some written by Rubess herself, others including Andrew Lloyd Webber's *Joseph and the Amazing Technicolor Dreamcoat*, in Riga. Her most adventurous works include an immersive production about refugees, staged on a beach, with actors, a choir, a baritone, and a naval marching band. After working in Toronto for many years with companies such as Nightwood, Theatre Direct, Tapestry Opera, the Great Canadian Theatre Company, and Theatre Passe Muraille, Baṇuta moved to Latvia in 1998. She returned to Canada in 2012. Since then, she has created a verbatim piece about love with choreographer Julia Aplin, and directed a site-specific mini-opera with Juliet Palmer's music, as well as the opera *Sweat* with Bicycle Opera. She teaches theatre at the University of Toronto and is currently focused on writing prose.

Julie Salverson is a writer, speaker, teacher, and workshop leader who has worked in professional and community engaged performance for many years. Her theatre, opera, and essays embrace the relationship of imagination and foolish witness to stories of violence. Her book *Lines of Flight: An Atomic Memoir* (Wolsak & Wynn) follows her journey tracing uranium from the Northwest Territories to Hiroshima while unearthing the secrets of her childhood, burning out as an activist, and finding beauty in haunted places. She runs workshops for groups practising resiliency through drama. She has published many essays about how to witness a terribly beautiful world, as well as the role of clown and courage in facing difficulty. She is a professor of drama at the Dan School of Drama and Music at Queen's University and is based in Kingston, Ontario.

Diana Smith's collaboration with R. Murray Schafer began in 1981 with *The Princess of the Stars* at Heart Lake in Brampton and continued with the epic Egyptian ritual music/drama *RA* in Toronto and Leiden, Holland. She later designed costumes for remounts of *The Princess of the Stars* in Banff, Alberta, and the Haliburton Forest in Northern Ontario. In *The Greatest Show*, her "surreal carnivalesque designs attested to her flair for period costuming as well as her industriousness" as over one hundred cast and crew members were clothed circa 1940 for this fairground extravaganza. Ms. Smith's "Kafkaesque designs" for *Requiems for the Party Girl* received a Dora Mavor Moore Award nomination, as did her work for Ann-Marie MacDonald and Nic Gotham's *Nigredo Hotel*. Other design projects include Schafer's *The Black Theatre* in Liège, Belgium, *The Black Theatre of Hermes Trismegistus* at Union Station in Toronto, *The Enchanted Forest*, and *The Palace of the Cinnabar Phoenix*; as well as dance productions by Denise Fujiwara, Judith Marcuse and others; Queen of Puddings's *Beatrice Chancy*; and *The Winslows of Derryvore*, *The Moodie Traill*, *The Great Farini*, and others at 4th Line Theatre in Millbrook, Ontario.

One of Canada's most distinguished music directors, **Wayne Strongman** is a champion of Canadian writers and composers. As founding artistic director of Tapestry Opera he commissioned and premiered over thirty Canadian operas including the Cantonese-English *Iron Road* (Brownell/Chan), *Elsewhereless* (Egoyan/Sharman), *Facing South* (Hannah/Smith), *The Shadow* (Poch-Goldin/Daniel), and *Nigredo Hotel* (MacDonald/Gotham). He conducted the premieres of Tapestry-developed operas: *Shelter* (Salverson/Palmer) for Edmonton Opera and *Elijah's Kite* (Chai/Rolfe) at the Manhattan School of Music. Strongman conducted the world premieres of *Dark Star Requiem* (Battson/Staniland) and *Sanctuary Song* (Chan/Richardson) for Luminato. He led opera creation projects at the Banff Centre, the National Arts Centre, and the Manhattan School, and projects with Vancouver New Music, Montreal's Centaur Theatre, American Opera Projects (NYC), and Scottish Opera (Glasgow). Many of his performances have been broadcast nationally on CBC. Early in his career, Strongman commissioned new works for the Bach Elgar Choral Society in Hamilton, where he was artistic director for fourteen years. His leadership of the Tapestry Singers was characterized by commissions from the senior echelon of Canadian composers. Major works include the premiere of Schafer's *Princess of the Stars* and Somers's *Chura-Churum*. Strongman also nurtured artists from the US, New Zealand, and the UK through Tapestry's new opera development programs. Relationships cultivated with English National Opera,

American Opera Projects, and Scottish Opera provided international exposure for Canadian artists. Named an Ambassador for New Music by the Canadian Music Centre, Strongman was invested into the Order of Canada for his innovative leadership of Tapestry and his volunteer work with children's choirs at the Regent Park School of Music.

Keith Turnbull has worked in Canadian theatre, opera, and music theatre as a producer, dramaturge, and director. He has been artistic director of the Manitoba Theatre Centre, Neptune Theatre: Second Stage, the NDWT Company, and Banff Centre: Theatre Arts. Keith has directed some hundred plays in theatres across Canada and developed and directed opera for Les Coup de Théâtre Festival (Montreal), NEXMAP (San Francisco), Norrbotten NEO (Sweden), Nouvel Ensemble Moderne (Montreal), Music Theatre Wales, Piteå Chamber Opera (Sweden), Taliesin Arts Centre (Wales), Tapestry Opera (Toronto), Welsh National Opera, and Vancouver Opera. Most recently, he was co-producer, dramaturge, and director of the much-acclaimed world premiere of *Under Milk Wood: An Opera* by composer John Metcalf with text by Dylan Thomas produced by Taliesin Arts Centre (Swansea), Companion Star (New York), and Le Chien qui chante (Montreal) in association with Welsh National Opera. The production opened in Swansea followed by a tour to four Welsh cities. It was chosen by the Royal Philharmonic Society as one of the top three UK opera productions of the year, by the *Guardian* as one of the top ten UK opera productions, and by the International Opera Awards as one of the top ten world productions. The double CD recording was selected by British Airways for their in-flight entertainment. Keith has translated seven Quebec plays and teaches regularly across Canada.

Victoria "Vita" Tzykun [tsee-'koon] is a production designer for stage and film. She has designed sets, costumes, and projections for companies such as the Bolshoi Theatre (Russia), Norwegian Opera and Ballet, Lyric Opera of Chicago, and Santa Fe Opera, among others. Her numerous film and TV credits include art direction for Lady Gaga, production design for several award-winning films, and commercials for leading entities such as PBS, DirectTV, and Qualcomm. Tzykun is a founding member of GLMMR, an interdisciplinary art collective that fuses the worlds of fine art, audiovisual technology, and live performance. Her work was showcased in a solo exhibition at the National Opera Center in New York, and in *Entertainment Design* and *Lighting & Sound America* magazines. Tzykun has also served as a panellist on the Opera Panel of the National Endowment for the Arts and was nominated for Best Design by the International Opera Awards.

Royce Vavrek is a librettist whose opera *Angel's Bone* with composer Du Yun was awarded the 2017 Pulitzer Prize for Music. His collaborations include operas with Missy Mazzoli (*Breaking the Waves*, *Proving Up*, *The Listeners*, and *Song from the Uproar*), David T. Little (*Dog Days*, *Vinkensport, or the Finch Opera*, and *JFK*), Ricky Ian Gordon (*27* and *The House Without a Christmas Tree*), and Gregory Spears (*O Columbia*); concert works with Paola Prestini (*The Hubble Cantata*), Julian Wachner (*Epistle Mass*), Ellen Reid (*Knoxville: Summer of 2015*), and Matt Marks (*Strip Mall*, *A Song for Wade (This is Not That Song)*); and a musical with Joshua Schmidt (*Midwestern Gothic*). Recent and upcoming projects include an adaptation of Carlos Reygadas's *Silent Light* with Paola Prestini and director Thaddeus Strassberger, developed at the Banff Centre for Arts and Creativity; *Crypto*, a contemporary dance creation with choreographer Guillaume Côté and composer Mikael Karlsson at the Festival des Arts de Saint-Sauveur; new operas with Julian Wachner (*Broadview Christ*) and Mary Kouyoumdjian (*Adoration*) for Beth Morrison Projects; a grand opera with composer David T. Little for the Met/LCT commissioning program; adaptations of Lars von Trier's *Melancholia* for the Royal Swedish Opera and Ingmar Bergman's *Fanny and Alexander* for La Monnaie / De Munt, both with Mikael Karlsson; and an adaptation of George Saunders's Booker Prize–winning novel *Lincoln in the Bardo* with Missy Mazzoli for the Metropolitan Opera. Royce is an alum of Concordia University (Montreal), NYU's Graduate Musical Theatre Writing Program, and American Lyric Theater's Composer Librettist Development Program. You can follow him on Twitter and Instagram at @rvavrek, or visit his website at www.roycevavrek.com.

Irish composer **Gareth Williams** lives in Scotland, where he makes work that seeks to find new participants and audiences for opera and music theatre, to shed light on stories and communities that have been overlooked, and to explore ideas of vulnerability in vocal writing. He was the inaugural composer-in-residence at Scottish Opera from 2012 to 2015, and his work has been commissioned by

Nov 28

ensembles such as BBC Scottish Symphony Orchestra, Red Note Ensemble, Plus-Minus Ensemble, and NOISE Opera, where he is currently Musical Director. His music is often site-specific and community-responsive, with performances happening in lighthouses, whisky distilleries, nuclear bunkers, and libraries. *Rocking Horse Winner*, produced by Tapestry Opera, premiered in Toronto in 2016, and was nominated for nine Dora Mavor Moore Awards, winning five, including Outstanding Musical Production. The work was recorded and released by Tapestry Opera in 2020. From 2015 to 2018 Williams collaborated with Oliver Emanuel to create the critically acclaimed 306 Trilogy, a collection of music theatre works telling the story of the British soldiers shot for cowardice during WW I, produced by the National Theatre of Scotland in partnership with 14–18 Now. The album *Lost Light: Music from the 306* was released in 2020. Currently Williams is creating *History of Paper*, a new musical with Oliver Emanuel; *Rubble*, a new opera for Scottish Opera to be premiered in 2022; and an album as a singer/songwriter. He lectures in Composition at the University of Edinburgh.